# THE POLITICAL ANIMAL

Studies in Political Philosophy
from Machiavelli to Marx

LEO RAUCH

The University of Massachusetts Press   Amherst, 1981

Library of Congress Cataloging in Publication Data
Rauch, Leo.
The political animal.
Includes bibliographical references and index.
1. Political science—History.  I. Title.
JA83.R34  320'.01'09  81-3070
ISBN 0-87023-338-6  AACR2

To Gila, Michael, and Daniel

The trees went forth on a time to anoint a
king over them; and they said unto the olive-
tree, Reign thou over us. But the olive-tree said
unto them, Should I leave my fatness, where-
with by me they honor God and man, and go
to wave to and fro over the trees?

And the trees said to the fig-tree, Come
thou, and reign over us. But the fig-tree said
unto them, Should I leave my sweetness and
my good fruit, and go to wave to and fro over
the trees?

And the trees said unto the vine, Come thou,
and reign over us. And the vine said unto them,
Should I leave my new wine, which cheereth
God and man, and go to wave to and fro over
the trees?

Then said all the trees unto the bramble,
Come thou, and reign over us. And the bramble
said unto the trees, If in truth ye anoint me
king over you, then come and take refuge in my
shade; and if not, let fire come out of the
bramble, and devour the cedars of Lebanon.
JUDGES 9:8–15

Zeus, who leads men into the ways of
understanding, has established the rule that
we must learn by suffering.

As sad care, with memories of pain, comes
dropping upon the heart in sleep, so even
against our will does wisdom come upon us.
AESCHYLUS, *Agamemnon*, 176

**Acknowledgment**   The typescript of this book was read by Professor Stephen Ellenburg of the Department of Politics at Mt. Holyoke College. His criticism was a model of what such criticism should be: thoroughgoing, superbly informed, and immensely helpful.
As a result of it, the book is better than it might otherwise have been. I am grateful to him.

# CONTENTS

# INTRODUCTION

## Failures and Successes

One of the earliest of the many definitions of man is as "political animal." Perhaps no phrase has been more suggestive, more powerful, in our speculation about human nature. "Political animal" seems to capture our collective essence as nothing else does: We are creatures whose essence it is to live in a *polis* and to find fulfillment in activity related to that unique setting. Yet, although that potentiality exists in all of us, as human, it comes to realization in only the rarest of circumstances.

Equally traditional is man's definition of himself as a "rational animal." We *are* rational animals, but that phrase defines us as solitary, which we never can be by nature. Our nature is inevitably social, and so "political animal" defines us as we are and *must* be.

"Political animal" is never far from "rational animal"—and that interrelation is what this book is about. That is, I shall be discussing some famous attempts to show that political man is also, and essentially, rational man. I say "attempts," because we can by no means speak of successes or achievements here. No one has as yet proved that our political lives are unalterably and inextricably bound up with reason. The twentieth century has exploded that illusion. And yet, throughout the long and intricate history of political thinking, attempts were made to show how, if the political present is not rational, it could be made so.

That goal, the rationalizing of political life, has many roads leading to it: from the absolutism of Plato's philosopher–kings to the iron hand of Machiavelli's prince, from Aristotle's constitutional democracy to Marx's classless society, from Hobbes's regime of a mortal god to Hegel's monolith of a state that is the process of reason itself in the world. All are attempts at demonstrating that it is possible for rule to be consistent with reason. None of these attempts has resulted in a conclusive answer, one about which no further doubts could be raised. Each of the theories pretends to be the final truth—but because none of them is indubitable they can be said to have failed, at least in this regard.

I believe there is an explanation for that failure. Each of the great classical theories establishes itself on a fundamental theory of human nature, and the political theory is then derived from its fundament (presumably as its logical outcome). Yet the concept of "human nature" is a skeleton that has to be fleshed out. We might regard man as essentially—what?—acquisitive, violent, law-abiding, a producer of goods, or whatever; a certain political system is supposed to follow as a foregone conclusion.

The fact is, however, that no primary theory of human nature encompasses man in *all* his possibilities. And so, any such theory is simplistic and will be contradicted by elements it has left out of account. To say men are by nature selfish overlooks their equally natural tendency to huddle and cooperate. To say men are essentially peace-seeking and clubby overlooks their centrifugal tendency toward individuation and privacy. To the genus *Homo* we can add a never-exhaustive list of differentiae, so that the notion of *Homo sapiens* or *Homo politicus* can never be derived from *Homo lupus, Homo faber,* or any other of the well-known models. And if we try to say that man-the-wolf, or man-the-maker, is the essence and that all else is the artificial veneer of civilization, the model merely shows itself to be incomplete and will eventually run afoul of other truths we have ignored.

In a nutshell, then, we can say that political theory has traditionally taken for itself the problem of coming to grips with human nature (variously defined) and then of showing how that nature can be reconciled with reason in a political setting. If these attempts have failed at proof, they have at least been noble failures, tantalizingly interesting failures—and, above all, tremendously influential failures. Their *impact* needs no proof: Locke's words find their way into the Declaration of Independence, as do Rousseau's in the ideology of the French Revolution; Marx's immense reach is obvious; and one scholar has gone so far as to say that the battle of Stalingrad saw the confrontation of two Hegelian armies, the Hegelian Right versus the Hegelian Left.

My selection of political theorists for this book can therefore be justified by looking upon them as shapers of ideology and political activity. It is not my intention, however, to discuss them in this light. What I shall do is to discuss their theories in and for themselves, that is, prior to their entrance into the world arena. But if the selection needs justification, I can say that these theorists seem to me the most vitally and dangerously interesting from the viewpoint of the last quarter of the twentieth century. They are still very much with us. There are also others I was sorely tempted to discuss: Plato, Aristotle (who coined the phrase "political animal"), Thomas Aquinas, Montesquieu, de Tocqueville, Bentham, the Mills, Dewey—but that would have made a far larger, and a different, book.

Machiavelli, Hobbes, Locke, Rousseau, Hegel, Marx. In discussing their theories, I shall have three aims in mind: I shall try to present their theories as completely and yet as concisely as I can in the space allotted; I shall try to show them responding to their predecessors (in Machiavelli's case, his implicit response is to Plato and Aristotle); and I shall try to give a fair evaluation to the present criticisms of these theories. That criticism has by now become so vast, especially in the case of Marx, that any attempt at compression is in for inevitable frustration.

Above all, there is frustration to be expected in trying to find some connecting thread between each of them. Although (as I said) I want to discuss each theorist in and for himself, they illuminate one another so remarkably that they cannot be regarded in isolation; and yet, when we try to connect them, the differences are much too complex to allow for one continuous line. We might say that their shared aim is to come to terms with man's nature (however diversely they may have defined that nature); the common challenge they confront is to use the idea of man's individual nature as the theoretical basis of his political life with others.

There is an obvious equivocation when we start to say, "Man is . . ." and see that collective entity as one male individual. When we say something like "Man is selfish," we mean all human beings, generically, and yet we visualize one person. The meaning is universal; the image is particular. The theoretical problem begins here, in this equivocation, although the equivocation goes unrecognized as such. It is also the source of the political problem for Machiavelli, who states the problem with which all subsequent political philosophy has had to deal—the problem of seeing man's individual (and individualistic) nature as the basis of his social life. If these two aspects negate one another in theory, the clash is even more resounding in the outer political world.

Machiavelli, Hobbes, and Locke are unmistakably atomistic—in their widely different attempts to understand society as composed of individuals, who are to be understood in the light of their personal motives. Even holists such as Rousseau, Hegel, and Marx, who reject the idea that the individual is comprehensible in theory and therefore take society itself as the most basic datum—even they can speak of the individual's need for society as justifying the holistic approach; or they equate society's activity with the individual's praxis; or they take the individual's reasoning activity and elevate it to social, even cosmic, rationality.

Accordingly, the challenge raised by Machiavelli still stands (although he raised it only implicitly): How are we to build a social–political theory upon man's nature as an individual?

We see that what characterizes Machiavelli as a modern is his search for a purely political (that is, secular, nonmoral) value, as well as the fact that he sees politics as an end in itself. The contribution of this study, concerning Machiavelli, is to show that we must consider the opposed standpoints of *The Prince* and *Discourses* together, in order to arrive at Machiavelli's real philosophy.

Subsequent philosophers fail to meet his challenge in that they arrive at no purely political value: Hobbes bases his politics on psychology, Locke on the religious tradition of natural rights, Rousseau on communal (as opposed to political) will, Hegel on cosmic reason. Marx meets the challenge in a way, at least to the extent of regarding all previous views (in their attempts to base politics on a foundation external to it) as forms of "religion." Only in regard to Marx (of the five theorists we discuss, after Machiavelli) is it true to say that the concept of the state is fully secularized and demythologized.

In seeing how Hobbes bases his politics on psychology, we see how he arrives at his political theory as a resolution of his personal fears. This connection between his inner and outer worlds is what enables him to postulate a connection between psychology and politics. Yet Hobbes wants to go farther and establish psychology on physics. We see the difficulty faced by modern interpreters in trying to detach Hobbes's politics and psychology from the physical base. We see how his political theory emerges in the interplay between moral and morally neutral ideas.

In contrasting Hobbes, Locke, and Rousseau, we explain how it is possible for one idea, the social contract, to be used in arguing for opposed political views. Hobbes uses the idea in arguing for total authoritarianism. Locke uses the idea in arguing for libertarian restraints on government and in justifying democratic revolution. Rousseau uses the social contract as a basis for the ideas of collective consciousness and the infallible consensus. We see how these views emerge from his negative criticism of modern civilization. Past writers have stressed the Romantic inconsistencies in Rousseau. We show Rousseau to have one consistent philosophy, based on models of the presocial and postsocial natures of man. Thus, man emerges out of nature and returns to it, but the "nature" is not the same, nor is man.

Hegel's political theory is shown to arise from his metaphysics, and we see how he uses the model of logical reason as the basis of the state. In discussing his *Phenomenology of Spirit* (especially the master–slave relation) and his *Philosophy of Right*, we see that his problem is to show how the individual is to be fulfilled as a member of society yet remain an individual. We discuss his concept of alienation as a constructive factor in civilization; the distinction between state and civil society; and the organization of the rational state.

Marx and the "Young Hegelians" aimed at finding an end to philosophy and at developing the idea of political praxis. We see how Marx uses his critique of religion as a basis for criticizing all society and all previous philosophy. We discuss his view of alienation and alienated labor. For Marx, man has lost his human nature, and the problem is how to restore that nature by political means. We discuss Marx's materialistic conception of history and its implications for politics and revolution. Finally, we discuss neo-Marxism and the attempt to reconcile Marx's thinking with views he would have found inimical.

What insights we can draw from these discussions, and apply to our own time, are probably more indirect than direct. If I had to state those insights in summary fashion, while standing on one leg, I would say that from Machiavelli and Rousseau we learn what the differences are between political health and political sickness; from Hobbes we see the outcome of holding life more precious than freedom; from Locke we realize that democracy is utterly and essentially Christian and European; and from Hegel and Marx we see how far the myth of human perfectibility can be taken. (And, if these discussions have succeeded in anything, it ought to be that they show such capsule characterizations to be practically useless and methodologically wrong.) What, then, is the result of these discussions?

I have not set myself the task of drawing conclusions for or against any of these political theorists. No one of them is finally "right"; no one of them is totally "wrong." What is of positive value in each of them, and what I have tried to show, is that each has illuminated one or more aspects of political life in its essence, and each has therefore contributed something of permanent value to the fund of political wisdom we can call upon.

# MACHIAVELLI

## The State as a Work of Art

The second panel of the Sistine Ceiling portrays God creating the sun and the moon. The face of God bears Michelangelo's typical *terribilità*. After this bit of creation, the figure of God is seen to float away, his back turned toward us. It is a gesture whose meaning was clear to the time: Turning one's back was an act of trust in an era when no man turned his back to another unless he trusted him with his life. God could trust the world because he had not yet created man. (That act of creation is shown two panels later.) It was in man's future to disappoint that trust—not only through Adam's Fall but also in the discovery of a human "nature." Whereas the *physis* of the natural world reflects God, the *physis* of man defies God and disappoints him. But it disappoints him for man's own reasons, not God's. Man's rational nature is seen as God-given. Yet his "nature" as a political animal—selfish, violent, with an intelligence bent entirely to the service of his selfish ends—this is not at all God-given. Man, in expressing that "nature," denies Creation. The truth that man has his own reasons, which are not God's—this is the discovery of the Renaissance.

The Sistine Ceiling and Machiavelli's *Prince* come out of the same years (1511, 1513). With Machiavelli we breathe the modern air. Not only does he foreshadow modern political thinking, he already thinks within the modern framework: There is his "amoralization" of politics, separating it from all considerations of personal ethics. Then there is his emphasis on the central importance of the nation–state, placing national security and existence above all else. And then there is his "secularization" of politics, treating it *sui generis*, without any basis in religion or metaphysics.

All this makes a sharp contrast with earlier philosophy. Protagoras (in Plato's dialogue of that name) says that a social nature is implanted equally in all men. Aristotle pronounced man to be a political animal—in the sense that it is man's nature to live in a *polis* and that he who does not participate in such an arrangement is not fulfilling his humanness. Both Plato and Aristotle believed in the contiguity of politics and ethics: The state is there to make men moral. The political system sketched in Plato's *Republic* is an extension of a metaphysical system whose ultimate basis is a visionary grasp of "The Idea of the Good." In Aristotle, the opening sentence of his *Politics* tells us that all human action is oriented toward some end; and, later, Aristotle tells us that the state arises to serve the needs of life but that its ultimate end is the good life.

Accordingly, when we say that Plato and Aristotle believed in the contiguity of politics and ethics, we mean that for them politics has a moral goal beyond politics itself. Man is somehow connected to the cosmos. This view is echoed in various ways by medieval writers. The Renaissance spirit, however, is expressed in Leonardo's drawing of the nude male figure, with arms and legs outstretched, standing inside a square inscribed in a circle. Man is now a cosmos unto himself, filling his world at all points.

For Machiavelli, in the same way, political life has no such higher *telos* as the equating of politics and ethics. Political life, rather, must be regarded as self-contained, with values that are altogether political. This has usually been expressed by saying that, for Machiavelli, politics must be value-neutral; that is, in politics there can be no "wrong" or "right" in any moral sense. Now, although this statement about Machiavelli is true, we ought to accept it with care. Some commentators say that he has no values at all. I shall try to show that he does have values, but they are political, not moral, ones. Indeed, he is the first of the moderns because he is the first to show that there is such a thing as a purely political value.

The three aspects just mentioned (the "amoralization" of politics, the emphasis on the nation–state, the "secularization" of politics) are not theoretically distinct but are three faces of Machiavelli's man-centered approach. There is no formally articulated system here. Rather, his approach is that of observation, and each observation confirms another in a loosely inductive way. What he observes is the political animal in his true nature. Throughout, Machiavelli seems to be saying: "This is the way men really are; I have seen them act this way, time after time." His experience is that of public servant and working diplomat in an amoral age, when popes, princes, and adventurers wage a deadly struggle for power. He reads deeply in ancient and modern history, but this reading only shows him the great distance between an ideal such as the Roman republic and the actuality of his own era, thereby substantiating what he has learned in his arduous experience of the present.

Thus, in the dedication to the *Discourses*, he says that he has written a book "in which I have expressed what I know, and what I have learned through long practice and continuous study in the affairs of the world."[1] In the dedication to *The Prince* he uses similar words, promising to impart "that knowledge of the deeds of great men which I have learned through long experience of modern events and continuous study of the past."[2] We must read the second dedication in the light of the first: His aim is not to take the past as a model but only to show us how to live in our own time.

His value to subsequent political thinking is, as I suggest, in the way he discusses the state in purely political terms. He does not need a wider philosophical system because he brackets out any concern that is not political. This poses a great challenge to political thinking thereafter, a challenge almost none of the subsequent philosophers could adequately meet. Indeed, it is as though everyone had learned from him how *not* to write a political theory, as though it were somehow wrong to base a theory of politics on political considerations alone: Hobbes based his politics on a theory of psychology; Locke based his theory of politics on an older metaphysical tradition of natural human rights; Rousseau tried to show that genuine political life is based on the morality of communal interest and consent, issues that Machiavelli ignores; Hegel tried to connect political life to cosmic rationality; and Marx inherited all these problems (most acutely those of Rousseau and Hegel) and had to come to terms with them. Yet the challenge for *our* time (as for Machiavelli's) is to deal with the concept of the state without such "external" connections. Whereas Hobbes and Locke, Rousseau and Hegel, may have rested their political theories on some nonpolitical foundation, we (for many reasons) cannot. Marx regards all such nonpolitical foundations as forms of "religion" (perhaps "idolatry" is closer to his meaning here), and then he urges us to think entirely in terms of "secular" values.

Another way of saying this is that we must avoid treating the concept of the state in mythic terms. The myth of the state is real enough out there in the world of conflicts and ideologies. But modern Western thought has allowed us to see past the myth. We can see its dangers—for example, that the State has its reasons which Reason knows not of. It makes its demands, forces men to obey, and even persuades them that that obedience is right and good. The persuasion usually consists of specious metaphysics, perverted religion, or demagoguery disguised as philosophy of history. Accordingly, this is the time to reduce the myth, cut it down to size, and treat the concept of the state in purely political terms. And this, as I said, is the aim of Machiavelli. Although his immediate aims were different from our own, this antimythic approach is his positive value for our time. (There is irony in the fact that, although the most powerful purveyors of the myth of the state have been avid readers of *The Prince* and firm believers in its doctrine of raison d'état, we can criticize their use of that myth—and the criticism can be found in Machiavelli himself.)

Before discussing this, I want to say something about the ideological function of myth in general. The concept of the state is one of the places in which man displays his values. He does this by elevating his current political situation to the rank of absolute truth. He does not first conceive of a state and then construct one on the basis of that conception—although this does happen in rare revolutionary situations. More often, he finds himself in a given political setting and then ennobles it as *the* way of life. His state becomes *the* state, the only way a state ought to be. In this way the state becomes a mythic entity, and we find ourselves speaking of it as though it had an independent validity, and a value higher than the individuals who comprise it.

We ought to distinguish myth from mythology.* Mythology can be defined as the representation of supernatural powers in natural terms. It is a descent from the higher to the lower, so that these powers become persons, demigods. Myth, on the other hand, works in the opposite direction, taking some aspect of nature and/or human nature and elevating it to the rank of the supernatural. Where the aim of mythology is to give the supernatural a human face, so that it can be approached and be appealed to, the aim of the myth is to

* See Ernst Cassirer, *The Myth of the State* (New Haven: Yale University Press, 1963), chaps. x, xi, xviii. Unfortunately, this very valuable book makes no distinction between myth and mythology.

deprive a human institution of its face, so that it is beyond approach (or reproach). A myth (such as the myth of the state) can exercise immense power when men do *not* recognize the object as a human fabrication. Then men can ascribe to it, and to its "commands," a transcendent importance. Modern political philosophy is capable of thinking of the state in mythic terms (as do Hobbes, Rousseau, Burke, Hegel), as well as in nonmythic or naturalistic terms (as do Machiavelli, Locke, Marx, and Mill).

Some recent commentary sees the mythic approach as beginning with Plato. This is altogether wrong. Plato never says that the state (any state, no matter what its form or purpose) has an importance over that of its individuals. Rather, he says that only pure philosophical wisdom would have such an importance—if, *per impossibile,* it could be embodied in an actual state. Its superior status would be based on the fact that such institutionalized wisdom could grasp a truth no individual, thinking alone, could grasp.

Actually, it is the naturalistic approach of Aristotle that gives the concept of the state its first impetus (but not a mythic impetus). He shows how the state grows out of such natural human institutions as the family and the village. These institutions are entered into merely for the sake of life. Yet for Aristotle the polis (as I indicated) has a higher goal: the good life. Human beings fulfill their humanity in the polis, and for this reason it is prior to the individual. I do not regard this view as mythic. The state is continuous with its natural origins yet is discontinuous with them because its purpose is "beyond" those origins, in morality. This is not to say that its purposes or interests are "beyond" those of its members (which is one of the typical ways of regarding the state as mythic).

Where Aristotle's concern with politics is moral, Machiavelli's concern with morality (namely, public morality) is entirely political. If he is concerned with it at all, it is only to the extent that it can be in some way relevant to the taking or retention of power. In every other respect, morality (public or private) makes no political claim. When he speaks of the Roman republic and characterizes it as having *virtù,* he is speaking not of virtue or of virtuous people but rather of something closer to political health or soundness. I shall discuss this later on. Here I just want to point out the moral neutrality of Machiavelli's political values. For this purpose, I offer the following contrast: Aristotle was the first to characterize man as, by nature, a political animal; that is, by their nature men are morally fulfilled in communal

life. For Machiavelli, too, man is a political animal; but to Machiavelli this means that man is a lover of power and that he fulfills this
need only by exercising power over others in a political setting.[3]

It has often been pointed out that the contiguity of politics and
ethics, in Plato and Aristotle, owes something to the way the Athenian
polis could merge the public and private worlds of its citizens. As a
political institution, the polis is finished by the time Plato comes to
his maturity; yet, if he can say, later on, that the state is the individual writ large, it is because the polis had already established that
identity. Four centuries later, in a part of the world where the polis
had never existed, we are told to render unto Caesar the things that
are Caesar's and to render unto God the things that are God's. For
a Greek, such an idea would reflect the breakdown of the polis; not
only would it mark the demise of participatory democracy, it would
also mean the sundering of public activity from private moral conscience. For modern man, this separation of the two worlds is the
price he is willing to pay for the separation of church and state. In
order to protect his freedom of conscience, therefore, modern man
must separate that moral conscience altogether from his political life—
and this means that the political world is outside the sphere of
judgment by any personal or religious morality.

A further point: When I stress that it is Machiavelli who first
separates politics from ethics, what I mean is that politics is a kind
of *technē* for him, the methodology of attaining and retaining power;
to such aims, moral considerations are irrelevant. He wrote *The Prince*
and the *Discourses* between 1513 and 1519, at a time when older
political values were being dissolved in the acids of social change and
political upheaval. This left the field wide open to political creativity—but "creativity" in the most cynical sense. Where there are no
prior standards serving as restraints, everything is permissible and the
politician is altogether free to experiment. It is in this sense that we
can speak of the state as a "work of art."[4]

It is a kind of creativity that is characteristic of so much of the
Renaissance: a value-neutral creativity like Leonardo's dissections and
(later) Galileo's astronomy. When Machiavelli comes to consider
morality itself, he sees everywhere around him a barefaced duplicity
and corruption—against which his amorality was moral by contrast.
All this was reflected in murderous political strife. With Italy divided
into five parts, the French armies were usually being called in by one
side and the Spaniards by another, and the only result was Italy in

chaos. The remedy was the unification of Italy under one power, and this needed one man strong enough to overwhelm all the others.* The immediate aim of such a man must be to seize power and maintain it. *The Prince* tells him how to do this, and why he must not let moral scruples stand in his way. Only after the ruthless extension of unlimited power could Italy expect to return to the republicanism of Roman times; but that end is so remote that Machiavelli regards it as being beyond reach for his own era.

With that end being unattainable, he could direct his attention to means, and *The Prince* is a book about means. The lesson taught him by his long experience is that the only point in doing politics at all is success, and this goal is attained only if politics is done as an end in itself—as though the means have become the end. Yet, if we must separate means from ends, then we see a political end that is not at all remote: The function of a state is to *be*, to maintain itself in power; to this end, all means are permitted, and they all rest on force. When Aristotle says that the proper goal of a state is the promotion of the moral good of its citizens, he declares that the law is the means toward that end, for the rule of law is the necessary condition of good government. Machiavelli agrees with this view when he speaks of Roman republicanism in the *Discourses*.[5] But in *The Prince* he is speaking about his own time, and he expresses the view (which makes a contrast with that of Aristotle but is not in conflict with it) that force is both a necessary and a sufficient condition for government of any kind.[6] He does, in a way, express the hope of an Italian rebirth following upon Italian unification. Yet everything hinges on national *virtù*, for a corrupt people, once freed, has little chance of maintaining its liberty.[7] Even if a superior prince comes along to give it freedom, this will last only so long as the prince is there to rule; afterward, the people will revert to their earlier corruption. And if a people is corrupt, even the best laws will be to no avail.

Contrary to an impression widely held, Machiavelli does recognize the difference between good and bad governments. He recapitulates Aristotle's division of governments (according to the rule of one, a few, or many, the good types are monarchy, aristocracy, and democracy; their corrupt forms are tyranny, oligarchy, and the lawless form of democracy).[8] There is nothing to prevent the degeneration from

---

* It seems that there is a *telos* here: national unification. (This aim is extolled in the final chapter of *The Prince*.) Yet, for Machiavelli, the game called unification is in no way different from the game of power politics; the method is the same.

good to bad if it is going to happen. The crucial question, as I said, is whether society is healthy or corrupt. Republicanism is not the best system under all circumstances. Republics "work" only for a healthy people; the corrupt need a strong autocrat to control them.

It has been pointed out often enough, in commentaries, that reading *The Prince* alone does not give us a complete picture of Machiavelli's thought. I would put it more strongly and say that the only way we can understand either *The Prince* or the *Discourses* is to read them together and try to reconcile the differences between them. Obviously, that reconciliation must be in Machiavelli's own terms. Thus, one of the false differences raised by some commentators is the difference between *The Prince* in advocating autocracy and the *Discourses* in advocating republicanism. Yet the difference is not at all difficult to resolve once we see that although Machiavelli's heart is with republics he realizes that the corrupt societies of his own time need strong autocrats. After the original lawgiver is gone, it is the republic alone that can go on living according to law and prosper.[9] And, in this setting, a rule by the many is to be preferred because the people are wiser and more stable in judgment than a prince; they are given to fewer excesses, and their mistakes are more easily remedied.[10] The Italians, however, along with the French and the Spanish, are in Machiavelli's view the great corrupters of the world.[11] Italy is the worst of all because it harbors a class of idle nobility, and this is why no republic can exist there. The Italian people have become so degenerate, he says, that no law can restrain them. This is why the only remedy is a ruthless prince who will curb the corrupting influence of the nobility.

Another source of corruption is the papal court, which has destroyed all piety and religion in Italy.[12] This we owe to the Church, he says, as we owe it our continued disunity. Moreover, the Church preaches a corrupt form of Christianity, emphasizing all the wrong virtues. The ancient Romans rewarded greatness with deification, whereas the Church extols humility. Roman religion emphasized action, grandeur, strength, excellence, achievement (all that which can be comprised by the Latin term *virtus* or the Greek *aretē*), whereas Christianity extolls only the strength to suffer. This has enfeebled us, so that we are easy prey for evil men. Machiavelli seems to identify *true* Christianity with such *virtus*; and the false interpretation of Christianity, by the Church, is yet another reason why there are so few republics. Further, our corruption is measured by the fact that we simply have not the love of freedom the Romans had—and only states that are free can be great.[13]

Machiavelli can go readily from a discussion of ancient Rome to Renaissance Florence because he believes that men do not change in any fundamental way. All history is contemporary, and whatever development might appear to occur, human character does not develop. This is why a modern leader can learn from history how to found a republic, maintain a state, form an army, fight a war, dispense justice, and extend his empire. Heaven, the sun, the elements, and men— these have not changed, he says.[14] This approach allows him to exhort the modern hero: "Let no man, therefore, fear that he cannot accomplish what others have done; for all men are alike in that they are born and live and die in the same way." [15] There is also the possibility of prophecy in this approach. Because men are basically alike, we can see by studying the past what is likely to happen in the future. Today's French are the same as the ancient Gauls, which is a good reason not to trust them.*

All men, always and everywhere, are animated by the same desires and passions. The one trait that seems patently universal is that men are after one thing: more. They are never free of ambition; their desire is endless. They desire everything but cannot get it, so dissatisfaction is inevitable.[16] This leads men inevitably into conflict unless there is a stronger force to restrain them. Indeed, human selfishness is such that a man will sooner forgive another for murdering his father than for depriving him of his inheritance! [17] Men will always be evil unless forced to do good.[18] Even when men can gain glory by establishing lawful regimes they are just as likely to choose tyranny. This is why Machiavelli condemns Julius Caesar so bitterly: He could have saved the republican constitution, but he chose to set himself up as tyrant.

Because men are so naturally inclined to evil, nothing much is lost when a ruler suppresses them; if, in suppressing them, he forces them

---

* *Discourses,* III:xliii (hereafter referred to as *D*); see also *D*, I:xxxix. Now see Thucydides, *The Peloponnesian War,* I:22: "human nature being what it is, the events of the past will recur in similar or analogous forms." And David Hume, *Inquiry Concerning Human Understanding,* sec. 8, part I: "Would you know the sentiments, inclinations, and course of life of the Greeks and Romans? Study well the temper and actions of the French and English: . . . Mankind are so much the same, in all times and places, that history informs us of nothing new or strange." For Machiavelli, we understand men of the present by studying men of the past. For Hume, we understand men of the past by studying men of the present.

to do good then that is a plus, and if they turn out to be evil they cannot be much worse than they were. This is why Machiavelli speaks so highly of Cesare Borgia's suppression of the lawlessness of central Italy. He had to resort to bizarre and rather cruel methods, but he was successful—and what criteria are there, other than success? Borgia made use of a fiendish individual, Ramiro d'Orco, whom Machiavelli speaks of as a "cruel and able man," [19] and he uses the words as terms of praise. Cruelty and ability are closely related because they have the identical opposite, weakness, which is the one unpardonable sin.

When the question arises, therefore, as to whether it is better for a prince to be loved or to be feared, the obvious conclusion is that it is better for a prince to be feared: When the people love their prince, that love is in their control and they can grant it or withdraw it. But when they fear their prince, that fear is not in their control but in his.[20] For similar reasons, when a prince conquers a new territory, he should bear in mind that men must be either cajoled or crushed, and although they can take revenge for slight wrongs they cannot take revenge for great ones. So the injury done a man should be such that his vengeance need no longer be feared.[21] The meaning of this is obvious.

Above all, a prince should combine the qualities of a man with those of a beast. (We might savor the impact of these words by realizing that they were written during the high tide of humanism.) For Aristotle, man as a social being is something between a beast and a god, yet neither one entirely.[22] In Machiavelli we find that scope narrowed, and the man-as-god is altogether ignored. Know therefore, he says, that there are two kinds of combat: law and force. The first is that of men, the second of beasts. Because the first way is usually inadequate and short-lived, we must know how to use the second. The prince must therefore be half beast, half man.[23] As to playing the beast, a prince should be both a fox and a lion: The fox can detect traps, as the lion cannot; the lion can frighten the wolves, as the fox cannot.

Regarding the conventional moral values, it is certainly laudable for a prince to keep faith, to be a man of his word, and so on. Yet those who have little regard for such matters are the ones who have achieved great things. The prince ought not to keep faith when it is not in his interest to do so. This would be bad advice if men were good, Machiavelli says, but they are not. Moreover, they are easily deluded by appearances. The prince ought therefore to *seem* to be merciful, faithful, humane, religious—but he ought not to be so, for then he limits himself and is consequently a danger to himself. He must know how not to be good and how to use such knowledge according to the dictates of fortune. That is, he must be ready "to act against faith, against charity, against humanness."[24] To the Italians who read this, the shock value of these words must have been enormous, setting up echoes that clashed with the familiar Latin words for the Christian virtues of faith, hope, and charity.[25]

If we ask what Machiavelli's own values are, we find them embedded in the foregoing paragraph. The first value is contained in the phrase about men who "have achieved great things"—this is the value he calls *virtù*. Another value is contained in the phrase about the "dictates of fortune"—*fortuna*. The meaning of *fortuna* is clear: It is the combination of luck, chance, circumstances, and opportunity. The meaning of *virtù* is rather more difficult to express: It originates in the Latin word for "man" (*vir*), so *virtus* refers to manly or warlike qualities. For Machiavelli, steeped as he is in the Latin writers, *virtù* means everything from extraordinary ability and energy to courage and resolution—but in such a way that these are separated from their objects, and from good and evil; that is, *virtù* is ability, energy, courage, and resolution but considered in themselves and not in an ethical light.[26]

These two linked concepts appear throughout his writings. The greatness of Rome, he says, was due more to virtù than to fortuna—due, that is, more to valor and ability than to circumstances.* The concepts must be regarded as interdependent: Fortune rules only half our actions and allows the other half to be governed by our abilities.[27] A prince who allows himself to be led by fortune is lost when fortune changes. Caution may be right in one case and wrong in another. Generally, because fortune is a woman she is best conquered through impetuosity. Yet what ruins men is that they are set in their ways and cannot adapt their methods and abilities to changing circumstances. Great men owe nothing to fortune except the opportunity it provides, which serves them as the matter to which they give

* *D*, II:i. This is undoubtedly in response to one of the classical views of Roman history—namely, that its greatness "was founded on the rare and almost incredible alliance of virtue and fortune." The historian is Ammianus Marcellinus (b. 330 A.D.), the last of the great Roman historians. Quoted by Edward Gibbon, *The Decline and Fall of the Roman Empire* (New York: Random House, n.d.), Vol. II, chap. xxxi, p. 140.

form by their actions. Without opportunity, their abilities count for nothing; and without such abilities as theirs, the opportunity is wasted on anyone else.[28]

Now this seems to clash with other things Machiavelli says. On one hand, as we saw, he places great emphasis on experience, on how much he has learned from it, and on how useful that experience (Machiavelli's) can be to a prince. We also saw that he emphasizes the uniformity of human character and the predictability of the future from the observation of human character in past history. And yet fortuna rules so much of our lives (at least half) that there can be little certainty in it, if any, and the method that is right in one case is totally wrong in another. Time brings forward all things, and it can as well produce good as evil, or evil as well as good.[29] But if this is so and there is no certainty to be had, then it is pointless to depend upon experience or to expect to learn much from it. The only way experience can teach us is if it is dependably repeatable. Thus, what is the point of telling a prince how to deal with his problems if the method one recommends can as easily be wrong as right? Further, if so much is chancy and subject to fortuna, then it hardly makes sense to say that the future is predictable. If there is no one method or approach that can be expected to succeed in the general run of things, then wisdom and experience cannot count for much, nor could we rely on the supposed uniformity of human character.

Of course, this inconsistency is never remarked upon by Machiavelli, although it might have occurred to him. Perhaps we ought not to demand a systematic consistency from him, for (as I pointed out) he does not have a system at all, and his historico-inductive method can really be used to prove almost anything. In actuality, however, this is neither method nor proof but illustration. There is nothing wrong with that, provided it is not expected to do more than it does: namely, to give concrete examples in support of convictions already held.

A possible way out of the inconsistency is to say that fortuna ought not to be regarded in isolation from virtù—although Machiavelli does treat them separately from time to time.[30] Yet if they ought not to be separated, then their meanings are mutually interdependent: fortuna is the "matter" to which virtù gives "form"; that is, virtù fulfills fortuna. Aristotle had said (although Machiavelli does not mention it) that neither form nor matter is ever found in isolation in nature. I cannot be certain that Machiavelli intended to give us nothing more than a series of illustrations, but if he did then perhaps we can take his use of the matter–form relation as nothing more than an illustration to show that abilities without opportunity are useless and opportunities without ability are wasted.

All this is used in the service of historic exhortation. Thus, he suggests that heroes such as Moses, Cyrus, and Theseus could liberate their peoples because these men could summon the virtù that would answer the challenge raised by fortuna. And he suggests that Lorenzo de' Medici (to whom *The Prince* is dedicated) is the man of virtù to exploit the opportunities Italy now provides.[31] Italy now is more enslaved than were the Israelites, more oppressed than the Persians, and more dispersed than the Athenians. Presumably, Machiavelli would have to say that the liberator of Italy must possess a virtù combining that of Moses, Cyrus, and Theseus. It is almost as though Machiavelli believes this—for his hero must overcome *all* limits, whether religious, moral, or civic.

The new hero, thus, would operate without guidelines. This is the positive side of the idea of political "creativity." (The negative side, as we saw, is embodied in the unscrupulous political criminal who is "creative" in the sense that he will stop at nothing, reject no possibility fortuna may present.) Another positive side of political "creativity" is expressed in the phrase *raison d'état*. For the sake of the country's safety, there can be no reservations regarding the justice or injustice, the humanity or cruelty, the honor or shame of an action or policy. The ultimate consideration can be only: What will preserve the life and liberty of the country?[32]

We need not have the dangers of such a doctrine pointed out to us. We can easily see the similarities between the positive and negative kinds of political "creativity" and how easy it is to go from the one to the other or invoke the one for the sake of the other. There is no question that Machiavelli's writings have contributed (with or without his intention) to the cynical and corrupt use of that doctrine in the *Realpolitik* of modern totalitarians. Regarding the totalitarian use of the myth of the state, I suggested earlier that the criticism of this can be found in Machiavelli himself. He would say that there can be nothing intrinsically wrong in the tyrant's exploitation of such a myth. What is wrong is in the people who accept it and take it seriously. This goes with what he says about men being easily fooled by appearances. But, in addition to this, if they are so lacking in virtù that they fall for this mythical line, then this only shows that people get the tyrant they deserve.

Considering political "creativity" on the positive side, Machiavelli says that a nation that will not sacrifice all for its life *and* liberty is not much of a nation, and again it deserves its inevitable tyrant. National life and liberty, then, are Machiavelli's highest values. (We are speaking of liberty from foreign domination, not personal liberty.) In the interest of those values, no possibilities should be left unexplored. And the man of virtù will have the vision and the courage to explore them.

Let me end with a note about methodology. I said that Machiavelli's work can best be understood as "illustration." Whether or not he intended it as such, I maintain that it can best be understood in that way. I know that the word "illustration" is vague, but I choose it for that reason, because its flexibility settles all sorts of seeming contradictions in Machiavelli's thinking. One of these is the apparent contradiction between description and prescription: The one side says that Machiavelli is only a political scientist; the other side says that he is only a political moralist. This artificial division has some unacceptable results, one of which, as we saw, is the view that Machiavelli has no values and is "purely" scientific. Yet there is evidence in his writings for both views, if we want to read him in this partial way. The point is, of course, that we must read him so that both views are there, come into conflict, and are reconciled.

I have quoted from his dedications to *The Prince* and the *Discourses,* showing his self-avowed aim of approaching his subject in a factual manner. In chapter xv of *The Prince* he repeats that factual aim, making a sharp distinction between it and any prescriptive ideal, the distinction between *is* and *ought.* Others may speculate about ideal states, he says, but my concern is to enter into the factual truth of the matter.[33] The disparity between the way men are and the way they ought to be is so great, he says, that "he who ignores what *is,* in favor of what *ought* to be, will accomplish nothing but his own destruction."[34] And yet this passage begins with his expressed aim of writing something useful, something that will help to direct a course of action—so that it is obvious that he does intend to prescribe. The resolution to this problem is that he *prescribes* from the standpoint of his view of what men *are,* not from the standpoint of what they *ought* to be. Thus, he prescribes descriptively (and this is where the "illustration" comes in). Think of the difference between persuading someone as to the truth of a factual description and persuading someone to follow a course of action. It is clear to me that Machiavelli does both of these separately; but in addition, as I said, he prescribes a course of action on the basis of his description (illustration) of what men are.* This shows us something of the complexity of his thinking—and also that the distinction between description and prescription may be not as sharp as we had thought.

Another point: What is missing in Machiavelli's use of the term *virtù* is, first, a definition of it and, second, a prescription as to how to achieve it. Virtù seems to be an imponderable, itself a thing of fortuna, to be neither produced nor expected as the result of prior conditions. Thus, we can speak of political "creativity" *chez* Machiavelli and of political values *chez* Machiavelli but not of the creation of those values nor of the creation of the circumstances in which such values would be found. They are not prepared for or produced, in the way that Plato's Republic is consciously designed to produce wisdom and justice. For Machiavelli, virtù and fortuna can merely be reflected in action—and this is yet another reason for regarding his work as "illustration."

Because he never speaks of values being produced, he does not construct a society that will produce them. And because he is not concerned with such a (hypothetical, prescriptive) construction, he has no theory of justice, of human rights, or of political obligation. The final challenge he lays down for subsequent thinkers, therefore, is to ask them to think of man in *purely* political terms, as a political animal and nothing more, and upon this base to construct a form of society that will of itself engender these purely political values.

---

* For this point I am indebted to the excellent introduction by John Plamenatz in his edition of *The Prince* and selections from the *Discourses* and other writings (London: Fontana, 1972), p. 13.

# HOBBES

## The State as Mortal God

**"Myself and Fear"** In the century and a half between *The Prince* (1513) and Hobbes's *Leviathan* (1651) the world underwent profound political and spiritual changes. Yet the atmosphere of passion and terror remained. Thomas Hobbes was born when his mother miscarried at hearing the news of the approach of the Spanish Armada in 1588. Later in life, Hobbes said that his mother gave birth to twins: "myself and fear."[1] This remark reveals much about the man. His twin never left him. Hobbes felt it necessary to flee to the Continent on a number of occasions. The world of his experience most certainly continued to support and reinforce his anxieties. Indeed, Hobbes's philosophical work can be seen as a lifelong relation to fear. This insight enables us to see how the various aspects of his philosophy fit together.

We see, to begin with, how the private fear and the public situation of uncertainty dissolve into one another—until the need for internal psychological security is expressed in his constant emphasis on the need for external political security. His highest political value is peace—at all costs—and the worst thing he can imagine happening, he says, is civil war. Perhaps this close connection between his inner needs and his outer demands explains why Hobbes sees such a close theoretical continuity between the sciences of psychology and politics. His political theory calls for repression because his psychological theory shows man to be a creature of violence; the political situation around him generated the psychological theory. This continuity between the sciences is one of Hobbes's basic axioms: A proper political theory, he says, must find its justification in a psychological description of man as an individual (and that psychology is ultimately reducible to a physics of motion): "the principles of politics consist in the knowledge of the motions of the mind."[2]

The form he gave to his philosophy came from the new sciences, which aimed at a unified theory to explain all of nature. Earlier, medieval science had heeded the words in Isaiah about there being two worlds and therefore two kinds of knowledge: divine and human, celestial and terrestrial.[3] Thus, there was a celestial physics and a terrestrial physics. Galileo overthrew this distinction entirely, maintaining that there is one physics governing the universe as a whole. Machiavelli had had a similar idea about political theory, namely, that there is no higher world, whether Platonic or Christian, to dictate the values men must hold to in their political behavior. The new astronomy and physics were to break all ties with theology; and in a similar way political theory, too, was to become scientific and secular. What was lacking in Machiavelli's theory was a basis in mathematics or in some other formal foundation. Hobbes was inspired by Galileo's achievements in mathematical physics, and he would try to provide such a formal basis for political theory.

Galileo, for the first time in history, had employed mathematics in describing physical phenomena such as the swing of the pendulum and the acceleration of a freely falling body. The ultimate aim was to describe *all* physical phenomena in mathematical terms, so that mathematics would unify all the sciences and give them absolute certainty. These aims were exactly what Hobbes was looking for in political theory: unity and certainty. Unity would give to political theory a foundation in another science, psychology. And certainty (wonderful dream!) would lead to the overcoming of differences between men, so that all political strife would finally be at an end. Naively or not, Hobbes saw in the certainties of geometry a way of overcoming the discord, the fear and insecurity, that plagued his era. Machiavelli had great historical insight and sophisticated common sense, but these alone would not do—they could provide no formal certainty. Only a science could provide this, and it would have to be a science going back to the most elementary principles, from which all else would be deduced with absolute rigor. What else but mathematics could convince men universally? What Hobbes aims for, then, is a rational reconstruction of society based on first principles.[4]

What are these first principles? Galileo's science of dynamics studied the point in motion, the unextended point traversing extended space. Puzzling as this idea might be, the mathematical formulation made the idea clear and unchallengeable to anyone who would just think. When, in 1634, Hobbes fled for his life to the Continent, he frequented the company of men such as Galileo and Descartes, among others, and was inspired by Galileo's example to create a similar science of the point in motion—but this time the point would be man.[5] Thus, Hobbes claims to do for political theory what Galileo had done for physics: In considering civil society, we break the thing down into its constituent parts, thereby arriving at a basic human nature as revealed in the individual, the point. Then we put the parts together again, to see how and why men form states. When we see men's real reasons behind this, we can then show them how to avoid trouble and confusion.

As to the idea of man as a point in motion, the picture Hobbes gives us is the same vision of the world as that given by the new physics: atoms moving blindly, bodies striking bodies, moved by impulse but with no goal. In man, the motivating impulses are desire and fear, and the result is incessant conflict. Following Galileo, Hobbes opposes the Aristotelian idea of things moving toward some goal and then coming to rest; on the contrary, things in motion tend to stay in motion.[6] When he applies these physical principles to man, Hobbes says that "there is no such thing as perpetual tranquility of mind, while we live here; because life itself is but motion, and can never be without desire, nor without fear, no more than without sense."[7]

In man there is a ceaseless motion and pulsation, a flow of desires. Perhaps Hobbes's friend William Harvey had suggested this with his discovery of the circulation of the blood in 1628. This, too, was an application of the Galilean approach, and the proof Harvey gave was mathematical also. The capacity of the heart as a pump, the frequency of its pulsations, and the quantity of blood in the body—all this could be explained only on the basis of the circulation of the blood. Here, then, is the quantitative connection between physiology and mathematics. Similarly, Hobbes attempts to establish a connection between psychology and physics, with the aim of basing political science on psychology. This would give us the continuity of the sciences, one leading out of the other, each deriving its mathematical certainty from the more abstract science. Political science would then be based on psychology, and psychology in turn would be based on physics.

Such a proposed continuity between the sciences would be considered highly questionable today. As early as 1637, Hobbes conceived of a unified system comprising the concepts of Body, Man, and Citizen, with three corresponding sciences—physics, psychology, and political theory—each in turn established on the one before, and all established on the basis of a single set of mechanical principles.[8] But we are soon led to wonder whether, for example, the physical law of inertia could be applied in any way other than figuratively to problems of psychology and politics. Concerning this dependence of political science on the natural sciences, the question usually raised is whether Hobbes sees it as a dependency of method or of material (that is, form or content) or both. As I have suggested, there is no doubt that Hobbes wants to follow Galileo's method of analysis and synthesis, breaking down a phenomenon and then building it up again.[9] But besides this emulation of the form of the physical sciences, Hobbes intends also to establish a continuity of content between physics and political science.

With this aim the trouble starts; for if we say that the value and cogency of Hobbes's political philosophy depends on the soundness of his physical theories (as Hobbes himself insists), then we must admit that we (today) cannot accept his rather simplified physical base for his psychology and politics. And then the continuity is exploded, and the political theory must therefore be valueless to us. It is not so, however. The fact remains that Hobbes's political theory continues to be of interest as one of the most lucid arguments for authoritarianism. But what can we learn from Hobbes if we do not take his system "whole," as he intended it?

I have a possible solution to this dilemma. We can accept Hobbes's intention of creating an interconnected system. Yet, although the foundation is descriptive (that is, rooted in physical and psychological description), the final political theory is not descriptive but prescriptive (in a very complex way, which I shall explain). And even the concept of "prescription" ought to be taken in a special sense here. That is, he is not telling us how political societies actually *are*, and he is not even prescribing how they *ought* to be (as I shall show); rather, he is prescribing only how some *concepts* ought to be used and how they might make sense—concepts such as authority and sovereignty, for example.

For this reason, his stress on the continuity of the sciences need not trouble us at all. It certainly has troubled many fine scholars. Peters, for example, says that Hobbes is making the mistake of reducing his political values to psychology and that this is the mistake of trying to base a prescriptive *ought* on a descriptive *is*, of trying to base a judgment of value on a statement of fact.[10] This is the mistake Hume says runs through most of ethical writing.[11] As I shall show later, Hobbes cannot be said to be prescribing in this sense, and so the charge against him is not justified.

Let us try to understand the continuity of the sciences according to Hobbes. For him, the difference between political science, psychology, and physics is a quantitative difference—a difference in scope, scale, and measurement. It is a shifting of lenses merely. That is, political science is merely a more complex version of psychology, just as psychology is merely a more complex version of physics. He argues: Are not all political beings also psychological beings, and are these not physical beings as well? We are looking at nothing more than three aspects of one and the same material reality. It is a small step from this view of a material continuity in the object to a formal continuity of explanation (so that the truths of each science are actually derivable from the truths of the others). Hobbes can be credited with one of the first expressions of the modern program of a unified science (outlined in other ways by Descartes and Leibniz). That program has turned out to be illusory. In our own time, there is little left of it but the view (held by Carnap and other physicalists) that psychological descriptions must be translatable, ultimately, into physical descriptions and that psychology is a branch of physics.

It should be emphasized that the aspect of Galileo's work that inspired Hobbes, and that Hobbes sought to follow, was not Galileo's experimentation and observation but rather his application of a process of Euclidean deduction to empirical phenomena. Hobbes probably has such a Galilean mathematics in mind when he says: "when we calculate the magnitude and motions of heaven or earth, we do not ascend into heaven that we may divide it into parts, or measure the motions thereof, but we do it sitting still in our closets or in the dark."[12] This, then, is his idea of what a science should be; science is not a business of empirical description but a process of pure theoretical reasoning.

His fascination with mathematics goes back to an earlier time, before his trip to the Continent and his meeting with Galileo. Hobbes's friend Aubrey describes how stunned Hobbes was, at age forty, upon "discovering" Euclidean geometry. He happens to open a copy of Euclid, reads the proof of the Pythagorean theorem, and swears roundly, "By God, this is impossible!" But he reads back to the propositions upon which this proof is based until he is "demonstratively convinced" of its truth. Aubrey says, "This made him in love with geometry."[13] It also served him as an example of what it means to be won over, absolutely and completely. And if such conviction is possible in mathematics, why not also in politics? Such formal truth, once demonstrated, cannot be shaken. All doubt is overcome. The paradigm of such truth is geometrical axiomatization, where all propositions are deduced from a handful of axioms. Axiomatization becomes, therefore, one of Hobbes's main aims for political theory, even though he does not achieve it and does not practice systematic deduction in any strict sense. Yet—as I began by saying—it is quite clear to me that Hobbes intends to achieve with his theory a certainty that would serve as the emotional counterbalance to the utter uncertainty of the age.

A further aspect of Hobbes's philosophical system is his combination of materialism and mechanism: Materialism is the idea that all real things are basically matter in motion and that all supposedly nonmaterial events (such as thoughts) can be explained only as material events; and mechanism is the idea that all phenomena are explainable only in terms of the antecedent causes working upon them, rather than in terms of any ultimate purpose after the event. These principles are of vital importance for him, because the continuity of the sciences is conceivable only if all things are the same in kind, that is, basically material. And if external political security can serve the purpose of providing internal psychological security, it is only because everything can now be given the same material explanation. To this materialism Hobbes adds a mechanistic view to show the causal interconnection between material objects. Man, too, is seen in this light as a machine: "life is but a motion of limbs, the beginning whereof is in some principal part within. . . . For what is the heart but a spring; and the nerves, but so many strings; and the joints, but so many wheels?"[14]

This is a naturalistic approach that usually rules out any reference to supernatural values. And yet Hobbes does speak of God as creator and speaks of the laws of nature as fashioned by God. What, then, is his purpose in presenting this mechanical image of man? Hobbes's purpose is revealed in a clause I omitted in the passage just quoted: "For seeing life is but a motion of limbs, . . . why may we not say that all automata (engines that doth move themselves by springs and

wheels as doth a watch) have an artificial life?" Then he goes on to
speak of human life as being artificial as well, because it is the artifice
of God! And if human life is artifice, then there is an even greater
work of conscious creation—the state, the great Leviathan—that is
artificial and the work of man. The purpose of all this is to establish
the material continuity between the world of material things, men
and states. And on the basis of this material continuity, there is the
continuity in the fact that all has been *made* (some of it by God, the
rest by man); and if the state, too, has been made, then it should
reflect certain elements of rational purpose. Let us see how that
rational purpose is revealed.

To see this, we must go back to what is natural, not artificial,
about man. We saw that Hobbes begins with certain postulates about
human physical nature, and these are immediately translated into as-
sumptions about human psychological nature. Let us recall his statement that "there is no such thing as perpetual tranquility of mind,
while we live here; because life itself is but motion, and can never
be without desire, nor without fear, no more than without sense."[15]
Notice the phrase "because life is but motion" (which Machiavelli
would never say, either as premise or as conclusion; he simply did not
feel that his political views needed a basis in another science). According to Hobbes, the physical motion that is characteristic of life
in general is matched by man's psychological restlessness. Sensation,
for example, is caused not by constant motion or rest but by *changes*
in motion.[16] Thus, I do not sense my clothing when its contact with
my body is continuous; sensation occurs only when the usual contact
is changed or interrupted.[17] Sensation and life itself are therefore
characterized by inconstancy. The law of inertia had already been
stated by Galileo as a law of all physical existence; Hobbes now
restated the law so as to apply to life—but to apply (as I said) in
only a figurative sense. Life is seen as inertia's opposite: Things tend
to rest or to move at a constant rate, but sensation and life are incon-
stant motion, the "alternate succession of appetite and fear." Notice,
also, in Hobbes's statement his way of not only associating desire and
fear but also of seeing both as aspects of motion.

Desire and fear alternate in us as though they were reflexes. Desire
drives us forward, bringing us into conflict with others, and as a result
fear then drives us back. When we have recovered from our fear,
desire drives us forward once more, and so on. This, for Hobbes, is
the human equivalent of Galileo's point in motion: The human point

is nothing but the individual in the grip of infinite and insatiable desire. For Hobbes this is fundamental and axiomatic: "in the first place, I put for a general inclination of all mankind, a perpetual and restless desire of power after power, that ceaseth only in death."[18]

The difference between desire and fear is that desire is irrational whereas fear is rational. Desire is destructive because it leads to conflict; fear is constructive because it leads men to take measures to preserve themselves.* In any case, both impulses are basic to man's nature, Hobbes says. Man shuns death "by a certain impulsion of nature, no less than that whereby a stone moves downward."[19] To save themselves from death men employ reason; reason is thereby seen as an instrument of natural fear.[20] And it is out of fear that men are led to create society and to erect all their social values.

This is not far from Machiavelli's view of man. But where Machiavelli lacks an elaborated theoretical basis for systematizing his shrewd observations, Hobbes now offers such a basis—so that further conclusions may be seen to follow from the truths already postulated, and so that that view may itself be seen as a conclusion from even more basic premises.

Thus, the concept of the point in motion gives us the concepts of desire and fear, as special cases of motion. Next, desire leads to conflict, whereas fear leads to peace—and in each case the connection is intended to be deductive rather than merely empirical and contingent. How does Hobbes arrive at these conclusions? Let us remember that he is still "describing" man in his natural condition, before society has been formed. In that condition, man is moved by desire, as we saw in the quotation above. The completion of that quotation explains how desire leads to conflict—"leads," as I said, in a logically necessary way:

in the first place, I put for a general inclination of all mankind, a perpetual and restless desire of power after power, that ceaseth only in death. And the cause of this, is not always that a man hopes for a more intense delight than he has already attained to; or that he cannot be content with a moderate power: but because he cannot assure the power and means to live well, which he hath present, without the acquisition of more.[21]

The words "in the first place" suggest that the "general inclination" is to be taken as axiomatic to what follows. The words about "intense

---

* One might stretch and reverse the Freudian terminology here and speak of desire as *thanatos*, the death wish, whereas fear is *eros*, the life force.

delight" show that Hobbes is not talking within the factual framework of hedonism; "desire" is more inclusive and abstract a term than is "pleasure" (because pleasure is only one of the things desired)—and though pleasure is variable and contingent, desire is seen by Hobbes as altogether fundamental. Further, the words "the cause of this" may possibly convey the impression that Hobbes sees desire as *following* from acquisition. Yet he tells us that men are always out for more because their desires are primary and because they cannot satisfy these desires without protecting them through further acquisition.

The reason for this is in the fact that nature has made men fairly equal in their strengths and abilities.[22] If one man happens to be superior in strength, he is not so superior as to be able to overcome a few men acting together against him. From this equality there arises equality of hope in fulfilling our desires. And this latter equality leads us into conflict with one another. (If one of us were sufficiently superior in strength to subdue all the rest, there would be no conflict but peace.) Therefore, as long as no man is strong enough to overcome all others in a conclusive way, there will be strife. As he says: "during the time men live without a common power to keep them all in awe, they are in that condition which is called war; and such a war as is of every man against every man."[23]

Thus, it is their equality of powers that turns men against one another and isolates them from one another. In such a situation there is no possibility of men living by their own effort and industry; there is no art or culture. There is only "continual fear and danger of violent death; and the life of man solitary, poor, nasty, brutish, and short."[24]

**"Every Man against Every Man"**   Where did Hobbes get this fearful picture of man in the natural situation? Obviously, he had merely to look around him, at his own era. The conflict between Royalists and Parliamentarians created a bloodbath in Britain. Undoubtedly it is this Britain, the Britain of his experience, to which he points when he describes life in the state of nature as a war of every man against every man. Yet this means that he is looking at the condition of his own society for a picture of man's condition *before* society. This is perfectly in order: Because he must ultimately come back to men as they now are, he begins with them and strips away all that is acquired (as artificial and inessential), in order to find man in his true nature. Take away the last remnant of civilization and you find man the wolf—*that* is his real nature.

In presenting a picture of man in his "natural" condition, the state of nature, Hobbes is not intending to describe the actual condition of men as they existed "before" they formed societies. He admits that there never was such a time when this warlike condition was the general situation of men everywhere—although he imagines that there must be some places (for example, America) where men live in this way even now. He says that he is merely showing what life *would* be like without civilization, what it would be like for men who *have* lived under government to degenerate into civil war.[25] He is offering us an illustrative model of the logical alternative to civil society—the way men would be if left to their natural inclinations. In the words of Macpherson, Hobbes's description of the state of nature depicts "the behavior to which men as they now are, men who live in civilized societies and have the desires of civilized men, would be led if all law and contract enforcement . . . were removed."[26]

This point is worth emphasizing, because so much of the criticism of Hobbes (from his day to our own) consists in empirical arguments to the effect that men never have actually lived in this way, that they never actually "formed" civil societies that made them human, because they are not men until they *are* in society, and so on. But this criticism is entirely out of place if what Hobbes is presenting is not intended as an actual description. I suggested earlier that Hobbes is not painting a factual picture but that he is following Galileo's method of analysis and synthesis. The picture is therefore not descriptive but hypothetical. According to Hobbes's own words (when he admits that the state of nature never was a general condition of mankind), he is offering us not an empirical picture of presocial man but only a theoretical model of how man (as we know him) *would be* if he were without society. The function of this model is to shed light on the meaning and purpose of a state, any state per se, and thus to show how we can make sense of concepts such as authority, obligation, and so on.

The trouble with Hobbes is that he claims for his system a greater deductive rigor than he actually achieves with it. He thinks of himself as the Euclid-*cum*-Galileo of political science. And *if* he had actually succeeded in establishing political science on purely rational principles, then it would be a science entirely independent of experience (like geometry or pure physics). There is no point in telling a geometrician that his science of perfectly straight lines and perfectly round circles is without a basis in experience. He would agree, of course, that he had never actually seen such things, but he would be right to remind us that he is not concerned with lines or circles as seen. Now Peters says that Hobbes's attempted formalism is misguided, especially as he aims at actually changing society.[27] Yet this concrete aim has nothing to do with the formal cogency (or incogency) of his argument. This is a matter of how he argues from his basic premises to his conclusions. It is the argument itself we must consider, regardless of its concrete applications and regardless of the polemical aims Hobbes may have had in view. With that in mind, we must agree with the statement by Leo Strauss: "The state of nature is thus for Hobbes not an historical fact, but a necessary construction."[28]

There is another question often raised in connection with Hobbes's depiction of man's nature. This question is of a deeper sort, questioning the consistency of Hobbes's picture of man as antisocial—in the light of the obvious fact that men *do* come together into societies. It is asked: If men are so warlike, how could they have got together long enough to form society? (I shall be dealing with this question a little later on, at a number of places in the Hobbes chapter.) Further, if it is in men's nature to make war, then how can Hobbes consider the repressively peaceful society to be more consistent with human nature?[29] And if the sovereign state is consistent with human nature, then how can there possibly be such a thing as political disorder?[30] Yet these are not questions about consistency, actually, but questions about factual possibilities. And such considerations are as irrelevant here as they would be, say, in connection with the master–slave scenario in Hegel's *Phenomenology*: Can we object to Hegel's discussion by saying that the relation, as he describes it, has never been observed?

The point of Hobbes's state-of-nature model, then, is to show that the essence of the state (although artificially constructed) arises out of human nature and human needs and not from some other source such as Divine Right. Further, it shows that the essence of *all* government is in being repressive. The answer to the questions just stated, therefore, can be found in Hobbes's own words: "I deny not that men . . . *desire* to come together. But civil societies are not mere meetings, but bonds, to the making whereof faith and compacts are necessary."[31]

As to the question of whether the presocial condition of man or the civil society is more consistent with man's nature, Hobbes (as we saw) speaks of the former as natural and of the latter as artificial or conventional. Yet both are consistent with man's nature, because of the endless interplay between irrational desire and rational fear— between a centrifugal (let us say Dionysian) individualism and the centripetal (Apollonian) drive toward the life of collective society.

In the war of all against all, men are not sociable by inclination. Only reason and the fear of death drive men into some sort of union— and only coercion through fear of the sword keeps them to it. Hobbes says that man is born unfit for society and that he has to be *made* fit for society. And this only society itself can do. The problem is how to pass from the fear of death to the rational realization that only in society is there safety. For Hobbes, these two aspects are complementary; this very fear is what leads men to seek the means to evade death. Of course, man's desire fights him all the way: "the dispositions of men are naturally such, that except they be restrained through fear of some coercive power, every man will distrust and dread each other."[32] For if we could imagine people submitting *without* coercion to the rule of society or to the rule of one individual, then we could (Hobbes says) imagine all mankind capable of doing the same—and then there would be no need of *any* civil government, "because there would be peace without subjection."[33] Yet we see that there is no peace without subjection (not as a matter of contingent fact but due to the essential nature of human desires), and in this universal truth man's nature is revealed. There are some creatures (bees, ants) that are naturally sociable, but man is not one of them. It is merely consistent with his *selfish* nature for him to want to protect himself by entering *society!*

Man would not enter society if he did not need it to save himself. In this light, Hobbes's picture of the political animal differs fundamentally from the pictures offered by Plato and Aristotle. Where Aristotle had stressed man's innate social nature, Hobbes believes that man is naturally competitive, aggressive, and selfish, so that his sociality is artifice and contrivance. Where Plato had depicted an ideal state in which public and private interests are united as one, Hobbes believes man is always in pursuit of his private good, even if he has to make use of social means to protect it.

There is an even greater contrast to be made: Plato had sought to give to social and ethical values a metaphysical basis in a transcendent reality. The "right" and "good" were seen as having an ideal status beyond time, prior to all life or human culture; and it is the special task of the philosopher–king to rule in the light of such values. Now Hobbes offers the greatest possible contrast to this view. Before society comes into being, there are no values, no right or wrong. Prior to the imposition of civilizing restraint, human rapacity is boundless: Every man desires everything, and every man in the state of nature has the "right" to everything. This means, in effect, that no one has any rights in the presocial situation, least of all the right of property— because I cannot *rightfully* exclude someone from appropriating what is "mine." Not even my body is my own, so that if someone enslaves me I cannot *justifiably* object. In this state of war, a man "owns" something only as long as he can hold on to it, and when it is taken from him he can have no *legitimate* claim or complaint.

This holds for all values: In the absence of a coercive power, there is no one to make a decision as to justice or injustice, and so there can be no sense in speaking of actions as being just or unjust:

To this war of every man against every man, this also is consequent: that nothing can be unjust. The notions of right and wrong, justice and in-justice, have there no place. Where there is no common power, there is no law; where no law, no injustice. . . . Justice and injustice are none of the faculties neither of the body nor mind. If they were, they might be in a man that were alone in the world, as well as his senses and passions. They are qualities that relate to men in society, not in solitude.[34]

In this connection, Hobbes draws an important implication: that governments have imposed peace only *within* the state, by controlling their subjects. Outside the state, however, it is a different matter. As long as governments are subject to no higher power to restrain and control them, they remain in a natural state of war regarding one another. This, too, is a war of all against all, even if there are no open hostilities. In the way that it was for individuals in the state of nature, so it is for civil states in their dealings with one another: They operate in a value–neutral framework; each has the "right" to every-thing; there is no right or wrong, no justice or injustice, in interna-tional relations, and presumably there can be no legitimate claim or complaint when a state is deprived of its territory by another. Be-tween states, such value notions have no meaning, because there is no higher power to impose such notions or enforce them. Again: "Where there is no common power, there is no law; where no law, no injustice."[35]

The point in all this is to show that moral values are not part of the universal fabric of things but are artificial. They are not natural predispositions or faculties in man: "If they were, they might be in a man that were alone in the world"—that is, in a man who never had had contact with other human beings—but it is ridiculous to imagine that he would have such "natural" values innately, without the inter-personal framework that produces them. If values, therefore, must be created artificially and must be imposed by a higher power, then it is ridiculous to expect governments (who are like men alone to them-selves) to observe moral restraints and hold to moral values toward one another on a "natural" basis.

How does Hobbes's picture of man's nature reflect on man's "moral" character? The fact that Hobbes is looking to his own society in order to form a picture of life without society is clear when he asks us to consider how our fears are operative even here and now: Does not a man arm himself when going on a journey? Do we not lock our doors and chests when at home?[36] And, in so doing, do we not im-plicitly accuse our fellow citizens? The danger is bad enough even when there is an overall power to protect us and to make transgressors of the law fear punishment. But consider how life would be without such an overall power. Without it there is war.

Yet Hobbes insists man's nature is not evil or sinful—because the values by which we would condemn men are created only within society. The law decides what is good and what is evil; so the law does not reflect any values existing prior to society, nor is it justified by such values—simply because there are no such prior values. Every-thing begins with society itself and with its law. This may be taken in a cynical light—as though a Creon or a Thrasymachus were to say that whatever the ruling power declares to be right is right. Yet in Hobbes this idea has a humanistic and a positive aspect: The religious tradition had said that man (Adam) is evil, even without society. This is the theological version of a "state of nature," as opposed to the subsequent "state of grace" that makes men good. But now Hobbes shows that man is morally neutral by "nature" and that it is possible for man to achieve happiness and goodness by his own ef-forts, without God's grace—and that such happiness and goodness are entirely a matter of men's ability to form society and control it rationally.[37] Thus, Hobbes's emphasis on the idea that the law is artificial and man-made (rather than of divine origin) can be seen as part of the general secularization of Western culture in the modern era and the liberation of man to his own responsibility.

For Hobbes, the consideration of man in his essence leads to the view that in the state of nature man's condition is riddled with uncertainty. That this is necessarily so serves to connect the state of nature with the idea of life in general. Inconstancy is what characterizes them both: The human tendency is neither toward rest nor toward steady change but toward violent and chaotic change. If this is natural to man, then the state must impose an artificial order and constancy. Given the selfish nature of man, that artificial order would have to be harshly repressive. But this is justified by the fact that there is only one alternative to such repression, and that would be the chaos that would make life itself impossible. It is part of Hobbes's limitation as a thinker, and yet a mark of his time, that he could envisage no other possibilities than extreme repression or extreme chaos.

"The Mortal God"   We have seen how the idea of man's natural condition, prior to the formation of the civil state, points to the idea of what the ultimate purpose of the state must be. Because war in the condition of nature is so destructive, the one and only purpose of the artificial construction known as the civil state is to make it possible for life to go on. But the question was raised: How can men who are by nature so warlike arrive at the point of cooperating in the formation of a state? The answer that Hobbes gives is that the desire and fear that divide men also incline them toward peace—if the fear and desire are combined with reason. It is reason that suggests to men how they can help themselves, and the solutions they come to are the dictates of reason. Indeed, Hobbes considers these conclusions to be so apparent to reason that he calls them Laws of Nature.[38] Before we go into these, there is another point to be made.

There is in each man the aim of self-preservation—and in this connection let us recall Hobbes's statement that it is as natural for men to shun death as it is for a stone to fall downward. The aim of avoiding death is therefore so basic that Hobbes calls it a Natural Right, and in Hobbes's view it is the one and only natural right we have. By giving that natural aim so exalted a title, he seeks to extend and validate it, so that it is no merely personal inclination and so that it is the right of each man to use *any* means to save himself. Corresponding to this Natural Right, there is the first of Hobbes's Laws of Nature, that forbidding self-destruction.

Now we shall see that all these Laws of Nature are stated in the form of prescriptions—that is, the prescription of means to serve the one and only end of survival. In each case, the prescription is not moralistic but instrumental, practical. Thus, it is a dictate of reason "that every man ought to endeavor peace, as far as he has hope of obtaining it; and when he cannot obtain it, that he may seek and use all helps and advantages of war."[39] Thus, the first Law of Nature (the obligation to seek peace where possible) is a reflection of man's Natural Right to self-preservation. This may seem so obvious as to be axiomatic—and that is exactly the status Hobbes wants to give this idea. It must be entirely obvious and self-evident, so that what follows from it will be equally unquestionable.

Life *thrusts* to maintain itself, and it is therefore simply contrary to life's own nature to destroy itself. Now we must regard all this in a value-neutral sense. We must stress that for Hobbes this obligation falls not within the scope of morality but merely within the scope of naturalistic description—as though we might observe (neutrally) that each living thing seeks naturally to promote its own life. This is why this first Law of Nature is almost abstract and skeletal. Yet it is of immense consequence for Hobbes: This bare and value-neutral idea determines the subsequent role and value of the state.

It is obviously impossible for peace to be secured or for life to go on in a war of all against all, where every man has the right to every-thing. It therefore follows as a second Law of Nature that men ought to give up their infinite right to everything, if others do so as well. It is therefore obligatory (not in a moral but simply in a practical sense) "that a man be willing, when others are so too—as far-forth, as for peace and defense of himself he shall think it necessary—to lay down his right to all things, and be contented with so much liberty against other men as he would allow other men against himself."[40] What this amounts to is that each man stands out of the other man's way, so "that he may enjoy his own original right." For the benefit of not being hindered ourselves, we give up the freedom to hinder another person.

Now any arrangement based on this idea alone would be extremely tenuous. How could we trust others to abide by this obligation? The problem arises in the phrase "lay down his right." It contains the germ of the social contract—but without enforcement no right has been laid down, no contract has been made, no peace secured. Hobbes merely enunciates the second Law of Nature at this point, in order to show that reciprocity is a "dictate of reason." This rational element will ultimately take its place in the establishment of the civil state.

The third Law of Nature is "that men perform their covenants made."[41] This law, like the second, also points forward to the eventual formation of the social contract, and it aims at showing that the contract as well as the observance of it are rational—even though the observance will have to be ensured by the sword. What it means is that all agreements are binding, even though they be contracted before the coming into being of the civil society that alone makes such things as contracts meaningful. A man would have no grounds for claiming, therefore, that the contract he made earlier, in the state of nature, is now invalid because he made it in fear or under duress. (Hobbes says that even such contracts are valid as when we are held at gunpoint and agree to pay a certain sum of money later on in exchange for life.) Nor could a man claim later that the contract is invalid because he was a mere savage when he made it. Without this third Law of Nature, men would implicitly retain their unlimited right to everything, and then any contract would be worthless and war inevitable. This third law, then, is the basis of justice: Without such a Law of Nature (in the natural situation), no right has actually been given up. The keeping of a covenant is dictated by reason and is therefore a law of nature—because the keeping of covenants is life-preserving.

There follow sixteen further Laws of Nature.[42] These are what might be called, in the parlance of modern metaethics, prima facie duties, except for this difference: Such duties have their moral obligatoriness written on the face of them,[43] whereas Hobbes's duties are obligatory because they are utilitarian in character, leading to the desirable end of the maintenance of life. Yet I would still call them prima facie duties here, because their reasonableness is so obvious in the light of the goal they serve. These are duties of gratitude, sociability, mercy, magnanimity, and so on. They are by no means central to Hobbes's system as are the first three; nor are they as fundamental and abstract, for they seem to rest on the first three. Their value to us, however, is that they shed light on what Hobbes regards as a law of nature: they are "commands of reason" in that we accept them when we "see reason," in the broadest sense of that phrase. Given the aim of peace, it makes sense for people to be cooperative, to avoid slandering one another, and so on, as the remainder of the Laws of Nature prescribe. And anyone who cannot see these as prima facie duties imposed by the need for peace in social life is probably blind to social values in general.

Although equality is the source of strife in nature, it is also the precondition of peace in society.[44] If men see that their equality of powers makes them helpless against one another, then they are more likely to agree to negotiate peace. It is in their own best interest, therefore, for men to acknowledge their equality with others—and this becomes a Law of Nature for that utilitarian reason only. It is this kind of reasonableness that leads to fair play and to not demanding more than others have. This sense of fairness leads also (when we "see reason") to equality of judgment in dealing with others. It is a sense of fairness that is particularly English (so English that Hobbes's seventeenth-century man can see reason in it, even in the state of nature and even though his world is too uncertain for him to put that sense of fairness into practice without the protection of the sword).

It is a Law of Nature, for example, that those things that cannot be divided should be enjoyed in common, and if they can neither be divided nor enjoyed in common then the sense of fairness demands that they be disposed by lot. We should recall that the Athenians considered the selection of public officers by lot the fairest method (because all Athenian citizens were considered equal and there was therefore no basis for choosing between them). The method of voting is less democratic and less fair, because it is selective and implies that one man is better than another. It may startle us to realize how much stress Hobbes places on fairness and democracy (because he is so clearly identified with authoritarianism).

It stands to reason, further, that as soon as we acknowledge the fact that men are guided by motives of self-interest we must agree that no man ought to be judge in a case where his own interests are concerned, as he cannot be truly impartial. This is so reasonable a view that it becomes another Law of Nature. Without true impartiality, strife arises. This shows us, again, that the justification for these Laws of Nature is finally utilitarian—and it will be important to bear this in mind later on, when we discuss the recent criticism seeing Hobbes as some sort of religious moralist. We do have his own words, moreover, to indicate the utilitarian character of his thinking in connection with these Laws of Nature. "These are laws of nature, dictating peace, for a means of the conservation of men in multitudes; and which only concern the doctrine of civil society."[45] There has been a lot of discussion as to whether Hobbes believes that there can be any moral laws in the state of nature and whether the Laws of Nature are moral laws. But it is clear from the nature and purpose of these laws, and from the last phrase of the quotation just given, that these laws concern men in a well-ordered social setting, not in the state of nature (where the opportunity of sitting in judgment never arises, let alone the possibility of judging fairly). As to whether these laws are moral laws, that question will be taken up in the forthcoming pages.

Let us return to our quotation, and let me point out that the utilitarian character of these laws is indicated by the words, "a means of the conservation of men." To make these laws comprehensible to the meanest intelligence, Hobbes compresses them into the single statement: "Do not that to another, which thou wouldest not have done to thyself." What this involves is the identification of another's interest with one's own, and in essence this can be taken as the central meaning of social life and of sociability itself. And this would be Hobbes's reply to the question of how man (who is naturally war-like and antisocial) can enter into society with others: His reason tells him that this is the only way toward his self-preservation. It becomes clear, then, that in these last sixteen Laws of Nature he is talking about the meaning of sociability—although he must resort to certain models and devices such as the presocial state of nature, the social contract, and laws of nature in order to make that meaning clear.

As to the obligatory character of these Laws of Nature, we have already elaborated on Hobbes's view that they are dictates of reason with a utilitarian end. He goes on to say, however, that these laws are obligatory to conscience (in foro interno). That is, we are bound to assent to them and to desire them in the "inner forum." But we are not bound to act on them (in foro externo) unless there is some external power to provide security and to guarantee that all men will be held to the observance of these laws. For to act on these laws when there is no such external security (for example, to be generous when your neighbor is your enemy and is not made to return such generosity) is to invite conflict and possibly one's own destruction. This brings us to the problem of established power and the social contract, for these alone make the Laws of Nature viable.

As I pointed out, Hobbes recognizes the fact that these Laws of Nature, although clear to reason, are nevertheless contrary to man's natural passions and are therefore useless for the purpose of shaping men's actions unless there is the power to compel them. Yet, although social life is contrary to man's *inclinations*, it nevertheless serves his deepest natural *needs*. His inclination is toward war; what he needs, however, is peace. Because the tension between these two poles is so great, only a very great force can span the gap. Peace, therefore, must be imposed upon men *against* their inclinations. This means that a social existence, too, must be imposed upon them against their inclinations—even against their will!

The only way in which a social existence can be imposed is for men to give up their rights. Is there not a conflict here between the ideas of voluntary surrender and involuntary imposition? No. The second Law of Nature tells men (when they see reason) that if they wish to live they must give up the infinite rights that brought them into conflict with other men. With this principle they can voluntarily agree *in foro interno*. But there is no way they can expect either themselves or others to stick by this agreement *in foro externo*, for the will is weak and the desires infinite. There is needed, therefore, some force, some sword, some person or persons standing outside the community of men (outside in the legal sense), to impose peace and compliance with the dictates of reason. Men then give up their rights and powers to this one man or sovereign assembly, so that the men who were by nature turned against each other now become one society, and the plurality of voices becomes one voice.

The common power that can restrain men is thus set up by men themselves. Hobbes makes much of this point because it serves to define the infinite obligations of the subjects to their sovereign and the minimal responsibilities of the sovereign to his subjects. When men confer their rights upon one man or upon one sovereign assembly, this sovereign becomes their *persona*, and they are the "authors" of what he does. This does not mean that they are constantly telling him what to do and say. Quite the contrary—they are the "authors" of his deeds in the very restricted sense that they once and forever authorized all his future deeds, so that the decisions concerning actions and policy are *no longer* in their hands. In this way, genuine unity is achieved, and all discord is overcome—although we could point out that the unity achieved is the spurious unity of repressive autocracy, and the discord overcome is actually the discord and dissent of free men!

The way men surrender their individual rights is by a covenant of every man with every other man, saying: "I authorize and give up my right of governing myself, to this man, or to this assembly of men, on this condition, that thou give up thy rights to him, and authorize all his actions in like manner."[46] We thereby create an artificial entity, something contrary to nature—a mortal god—to ensure our peace and defense.

This is a deliberately instituted arrangement. But even when a man conquers a territory and subdues the inhabitants, granting them their lives in exchange for their obedience (what Hobbes calls a "commonwealth by acquisition"), the arrangement must still be considered a *voluntary* contractual authorization. Obviously, Hobbes is speaking here in terms of his model; he is not speaking literally or he would not have called the commonwealth by acquisition voluntary or contractual. This is crucial: If Hobbes is taken to be speaking factually, then it is simply not true that such an arrangement is voluntary—any more than that the authority can be indefinitely authorized. We must conclude, therefore, that Hobbes is speaking not in terms of facts but in terms of some analogical model. The contract model is intended to show us that *all* government (whether voluntarily instituted or imposed by the sword) involves the surrender of self-rule on the part of the individual as well as the suppression of internal dissent by superior force. Above all, for Hobbes, the contract model shows that *all* government is government by *consent*—certainly not the subject's consent to the sovereign's day-to-day decisions but consent in the sense that we are tacitly agreeing to gain our lives in exchange for obedience.

The sovereign is "one person, of whose acts a great multitude, by mutual covenants with one another, have made themselves every one the author, to the end [that] he may use the strength and means of them all, as he shall think expedient, for their peace and common defense."[47] What is created thereby is a legal fiction, a legal persona having no liability at all because *he* did not obligate himself to the people in any way—an artificial authority with ultimate power. It is in this sense that Hobbes speaks of "that great Leviathan . . . that mortal god." His authority is the same whether we voluntarily authorized it or it was forced upon us. And because the sovereign is not himself a party to the contract but remains outside in the state of nature, he is not bound to perform any service or to provide benefits of any sort. It is we who sign over our rights to him; *he* is not a signatory to the agreement.

Nor are we (or subsequent generations) entitled to break the contract on any grounds whatsoever. This follows from the third Law of Nature, "that men perform their covenants made." Subsequent generations might wish to say that because they were not signatories to the contract they are not bound by it. The answer to this is to point out that such an objection appeals to fact and is therefore irrelevant—Hobbes is speaking not of a historical contract but rather of a theoretical model that is intended to show us that man's existence in *any* society involves his submission to authority.

Accordingly, no dissent can ever be justified, because it was "we" ourselves who authorized the sovereign's actions, even though the "authorization" never took place in time (let alone our lifetime). And for the same reason, no revolution can ever be justified, because it violates the undertaking "we" ourselves have "committed" ourselves to uphold. Nor can a subject justifiably accuse the sovereign of *anything*, for the sovereign is above the law, is empowered to act "as he shall think expedient," and is not obligated to his subjects in any way. The sovereign might commit iniquities, Hobbes says, but nothing he does can ever be regarded as an injustice. This is because the sovereign alone is the judge of what is just—for so he was authorized by us—and therefore he cannot be judged by us. And, because he is the only judge of what will best serve the cause of peace and security, he has the right to pass on all doctrines taught in schools and churches and to decide what shall constitute good or evil, what shall be lawful or unlawful.

*Every* commonwealth (whether instituted by us or imposed on us) is thus representative of us.[48] This is because the actions of the sovereign are authorized by us all—by those who vote "for" as well as those who vote "against." Thus, the covenant involves either tacit or explicit agreement with all of the sovereign's actions, as if his actions were the actions of each of us individually when we act for our own private ends of peace and security. This certainly has some momentous implications for the problem of collective responsibility and collective guilt. But the more immediate consequence is that, in place of a war of every man *against* every man, we now have an agreement of every man *with* every man. Our individual purposes are maintained, but they are now acted upon by our representative.

If anyone is punished by the sovereign for insurrection, the person who is punished is the "author" of his own punishment, because he is the author of whatever the sovereign may do. Even if I disagree with the policies of the sovereign and seek to depose him, I nevertheless "authorize" him to punish me for trying to depose him. Hobbes sees the paradox in this, but in his view that paradox recoils upon the dissenter and makes *his* actions paradoxical. Because the agreement is not between the sovereign and ourselves he cannot be accused of breach of contract. Therefore, nothing he does is wrong—and that is another reason why no revolution is justified.

Further, because each man has agreed with the others to abide by the will of the majority in setting up the sovereign, no dissent can be justified—even if the present sovereign is not the choice of the majority. Each man must accept whatever the sovereign does, or else that man shall be "justly destroyed by the rest." Whether or not his consent is asked for or given, he must submit or else consider himself outside the law, in a state of war with society, a war "wherein he might without injustice be destroyed by any man whatsoever."

And yet, although no revolution is justified—and although the peace that comes even with tyranny is always preferable to the war of all against all—the obligation of the subjects to their sovereign lasts only so long as the power lasts with which he protects them. If, therefore, the sovereign is too weak to protect himself from internal revolution or from takeover by an invading power, then he is obviously too weak to protect his subjects. And then the contract is at an end, the subjects are absolved from all obedience to him, and men revert to a condition of nature.[49] This means, in effect, that no revolution is justified—unless it succeeds! And then the new regime (*whatever* it may be) becomes the rightful one. Thus, Hobbes approves of any government that exists in fact, and he denies the legitimacy of any deposed government such as a government-in-exile.

Hobbes's theory has been called "representational absolutism." It combines the idea of representation (that is, "authorization") with the idea of absolutism (that is, the sovereign's authority is above the law and is unlimited). As a result, Hobbes offended the Royalists, who claimed that the authority of their absent king was based upon Divine Right. (To this claim, Hobbes says that a king without power has no legitimacy whatever.) And he offended the Parliamentarians, who aimed at limiting the authority of the sovereign in a constitutional monarchy. (To this view, Hobbes says that the authority of the sovereign cannot justifiably be limited by any law made by his subjects.)

Against the Royalists, the Parliamentarians argued that a proper government should be by consent. To this, Hobbes replies that all governments already rule by consent because we ourselves have "authorized" them. Even if we happen not to agree with a particular government, it nevertheless has our implicit consent by virtue of the fact that we continue to live under its laws. Against the Parliamentarians, the Royalists argued that the king rules by divine will. To this Hobbes replies, first, that no one can know what God's will is, and so no one can claim to know that God wants him on the throne. Second, Hobbes says that a deposed king is without a claim because there can be no such thing as a government de jure that is not also a government de facto. The mere existence of a government is both the necessary and the sufficient condition for its legitimacy. Any regime that *is* is legitimate. Hobbes thereby attacks the idea that there is a difference between legitimate and illegitimate government, as well as the difference between government de jure and de facto. A government is a government de facto, or it is no government at all; in either case, the question of its being de jure or legitimate is irrelevant.

From our point of view, these are concepts and differences we would certainly wish to retain. Hobbes's contemporaries felt this way about the matter, too, to put it mildly. Hobbes thereby put himself in the unenviable position of being opposed to all the ideologies of his time and being the partisan of none. This got him into trouble on all sides, and he feared for his life once again. As I suggested at the beginning, the world continued to support his fears, and all that happened around him confirmed for him the correctness of his philosophy. It is of historical interest that the times were so desperate and chaotic that this man should be willing to give up almost every right for the sake of peace (and not necessarily the kind of peace in which he might be sure of the chance to pursue his personal happiness). We must note, however, that the danger did not lead him into taking the obvious path to safety—silence. His courage is undeniably there, despite his desperation and fear. It is out of this desperation and fear that he developed a theory of absolutism justified by a picture of man's violent nature.

**New Interpretations**   There are a number of new and interesting interpretations of Hobbes that have generated quite a bit of literature—all shedding some valuable light on what it is that political philosophy is supposed to do. The central issue seems to be the moral status of Hobbes's ideas. Was Hobbes being ethically neutral in setting out his Laws of Nature? Or could these have been intended by him as moral laws? And, quite apart from what *he* intended, must *we* regard these laws as moral laws in order to make sense of them? If they were intended by him as moral laws, then is he not committing the fallacy of trying to derive "ought" from "is" by trying to base these moral laws on psychological facts?

The surge of new interpretation was in a way brought about by Hobbes's own emphasis on the systematic consistency of his philosophy. He claims to have based his political philosophy on a theory of human psychology. But this psychology is so questionable, and the basic claims made by his view of human nature so dubious, that his political philosophy had to be logically detached from that base in order to be acceptable itself. If it could not be detached (so says the modern interpretation) and if the political theory were to rest only on his theory of human nature, then we should have to reject his political theory as being unworthy of serious consideration.[50] Yet Hobbes's political theory does continue to engage our interest, thereby making the divorce from his theory of human nature necessary. We therefore need a way of rejecting his psychology without endangering his political theory, because that political theory is still of great value in any discussion of basic political concepts such as authority, obligation, and dissent.

If we try to devote our attention to his political theory alone, apart from its dependence on his psychology, we lose the sense of the totality upon which he placed such value—the sense of deductive certainty and consistency in the way his political theory follows from his psychology and physics. In order to retain this sense of totality, therefore, the recent interpreters of Hobbes hit upon the idea of (a) showing that his political theory is complete and independent in its own right or (b) basing his political theory on a foundation other than his psychology.

These are the two lines in the new interpretations of Hobbes. There is (a) the Strauss thesis, which says that Hobbes's political ideas were already complete before he "discovered" geometry and that the "discovery" inspired him to give his ideas a systematic base they did not need. And there is (b) the Taylor-Warrender thesis, which says that there is no logical dependence of Hobbes's theory on his egoistic psychology; rather, his political theory is regarded as actually based on (of all things) theology. The first thesis is a historical theory of how Hobbes's ideas in fact evolved. The second thesis is a hermeneutic theory of what Hobbes *ought* to have said in order to give his system its consistency and completeness.

a. Let us recall that through his "discovery" of Euclid Hobbes was led to seek a deductive certainty for political theory as well. Apparently Hobbes felt the need to deduce his theory *from* something, namely, psychology. Yet, according to Strauss, his theory was substantially complete before the "discovery."[51] Hobbes's "pre-Euclidean" philosophy emerged out of his extensive study of Thucydides' *Peloponnesian War*, of which he did a translation. It was here Hobbes derived the first version of his antidemocratic ideas. In seeing the kind of certainty geometry could achieve, however, Hobbes left his work in history to turn to philosophy. Yet his political thinking was adversely affected by his subsequent philosophizing, Strauss claims. Let us see why.

First, let us point out that the earlier influence of his historical researches persists in Hobbes in a variety of ways. In the idea of a state of nature, for example, his philosophy reflects a quasihistorical character in speaking of a transition out of one state into another. Yet the idea stands above any particular historical era. In this way, history is rendered superfluous for him: Political philosophy takes the place of history and itself becomes history—"a typical history."[52] Hobbes's philosophy is historical also in showing that the social order is not unchangeable or eternal, Strauss says, but is the product of human volition and human making. Man's world is thereby shown to have no theological foundation or metaphysical significance. There is only a historical significance; in seeing the transition from the state of nature to civil society, we see how it is possible to go from a defective order to a better order through the aid of reason. Thus, the fact that progress is possible is due to man himself. Yet the impotence of his own reason (in the attempt to create a sound theology or metaphysics) means that it is no longer possible for man to turn to a transcendent order for guidance. Thus, neither Plato nor Aquinas presents viable possibilities. This turns philosophers to history and leads to the "historicizing" of philosophy itself.

In the view of Strauss, Hobbes developed his moral philosophy (which is the basis of his political philosophy) *before* he turned to the mathematical-scientific approach.[53] Now, since the *Leviathan* is dominated by that approach, it is *not* the best presentation of Hobbes's moral philosophy! This is why Strauss feels that Hobbes's scientific approach obscures his moral philosophy—and his political thinking. We can give only a sketch here of that earlier theory: Hobbes is the first to make "natural right" (the justifiable claim of the individual to his continued existence) the basis of political philosophy, without reference to natural or divine law in their traditional forms. For Hobbes, the state is based on "right," of which "law" is a mere consequence. This is why (according to Strauss) Hobbes distinguishes between Natural Right and Natural Law in *Leviathan*, chapter xiv.

It is possible, however, that Hobbes has another purpose or purposes in setting up this distinction: In seeing the motive of self-preservation as a basically human *end* (and thus a Natural Right), and justifying any *means* toward that end (as a dictate of reason, or Natural Law), there could be the purpose of showing the means–end relation to be the paradigm of rationality in political thinking. For Strauss, however, Hobbes's innovation consists in the subordination of all law and all legal or moral obligation to this one natural right, the right to exist. Yet it is hard to see why this must be given a moral coloring. We have seen Hobbes capable of the ethically neutral observation, first, that the drive toward self-preservation is basic to all life and, second, that men using reason have been able to evolve certain practical (and not necessarily moral) imperatives to serve that end. Man makes all, placing himself outside nature and opposing it. This is reflected in *Leviathan*'s notion that the state is "artificial"—in the antithesis between man's natural condition and the constructing of a civil society. Yet this stress on our creative freedom is hindered and obscured (Strauss says) by Hobbes's materialistic-deterministic philosophy.[54] This philosophy is monistic and reductive, so that man is part of nature once again. In this way, the materialistic-deterministic philosophy rejects the man–nature duality implicit in Hobbes.

I see this as Strauss's best point. He thereby shows that Hobbes stands opposed to his own deepest purposes. This has the salutary effect of making us turn back to Hobbes and read him more deeply. In the meantime, however, the effect of the Strauss thesis is that Hobbes's chief work, *Leviathan*, is lopped off the corpus of Hobbes's system. *Our* problem, however, is with that work itself in its attempt to present a consistent system—and it is precisely this attempted systematization that has made the new interpretations necessary. We may be inclined to go along with the separation of the politics of *Leviathan* from the psychology of *Leviathan*, but it is impossible to accept the separation of Hobbes's moral philosophy (à la Strauss) from *Leviathan* as a whole. Thus it is Strauss's aim to show that Hobbes's political theory is complete and independent in its own right—but the cost is too high if that means introducing a moral component that was not there or (worse) truncating Hobbes's theory in a way most of us would find unacceptable.

*b.* The Taylor–Warrender thesis has stimulated much controversy and subsequent commentary. As I indicated, it is the attempt to lift Hobbes's political philosophy off the base of his egoistic psychology and to place it on the base of theology. It began when A. E. Taylor suggested in an article that there really are two questions before Hobbes:[55] First, there is the *practical* question of what inducements there are for me to be a good citizen and obey my sovereign. To this question, Hobbes answers that it is in my own best interest to do so, for otherwise there is conflict and strife. Second, there is the *ethical* question of why I ought to behave as a good citizen and obey my sovereign. Hobbes's answer (according to Taylor) is that I have obligated myself in the third Law of Nature to perform the covenant I made. The first question is not an ethical question, and its answer comes from the egoistic psychology that says that I always pursue what I consider to be in my best interest—and so the aim of Hobbes would be to enlighten me as to what truly is in my best interest.

The second question, in being an ethical question, is such that its answer has no logical connection to his egoistic psychology. It says that I ought (morally) to behave in a prescribed way because I have given my word to do so, expressly or tacitly. The answer is thus strictly deontological in character, suggestive of Kant, in that it derives its moral obligatoriness not from any practical consequences (as in the first question) but from the nature of my self-obligating act itself. Yet, as if this were not sufficient as a moral warrant, Taylor says that the Laws of Nature are to be obeyed because they are dictates of God. This is the only way (he feels) we can overcome the pragmatic consideration in "Why should I obey?" and thus make the answer moral rather than instrumental. According to Taylor, then, the Kantian aspect is not enough, and Hobbes needs a theology in order to make his system complete.

The problem under discussion is not merely concerned with the interpretation of Hobbes; rather, it touches on the all-important matter of civil obligation. Why should anyone obey any government? To this question, Hobbes has given some very meaningful answers, and it is Taylor's aim to preserve their meaningfulness. Now there is simply no space here to discuss all the ramifications of Taylor's view. So we must be aware that we are inevitably doing that view an injustice by compressing it. Yet a number of doubts can be raised, even in compressed form. First, when Taylor says that Hobbes's system needs a theology to complete it, Taylor is declaring what he thinks Hobbes *ought* to have said, and this approach is of questionable value for our understanding of what Hobbes did say. Further, Hobbes's very obvious antitheological and antischolastic temper certainly indicates that he had no intention of creating a system that would depend for its completeness on the concept of God's will. Hobbes would then have been too close to Divine Right royalism for his own comfort. We saw that it is a declared principle of Hobbes that all we can know about God is that he exists and that we cannot know his will or his intentions concerning man. It is therefore unlikely that Hobbes would have accepted the view that we *can* know God's will as expressed in the Laws of Nature. Hobbes explicitly says that our "rational knowledge of God is limited to the fact that he exists" and that the Laws of Nature are "deduced neither from the attributes of God nor from the character of divine sanctions, for a substantial knowledge of these is impossible."[56]

Despite all this, the question raised by the Taylor thesis is whether the Laws of Nature are to be regarded as *morally* binding and, if so, whether they are morally binding *because* they express the will of God. I hope I have shown that Hobbes is quite clear in regarding these laws as dictates of reason with the purpose of helping man to save himself.[57] Against the Taylor thesis, then, we must say that these laws are rational (not theological) and pragmatic (not moral). Hobbes says that, *if* we wish to consider these dictates of reason as dictates of God, then they are properly called laws. Yet they ought not really to be called laws at all but rather "conclusions, or theorems concerning what conduceth to the conservation and defense of [men]"—whereas law is, properly speaking, "the word of him that by right hath command over others."[58] It follows that if Hobbes does not consider them to be laws in any literal sense then he cannot regard them as commands of God or of anyone.

Further, Hobbes does not consider these laws to be dictates of God, or he would not have given them this utilitarian justification. Taylor cannot be right, therefore, when he says that Hobbes needs the concept of God. Hobbes's system requires no further completeness than the law dictated by reason and making good sense because it promotes life. The laws are compelling, Hobbes says, because to defy them leads to war, and war is destructive of life. (Why should we want to preserve life? We do not need God to tell us. It is a natural impulse in all men, the way stones fall downward.) Other men have praised justice, gratitude, modesty, equity, mercy, and so on (Hobbes continues), but they have failed to see what makes these things good.

They are good because they are "the means of peaceable, sociable, and comfortable living." A more decidedly utilitarian statement could hardly be imagined.

On the basis of Hobbes's own words, therefore, I would say that it is impossible to consider his values (in the state of nature) as anything other than instrumental. They can in no sense be called ethical or moral; and, if they are not ethical or moral, then they certainly do not need the concept of God's approval to give them their force. Only if Taylor were prepared to say that *all* instrumental philosophies need the concept of God to complete them (and I cannot see how he could say such a thing, nor does he) would he be correct in giving Hobbes's Laws of Nature this deontological interpretation and basing them on divine command.

Other objections to the Taylor thesis have been put forward by Watkins,[59] and we can summarize them as follows: Although Taylor maintains that, according to Hobbes, political authority must rest ultimately on God's commands, it can be shown that this is precisely the view Hobbes attacks when he says that political authority originates in the individual's desires. Further, it is Hobbes's aim to offer a rationally demonstrative argument against the religious zealots of his day, and for this reason he does not regard his laws as theistic. If he had, then any Puritan could have maintained that he understands God's will better than Hobbes does, and Hobbes's argument would have lost its effect. Hobbes's only tenable position, therefore, is that God's will cannot be known and that we must consequently rely on reason.

An even more important point is this: If Taylor is correct in saying that these Laws of Nature are moral laws, then this means that a system of moral laws already exists in the state of nature. Yet Hobbes is explicit in saying that there are no moral rules until they are commanded by a sovereign in a civil state. Thus, for example, he does not blame man for his selfish nature because nature itself is value-neutral:

The desires, and other passions of men, are in themselves [that is, in the state of nature] no sin. No more are the actions that proceed from those passions, till they know a law that forbids them: which, till laws be made, they cannot know; nor can any law be made, till they have agreed upon the person that shall make it.[60]

Further on the same page there is the passage I quoted earlier to the effect that in the state of nature nothing is unjust because there is no restraining power and no law. In Hobbes's view, then, the presocial state of nature can have no moral component, no sense of right or wrong. There are merely the Laws of Nature that are dictates of value-neutral reason, showing us how to save ourselves from death. Taylor is clearly wrong, therefore, in saying that the Laws of Nature pose an ethical question.

c. The Taylor thesis has been given very deep analysis and support by Warrender.[61] His intricate and exhaustive argument has been summarized by Watkins as follows:[62] (1) The Laws of Nature persist through the state of nature into civil society. (2) They are essentially moral laws prescribing one's duties to society, and they are morally obligatory because they are commanded by God. (3) Therefore, moral laws are not created by the sovereign.

Watkins agrees with Warrender's first point, and it is clear that Hobbes would agree also, because the dictates of reason do not cease being dictates of reason when we emerge out of the state of nature and enter civil society. It is easy to disagree with the third point, because Hobbes explicitly says (as we saw) that morality *is* created by the sovereign and that there is no morality until the sovereign creates it. Warrender maintains that the sovereign merely sets his seal upon a *moral* code already in force in the state of nature; but this is so contrary to Hobbes's principle that all morality stems from the sovereign[63] that we can hardly see how the third point is even what Hobbes *ought* to have said, once we admit that he did not.

The real point at issue is the second: whether the Laws of Nature are moral laws prescribing duties. That question can be broken down into two parts: In setting out these Laws of Nature, was Hobbes actually prescribing? And, if so, was he prescribing moral rules? My answer is that Hobbes could be said to be prescribing *if* he were talking to men who actually found themselves in a state of nature and if these men were deliberating how to act and whether to accept the social contract. Obviously, the state of nature does not exist in the midst of British society (even if the current situation shows Hobbes what the state of nature would be like, if . . .). And obviously, therefore, as Hobbes is not talking to men in a state of nature, he cannot be prescribing a course of action to his readers or telling them how *they* ought to behave.

He says that although there are certain places (in America) where people live in such a presocial condition of war, "I believe it was never generally so all over the world"; that is, it was never an actual condition of mankind in general. What he gives us, therefore, is not a description of man as he actually was but rather a hypothetical picture of what man would be like, *if*—after having been in society—he were then to be stripped of everything he had acquired in society and had reverted to his natural condition. Thus, "it may be perceived what manner of life there would be, where there were no common power to fear, by the manner of life which men that have formerly lived under a peaceful government use to degenerate into a civil war."[64]

The aim of all this is to show how society, as an artificial construction, is meant to cope with human presocial nature: If man is naturally selfish, then such-and-such is what society must be. Thus, Hobbes is not telling his readers what to do or how to behave. He is only saying that, *if*—given this hypothetical model of abstract man living outside society—such a man wanted peace, then this-and-so is what he ought to do. What sort of "ought" is this? Because, by Hobbes's own stipulation, there is no morality in that presocial world, the "ought" is entirely hypothetical (that is, if x is what one wants, this is what one does to get it). The "ought" is practical, nonmoral, and is not a prescription *to* men of Hobbes's own society in any literal or immediate sense.

Yet that hypothetical, nonmoral "ought" is here transmitted to subsequent societies as revealing the essence of social life: The idea is that social life is based on some sort of concord or agreement, whether implicit or explicit, and that we ought to stick to it (namely, "perform covenants made"), for the alternative is a return to deadly strife. If Hobbes can therefore be regarded as prescribing a course of action by setting down certain rules, it is not (as I said) in any literal sense of prescribing. Just as he says that his laws are "laws" in only a figurative sense, so he is prescribing in a figurative way to an abstract model of presocial man. And therefore, if Hobbes's prescription is not a moral prescription, then his philosophy is not a system of ethical precepts in any literal sense.

Is there, then, a moral philosophy in *Leviathan*? Hobbes does use the phrase "moral philosophy,"[65] but in the same paragraph he shows us that he uses the words "moral," "good," and "evil" entirely as nonmoral terms—as evaluative terms standing for certain appetites and aversions. He relates to them from the standpoint of what men *call* "good" or "evil" rather than what *is* intrinsically good or evil. These terms are not given a moral sense by Hobbes but are part of his composite psychopolitical philosophy of human nature. I therefore reject Warrender's main point: that the Laws of Nature are moral laws. Far from their being moral laws of a Kantian sort (as Taylor and Warrender wish to maintain), Watkins goes so far as to refer to them in terms Kant considered nonmoral: They are assertoric hypothetical imperatives, like "doctor's orders of a peculiarly compelling kind."[66]

Let us come to a tentative summary of these points: Hobbes's Laws of Nature are not moral (categorical) imperatives, and so he is not a Kantian. (Watkins says: "Hobbes's laws of nature do not have a distinctively moral character.") And if his imperatives are not moral ones, then (Peters to the contrary) Hobbes has not committed the fallacy of deriving a moral "ought" from a factual "is." All this emerges out of the special meaning I have tried to give to Hobbes's "prescribing." He is "prescribing" to his model of presocial man, saying: This is the reasonable way to behave—keeping covenants, accommodating yourself to others, expressing gratitude, extending pardon, and so on, and so on.[67] Yet, if a person were living in the state of nature, he could not be living with such values because he could not possibly recognize *any* values as morally binding. He could only gaze upon them from the far shore, so to speak, and his reason would urge him to enter into a social contract with other men in order to make such a rational life possible. In the state of nature he would also see (with the same eye of reason) that without an established power no such values could be *made* morally binding. They could only be, let us say, morally "attractive."

The main point to be made against the Taylor–Warrender thesis, therefore, is that these laws are *not* binding, and certainly not *morally* binding, on the solitary man in the state of nature. Hobbes says: "These are the laws of nature, dictating peace, for a means of the conservation of men in multitudes; and which concern only the doctrine of civil society."[68] In the same chapter, Hobbes tells us that in a state of nature such laws bind the inner conscience only, not the outer action. Here, then, is the crux of Hobbes's own opposition to the Taylor–Warrender interpretation of Hobbes. The Laws of Nature obligate us *in foro interno,* not *in foro externo*—because it would be suicidal to act on the basis of such laws if no one else did. Acting on such laws in a state of nature would thus be *against* the purpose of all Laws of Nature: self-preservation. Only in society (where we do have the security of knowing that other men will observe such laws) would the nonobservance of such laws lead not to peace but to war.

It would therefore be *unnatural* to observe these laws in the state of nature, where there is no enforcing power, yet it would be right to observe such laws in society if we were commanded to do so.

This goes against Warrender's view of the continuity of these laws, as moral laws, from the state of nature to civil society. There would be such a continuity if the laws were immutable, eternal. These laws are immutable and eternal, Hobbes says, only in the clearly pragmatic sense that their opposites lead to war, and "it can never be that war shall preserve life and peace destroy it." This, then, is the only "moral" philosophy in *Leviathan*—namely, the study of good and evil, understood as nothing more than appetites (good) and aversions (evil). And, although men will disagree as to the content of what they call "good" or "evil," they must agree that life and peace are good in an ultimate sense needing no justification by God but, rather, justifying all else.

How does God fit into all this, and how do Taylor and Warrender arrive at the mistaken impression that Hobbes's theory could be made to fit onto some sort of theological base? I indicated that Hobbes refuses to regard these Laws of Nature as "laws" in a literal sense. They are laws only if, failing all else, we *must* think of them as commanded by God in order for us to accept them (even though their true power is as dictates of reason). This is where Taylor and Warrender derive the idea that these "laws" *could* be commanded by God. Yet Hobbes points out that what makes them commands is not that God commands them but rather the fact that they are commanded at all. Indeed, they *are* commanded by the sovereign, once the civil society is established—whereupon they are declared to be moral laws and ought to be taken as such—but not before.

Hobbes has his proper doubts as to the compelling power of reason. In the absence of a sovereign to command them, these laws are mere dictates of value-neutral reason (as we saw). But because we cannot be sure how strong the influence of reason can be (upon ourselves or upon others), the authority of God may be evoked as a propaganda device—if, that is, we must give them the status of commands.

It seems to me that Hobbes is sufficiently sophisticated to demythologize the concept of God, whereas Taylor and Warrender want to push him back into the myth. For Hobbes, God's authority is a paradigm case of all authority, including human authority. But it is a mere paradigm and not the actual source of authority. Thus, in the last chapter of *Leviathan*, part II, we read:

To those therefore whose power is irresistible, the dominion of all men adhereth naturally by their excellence or power; and consequently it is from that power that the kingdom over men, and the right of afflicting men at his pleasure, belongeth naturally to God Almighty; not as Creator, and gracious; but as omnipotent.[69]

I would call this idea thoroughly Thucydidean!*

As an idea of power in general, therefore, the idea of God's authority is secondary to and dependent upon the idea of human power; and the idea of human power eventually replaces it. The idea of God as a source of command is replaced first by reason, if reason is strong enough. But the idea of God is replaced quite definitely by the earthly sovereign—the Leviathan, the mortal god. He, not God Almighty, is the source of values. The obligation imposed by God lasts only so long as other power is lacking, such as the power of reason or the power of the sword. The absence of all authority in the state of nature is what makes it necessary to appeal to ultimate power. But, once the sovereign appears on the scene, it is for him alone to "interpret" God's will. This means, not that the sovereign's authority rests on God's will (precisely the Royalist idea Hobbes was opposing), but rather that God's will rests upon the sovereign (in the sense that he alone declares it).

What this is intended to signify is that when men are sufficiently rational to enter consciously into a social arrangement, the creation of values becomes possible—and those values are in the hand that holds the sword. At that moment, the dependence upon God as a source of values becomes unnecessary, redundant, otiose. As Plamenatz puts it, "God is very much present in [Hobbes's] scheme of things, but is also, at bottom, superfluous."[70] In discussing the first Law of Nature, Hobbes says that "it is a precept, or general rule of reason that every man ought to endeavor peace." He does not say that "it is the will of God that every man ought to endeavor peace." Hobbes could have saved himself considerable friction with the Puritans had he said this. Cromwell could have wished for nothing better from Hobbes—for it would have shown that God approves of *all*

---

* It is particularly Thucydidean if we consider the Melian dialogue in *The Peloponnesian War*, XVII:104. When the Melians invoke God and justice, the Athenians answer, in the best tradition of *Realpolitik*: "Of the gods we believe, and of men we know, that by a necessary law of their nature they rule wherever they can." Obviously Hobbes did more than translate the work, he ingested it.

men's submission to Cromwell. Yet, had Hobbes said this, he would have had not a self-contained philosophical system but a system pointing outside itself to theology—that is, an ideology!

The Strauss and Taylor–Warrender theses are movements toward "revisionism," and such things are always a sign of the vitality of a thinker or a philosophy—its power to inspire us to think it through. Yet, in my view, these new interpretations of Hobbes arise from the mistake of taking him literally when he himself warns us not to. As I have tried to show, Hobbes's aim is neither to describe (in a factual sense) nor to prescribe (in a moral sense). Factually, Hobbes is wrong, so that if we take him literally we are forced to the antidote of the Strauss thesis, which tries to see Hobbes's politics as complete in itself. In moral terms, Hobbes is incomplete, so that if we take him literally the answer is the Taylor–Warrender thesis, which tries to complete his system with the idea of God.

I have tried to show that Hobbes's "prescription" is to an abstract model of man, in order to show us what social life *is*, not in its momentary actuality but in its essence. In this light, Hobbes's philosophy, if it is neither descriptive nor prescriptive, must be seen as *analogical* in character. Once we do see this, the various antidotes become unnecessary. If his political theory does not make a factual claim, then we need no longer try to detach it from his psychology (regardless of whether that psychology is true or false). And if he does not make a moral claim, then there is no longer a need to base his philosophy on the authority of God.

Let me now sum what I take to be Hobbes's contribution to political philosophy (not at all an easy task, for the questions he raised are of the most fundamental importance, his answers to them are unique and challenging, and the influence he has exerted has been immense). To compress it all into a few sentences, I would say, with Plamenatz,[71] that Hobbes's contribution has been to show that men are not born sociable but are made so; that justice is man-made; that there is no justice without law; and that there is no law without force. To all this, his contribution has been to elicit these ideas from a well-coordinated system embracing the concept of human nature in its widest dimension. That is, he does not simply put these ideas before us as a series of declarative propositions (true or false) but reveals the cogency of these ideas by means of an imaginative model of man as he *would* be, if he were without law and without a social order.

Taking a hard look at his model of man's nature, he asks the question: How much ought we to give up for the sake of peace and order? And his answer: Everything. For us—in an age when violence has become the norm in our communities and between nations, and when it seems as though only some restraining superforce in the shape of a subhuman computer or a cynical Big Brother could restore the world to peace and order—Hobbes's question is more than relevant. It is a burning issue.

# LOCKE

## The Individual as Atom

**"In the Beginning, All the World Was America"** It is interesting to see the widely different uses for the idea of the social contract. Apparently, we can use it to argue *for* complete authoritarianism (as Hobbes does) or to argue for our right to rebel *against* authoritarianism (as Locke does). Does this mean that they are contradicting one another and that at least one of them must be wrong?

Hobbes uses the idea of a social contract to justify the absolute power of the state. In his view, the contract is a rather one-sided arrangement in which the individual gives up all his rights for the sake of peace. Whatever "rights" he has in society are those the state grants him, and it is the prerogative of the state to grant them or not. The individual is a subject, and he is to adopt an attitude of complete submission. Because he has no "rights" against the state, there is nothing the state may not do to him with complete justification, and he therefore can have no claims or grievances against it. Above all, no protest or rebellion against the state can ever be justified. The power of the state—that "mortal god"—ought to be practically unlimited. And the idea of the social contract is used as the device that demonstrates all this.

Locke, however, uses the idea of a social contract to argue for the limiting of the state's power with respect to the individual. In his view of the contract, the individual gives up very little—merely the right to take the law into his own hands. In the state of nature, the individual already has certain natural rights (namely, the rights to life, liberty, and property), and the ruler is obligated to safeguard the rights of individuals when they become his subjects and subjects of civil society. If the ruler fails to fulfill his task of safeguarding individual rights, the subjects are justified in rebelling against him. The aim of Locke's *Second Treatise of Government*[1] is primarily to provide a rational justification for revolution: Its last (and longest) chapter is the climax of the work as a whole, and its title is "Of the Dissolution of Government." Where Hobbes can therefore be said to provide the classic argument for authoritarianism, Locke can be said to be the spokesman of liberalism and of revolution on libertarian grounds. Locke can rightly be called *the* philosopher of England's Glorious Revolution of 1688—even though the *Treatise* was not published until 1690, and anonymously.* Because his work came after the revolution, he cannot be said to have inspired it, only to have attempted to vindicate its aims in a rational manner. He was, however, read eagerly and enthusiastically by the Americans in the next century, and it is clear that his writings played a significant role in shaping American revolutionary thought.

There are all sorts of ways in which one might try to justify a revolution after it is over. But the type of justification would surely owe a great deal to the type of revolution one was seeking to justify. If it was a violent revolution, then the justification would likely seek to show that the situation beforehand was itself so violent and oppressive as to call for a revolution of that kind, using violence and oppression in order to do away with unbearable conditions. But if the revolution was rather peaceful and orderly, as the 1688 "bloodless" revolution clearly was, then one could try to show that all social life is by nature peaceful and orderly and that the social situation of one's own time was that way, too, until someone came to threaten that peace and order, thereby making a revolution necessary.

It is obvious that the relatively safe atmosphere of the 1688 revolution is reflected in Locke's vision of the state of nature—just as the chaos and danger of Hobbes's time are reflected in his picture of man in the natural state. The difference between the two thinkers, accordingly, is in their respective ideas of man's natural tendencies. Hobbes

* Locke did not acknowledge authorship until 1704, when making his will. See E. S. De Beer, "Locke and English Liberalism: The *Second Treatise of Government* in Its Contemporary Setting," in J. W. Yolton, ed., *John Locke: Problems and Perspectives* (Cambridge: Cambridge University Press, 1969), p. 35. See also the article by John Dunn in the same anthology, as well as John Dunn's book, *The Political Thought of John Locke* (Cambridge: Cambridge University Press, 1969).

saw man as being by nature aggressively competitive, thereby being led into a war of all against all. Locke sees man in his natural condition as a being who is naturally social, inclined to live in peace in an atmosphere of equality, freedom, cooperation, and observance of the Golden Rule.[2] Where Hobbes believed that society is an artificial construction, imposed upon men in order to inhibit their natural combativeness, Locke believes that society is entirely natural to men and that the civil state is merely an extension of that natural sociability. Men in the state of nature already live together according to the dictates of reason, and the only thing they lack is a "common superior on earth."

Hobbes regarded the state of nature as so violent that all sensible men eventually will seek peace merely in order to survive. And it is in the interest of survival that they give up all their rights. For Locke, however, the natural tendency of man is harmony, and so Locke's one law of nature is that because all men are equal "no one ought to harm another in his life, health, liberty, or possessions."[3] Where Hobbes had said that the equality of men is what led them into conflict, Locke quotes his favorite author, Richard Hooker (1594), who says that the equality of men rather makes the observance of the Golden Rule a duty.

Thus, Hobbes saw the natural state of man as being empty of values and exhibiting nothing but natural drives (and all values are to be decided by the sovereign, once the state is established). For Locke, however, the natural condition of man is one in which he already has a sizable battery of values, although that battery may not be complete. Indeed, the natural man is so much aware of his values that he punishes violators of them.[4] Even in the state of nature, those values are based on reason and on the idea of equality derived from the deeper idea that we are all the creatures of God. For Locke, then, the state of nature is a theater of Judeo-Christian values. These values are not, however, to be regarded as the temporal products of any given society but are rather beyond any such connection: "for truth and keeping of faith belongs to men as men, and not as members of society."[5]

From the point of view of rights, we saw how Hobbes had characterized the natural condition as one in which each man has a right to everything—which is an elliptical way of saying that there are no rights (except the right of survival). Locke, however, specifies the numerous rights men have in a natural condition ("life, health,

liberty, . . . possessions"), and he also proclaims the right of every
man in the state of nature to punish any infractions of natural law.
It is natural for a man to protect himself against someone who uses
force against him and to kill him as he would an animal, because he
is beyond all appeal to reason. The transgressor against natural law
(and thus against reason) puts himself outside the natural community
(so real is the sense of community), and he is therefore a danger to
all men. If a man steals my money by stealth, in organized society,
I may not kill him but must appeal to the law. But if a man steals
from me at gunpoint, whether in the state of nature or in society, I
have a perfect right to kill him, because his attack is a threat to my
life that even the law cannot restore should he take it.

This means that for Locke there is a retention and continuation of
values from the state of nature into society. The state of nature differs
from society merely in the absence of an authority to make judgment
and enforce it. The two situations—the state of nature and civil
society—can therefore be identically peaceful. Whereas Hobbes sees
a necessary equation in nature = war and society = peace, Locke
breaks that logical tie, because violence can be experienced in nature
as well as in society. It is this violence, not the absence of a social
contract, that defines the state of war. "Want of a common judge
with authority puts all men in a state of nature; force, without right,
upon a man's person makes a state of war, both where there is, and
is not, a common judge."[6]

A very valuable point is made by this idea that the state of war
might be found in the condition either of nature or of society: What
characterizes the state of war is that there is no possibility of appeal-
ing to justice. If, therefore, the state of war involves a condition of
violence against which I have a right to protect myself, then we must
agree that *even in society* when justice is perverted, so that no appeal
to justice is possible, that too is a state of war. Thus, when a monarch
perverts justice he puts himself in a state of war against his subjects.
If he seeks to deprive them unjustly of their lives or freedom, then
that is war, and their only alternative is "an appeal to Heaven"[7]—
meaning rebellion. With only the beginnings of his theory, therefore,
we see Locke arguing the case for justified revolution.

What we ought to ask ourselves, through all this, is the basic question of just what kind of argument Locke is giving us. If he is trying
to convince us of the justice of a certain course of action, then this
question of argument is of the greatest practical importance. The

main element in his argument so far has been the idea of the social contract. The fact that the idea of the social contract can be used to argue for authoritarianism or against it shows us that the idea taken in itself has no intrinsic content associated with it. It has no demonstrative force in one direction or another. There are no conclusions following from the idea alone, and nothing can be deduced from it as an argument for libertarianism or authoritarianism. If the idea did have some intrinsic content associated with it—the idea of the social contract alone, I mean—then either Hobbes or Locke would be in the wrong. *Something* would follow from the idea, and that something would tend to support either the one side or the other but never both.

Now we might want to say that neither one of them is right in what he believes. Yet we cannot say that either one of them is contradicting himself. This means that both these diametrically opposed standpoints are consistent with the basic idea of the social contract. And the only way that this is possible is if the idea itself says nothing, implies nothing! I have been arguing (in the Hobbes chapter) that the idea of the social contract is a bare, skeletal model that must be fleshed out with content in order to become meaningful.

If, for example, we take this bare structure and attach to it the *further* idea that the sovereign is *not* a party to the contract, then we can draw the conclusion that he is under no obligation to his subjects—and that conclusion can then become a basis for arguing for authoritarianism (that is, if he has no obligations toward his subjects, they can make no justifiable claims against him). If, on the other hand, we attach to it the idea that the sovereign *is* a party to the contract, then we can draw the conclusion that he is obligated to the other signers in one way or another (for example, to protect their rights or property or to promote their welfare)—and that conclusion can then become a basis for arguing against authoritarianism and for the limiting of state power. This is why I began the second sentence of this chapter with the word "apparently." It is not the *same* idea that is being used to argue both for and against authoritarianism. Rather, it is the differing ideas of natural right and law, of authority and consent, that do the actual arguing—and these are the ideas we attach to the bare frame of the social contract, the way a sculptor puts clay on a wire armature.

Before we turn to some of these "outer" ideas, such as property and consent, we must say something more about the inner frame. The approach just suggested must lead us to reevaluate the role played by the concept of the state of nature within whatever philosophy it appears. If we turn to Hobbes, we see that the traditional approach of his critics has been to assign a central importance to the concept of the state of nature: It is this concept they attack first, as though all else rests upon it. Perhaps they do so because they feel that in the unified world system Hobbes offers—a system combining physics, psychology, and political theory—the concept of the state of nature serves as the connecting link between psychology and political theory. That is, it shows the political consequences of his psychology as well as the psychological foundation of his political theory. It would seem, therefore, that the concept is of crucial importance to Hobbes's system. I have tried to show, however, that if we do not expect his political theory to make any factual claims (that is, if we regard it as analogical rather than as prescriptive or descriptive) then there is no longer any problem of trying to make it consistent with his descriptive psychology. And, therefore, the question so often raised by his critics as to whether there ever was, in fact, a condition such as Hobbes's state of nature is a question that need not be asked, because the answer is irrelevant. Hobbes himself makes this "factual" problem far less crucial than his critics do when he suggests that the state of nature never actually was a universal condition of man.

When we turn to Locke, the question is even less problematic. One reason why it is less problematic is that Locke does not venture to present a unified world system, so there is far less riding on the one concept of the state of nature. Indeed, nothing falls if that concept falls. His view of natural law, of property right, of the role of reason in deciding such values as the obligation of the state to the individual—all this would still be the same for Locke with or without the concept of the state of nature. But another reason why the "factual" question is less problematic for Locke is that his use of the concept of the state of nature itself makes a more modest claim. He does not need to rely on it to assert the uniformity of human nature, because he asserts that uniformity in other ways (as we shall see).

He uses the image of the state of nature to show us men very much like ourselves, so that there is little that is controvertible in his use of that image, and there is far less strain on our credulity (if any) than there is when Hobbes talks about the state of nature. Locke is talking about men who live in a more primitive setting than our own, but it is primitive only in lacking the kind of organization that brings law and authority. In all other ways, the men in the state of nature share all the values, the rationality, and the linguistic capacity we enjoy. (The American West, before the territories were settled and became states, fits Locke's picture nicely.) Locke must make his state of nature as rich and complete as possible, so that we have more to safeguard in joining organized society and so that the obligation of the state to safeguard what we have will be that much the greater. We are not bargaining over life and death, as in Hobbes's state of nature. Locke's men are already living together in society, and they are by no means uncivilized.

The question, therefore, as to whether there actually was a state of nature is for Locke hardly a troublesome question. He even speaks of parts of America where Indians live in societies without the elaborate structure of law and society.[8] And, if he wanted examples of social contracts being agreed upon within society and other social organizations being set up, he had only to turn to the Bible.[9] But there was also the Mayflower Compact of 1620, as well as many other colonial charters and agreements. And as recently as 1689 the Whigs had declared in the House of Commons that James II had broken "the original contract betwixt king and people"—so much was the idea of the social contract a part of the political parlance of the era.

We must say, therefore, that although Locke does consider his description of the state of nature to describe a factual situation,[10] this is not at all opposed to the prescriptive use he makes of it (because he uses it to shed light on such political ideas as revolution and consent). And, as I have said, his actual discussion of concepts such as consent in no way depends (even in his own eyes) on the actual existence of the state of nature.[11] He makes what appears to be a factual claim when he says, "in the beginning, all the world was America"[12] (meaning that there was no settled organization and no money). But, although the state of nature is a fact for Locke, he uses it as an illustrative device.

Most important, Locke uses the concept of the state of nature in order to illustrate man's capacity for rationality and freedom. The task of civil society, therefore, is to preserve that rationality and freedom and to keep human nature as it is (whereas Hobbes saw the proper aim of society to force man to overcome his human nature). One of the "outer" concepts we can thus attach to the frame of the state of nature is the concept of the uniformity of mankind, with which we can then go on to the idea that there are certain natural requirements all governments must fulfill, so that that universal rational nature might be served. And, from that sense of what it is universally right and proper for a government to do, we can then draw the implied criticism of present government and say that the authoritarian oppression by James II is unnatural and that any resistance against him is right.

For Locke, it is man's capacity for rationality that makes human nature uniform. The *Treatise* is filled with this idea: "reason . . . teaches all mankind, who will but consult it," and "Reason . . . the common bond whereby humankind is united into one fellowship and society," and "reason, which God hath given to be the rule betwixt man and man, and the peaceable ways which that teaches."[13] And in Locke's *Essay concerning Human Understanding* we find: "He that will look into many parts of Asia and America will find men reason there perhaps as acutely as himself, who yet never heard of a syllogism."[14] That this is ultimately connected with man's social capacities is expressed thus: "God having designed man for a sociable creature, made him not only with an inclination, and under a necessity to have fellowship with those of his own kind, but furnished him also with language, which was to be the great instrument and common tie of society."[15] There would hardly be any point in trying to argue against this view on the grounds that the existence of God is after all in doubt and that it is even more doubtful whether God ever *gave* reason to man. Such objections in no way touch the meaning of Locke's belief in man's rational capacity—for that belief is there, with or without the idea of God. Indeed, we can even go so far as to say that Locke's belief in man's rationality is independent of any belief in God, even though Locke uses the idea of God so that it is connected in many ways with the idea of human reason. In the very same way, we can say that the idea of man's rationality is independent of the concept of the state of nature; and that, because all men are pretty much the same in their nature, we need not scruple as to whether, when, or how the social contract was actually signed or whether the state of nature ever actually existed.

A concept Locke attaches to the frame of the state of nature is the concept of divine law. Like the idea of the social contract, the concept of the state of nature taken alone gives us nothing, until we begin to describe it as violent or peaceful, and so on. But, when the concept of divine law is attached to it, we have an argument for resistance against despotism. The values that are held by men in the state of nature are referred to by Locke as divine law, "whereby I mean that law which God has set to the actions of men, whether promulgated to them by the light of nature, or the voice of revelation."[16] For Locke, it follows from this (and from the idea of the uniformity of human nature) that men can know these values, whether men be in society or not. Thus, the *continuity* between the state of nature and civil society is shown by the fact that men are as capable of using reason in the former as in the latter and are as capable of having reason guide their conduct. To the extent that they allow themselves to be guided by reason and the law of nature—to that extent they do not need any positive law to lean upon. This, then, is the deep authority of natural law: that if any ruler or government act in a way contrary to such law, the people have the right to rebel, so that they might thereby return to the kind of peace and rationality they knew in the state of nature.[17]

**Possessive Individualism**   The two most vitally important concepts illuminated by Locke are property and consent. They are interrelated concepts,[18] because a man's right of property is a right that obligates any and every government to keep its hands off his property unless he gives his consent. And the consent a man gives when he enters society (namely, consent to abide by the will of the majority and consent not to take the law into his own hands) is a consent given for the primary purpose of safeguarding his property. Now these two ideas are made interdependent by Locke when he attaches both of them to the state-of-nature framework.*

He does this by giving us what can be called a genetic account of property. That is, he aims to show how property came into being, and from that loosely "descriptive" account he will try to derive property's status as a right in a prescriptive sense. Thus, from a quasi-factual account of what a man actually does when he acquires property, Locke seeks to end up with the idea of what a government ought not to do with regard to the individual. This certainly seems like a case of the is/ought fallacy, in which we try to derive values from facts. Yet Locke's mistake (if it is one) is certainly mitigated by the

* Two fine discussions of Locke's view of property are John Plamenatz, *Man and Society* (London: Longman, 1963), I:241–49, and J. W. Gough, *Locke's Political Philosophy* (Oxford: Clarendon, 1956), pp. 73–92. There has been a provocative reevaluation of Locke's theory by C. B. Macpherson, whose views I shall discuss below, in the section, "New Interpretations."

consideration that he is not describing the ordinary day-to-day acquisition of property, in an organized legal setting, but rather the theoretically "first" acquisition of property in the state of nature. Thus, he is going back to the aboriginal model of ownership—to its *Ursprung* or *archē* (if we take these terms in the senses, both, of principle and beginning). The possible mistake also is mitigated when we realize that Locke uses the word "property" not only to mean possessions but in the wider sense that includes all that belongs to (or is "proper" to) a man—his life, liberty, and possessions. In his discussion of property rights,[19] he therefore makes property the model of all rights.

In order to do all this, Locke takes us back to the state of nature to show us that, like all rights, property is prior to government. The right to property is then seen as man's God-given right to do with himself and with what is his whatever seems best to him.[20] This property theory shows us Locke's basic individualism.[21] That is, a right is always something possessed by an individual, and it is usually expressed as some limitation of the powers of society toward him, in terms of something the state may not do to him. This idea of limitation is characteristic of liberalism in general.

If rights are natural to man, then he must already have them in the state of nature; and if he has any rights at all in the state of nature, then he must have the right of property. But, in order to have the right of property, there must at least *be* such a thing as property in the state of nature. Hobbes maintains that no one can own anything in the state of nature and that I can have no valid complaint if a thief takes something from me. Indeed, there could not really be such a thing as an act of theft in the state of nature, because there is no legal ownership that would exclude someone from using what is "mine." The right of every man to every thing includes the other's right even to my body. According to Hobbes, then, slavery would be entirely natural in the state of nature, because there is no property. What Locke wants to show is that the exact opposite is true: Freedom is natural, precisely because there is such a thing as property in the state of nature. This, then, is why Locke focuses his attention on the right of property and why he seeks to show that such a right already exists in the natural state, prior to any legal confirmation. It is on the basis of this prior right that we expect governments to consider themselves obligated to protect our rights, and this is why we consider our grievances against them to be *legitimate* if they fail in this task.

How can a man be said to own something in the state of nature?

To begin with, every man has the right to his own person, and no one else has a right to it. There is no way in which Locke establishes this point. For him, it is tantamount to saying that one's body is part of one's identity, part of what is "proper" to one. And, therefore, to ask whether a man has a right to his own identity is like asking whether what is his *is* his. To say that what is his is not his is a contradiction. Therefore, to say that what is his *is* his is a self-evident tautology: "every man has a *property* in his own *person*. This, nobody has any right to but himself."[22] From this point, Locke goes on to say that a man's labor is his own as well—because one's labor is the extension of one's body. Now from this he goes on to conclude that if I therefore take something out of the state of nature, something that belongs to no one (for example, fruit found on an uninhabited island), then by taking it (that is, picking it off a tree) I mix *my* labor with it and thereby make that thing mine. In the literal sense I have "appropriated" it, made it something that belongs to this self. (By the phrase "my labor" he means not only the labor exerted by my body but also the labor of any other body belonging to me, such as that of a servant.)[23]

Of course, there are limits to the right of appropriation, and these are limits suggested by fairness and good sense: I may take only as much as I can use without its spoiling. Beyond that limit, I am invading the possible share of another person. The same restriction applies to the acquisition of land—I may rightfully take only as much as I can practically use.[24] At another point, he says that selling something is one of the uses of it and one of the ways of "using" it. Yet this would mean that I would therefore have the right to appropriate vast tracts of land, some of which I would till and some of which I would sell, and both of these cases would be the taking of what I can "use." But this is clearly not the way he uses the word "use" in this earlier definition, where it is plainly associated with physical labor. Under this literal labor definition of "use," I could not justifiably enclose a huge acreage, leave it idle, and call it mine. Only the actual labor can be the basis of appropriation.

Locke gets himself into difficulties with this pivotal concept: If "right" involves the choice of doing whatever I like with a thing, then certainly my right to a thing must include my right to sell it. But that right of sale would appear to conflict, as we see, with the *basis* of right in labor. The difficulty arises precisely because Locke's justification of right is a genetic one, whereby a right is established on the basis of how the right is acquired. And it must be admitted that there is no logical connection between these two. Thus, it has been pointed out[25] that just because I may have the sole right to the use of my body it does not follow from this that I therefore have the right to exclude someone from using the things I have made with my body.

The difficulty of trying to square the right based on labor with the right of sale is that the former right would limit my possessions to my physical capacities to exploit them, whereas the latter would remove all limitations as to what (and how much) I could rightfully possess. Locke suggests that money was invented in order to overcome just this problem. That is, money was devised as an article of exchange that would not spoil and that would retain its assigned value.[26] (I should add a point that Locke overlooks: Money would also have to be something that could not itself be used or consumed.) The advantage of money, then, is that it allows men to increase their possessions beyond what is immediately usable. Presumably, therefore, Locke's restriction of property (in the state of nature) to that which can be used immediately is a restriction applying only to the "first" or aboriginal acquisition, after which time we go into the wider meaning of "use," which includes sale. Yet Locke does not make this distinction explicit; we must read between the lines to find it. Nor is he aware of any conflict between the two senses of "use."

The theory does serve, however, as a basis for the idea of consent—for, as I pointed out, Locke believes that men enter into political relations only in order to protect their property (in its wider sense of life, liberty, and estate).[27] The labor theory of value, as it came to be called, became a commonplace in eighteenth-century economic thinking;[28] but it also had certain very practical consequences later on—for example, the Homestead Act of 1862, in America, where the size of the land allotted was definitely limited to the work capacity of the people living on it. The theory had no effect, however, on curbing the slave trade (even though the people enslaved were presumably in a state of nature, and therefore the work of their bodies was their own). Nor did Locke intend the theory to curb the slave trade; he does justify slavery if a "lawful" conqueror agrees to spare a man's life in exchange for his enslavement.[29]

(It is interesting that the labor theory of value found its way into Karl Marx's theory of value, after many changes and shifts in meaning. The point in common between them is Locke's statement that 99 percent of the value of a thing is traceable to the labor that went into the making of it;[30] but the difference between Locke and Marx on this question is that Locke believes that this is actually so at present, whereas Marx feels that this is the remote, postrevolutionary ideal and that in the meantime most of the economic value of a thing is made up of "surplus value" above and beyond the cost of labor.)

The concepts of consent and social contract illuminate Locke's vision of political society and its purposes. Man, the atomic individual, seeking to preserve his property ("that is, his life, liberty, and estate"),[31] enters into social relations expressly for that purpose. The social contract is tacit; Locke nowhere gives it an explicit formulation, as Hobbes does. The "contract" consists in a certain involvement of the individual in society whereby he surrenders his right to make judgments on his own or to execute judgment. With the social contract, such right and such power are held by society. Accordingly, Locke defines a civil society as a union of men having a common established law and judicature, together with the authority to decide controversies and to enforce decisions. Where there is no such arrangement, men are in a state of nature. This idea is immediately translated by Locke into an explicit criticism of absolute monarchy (but not of monarchy as such).

Absolute monarchy is "inconsistent with civil society,"[32] he says, because in it men have no judge to turn to for redress of injuries suffered at the hands of the monarch—and this is precisely the situation of the state of nature, as well as the reason why men should leave the state of nature to enter civil society! More than this, the subject in an absolute monarchy has lost even the freedom he enjoyed in the state of nature, to be his own judge and to defend himself. Where Hobbes had said that no tyranny can be as bad as the state of nature, Locke says that tyranny is far worse. Indeed, under a tyrant, even to ask for defense, or to seek defense against one's injuries, is counted as treason. (Locke had obviously read his Suetonius.) In this light, Locke seems to be challenging Hobbes by wondering how men could ever be so foolish as to enter into a contract that limits their own powers while leaving the monarch with unlimited powers in the state of nature. As he says: "This is to think that men are so foolish that they take care to avoid what mischiefs may be done them by polecats or foxes, but are content, nay, think it safety, to be devoured by lions."[33]

The main thing, then, is to place limits upon absolute power. And the way to do this is to erect the apparatus of consent. The freedom, equality, and independence of the individual are declared in the principle that he cannot be deprived of his property or be subjected to the political power of another without his own consent.[34] Now this principle of consent comes into play only with the establishment of a state by means of a social contract. By these means, one body politic is formed "wherein the majority have a right to act and conclude the rest." Because it is to be *one* body, it must follow the will of the majority and move in the direction to which "the greater force carries it." Thus, in addition to giving up his right to be his own judge, the individual consents to comply with the will of the majority. These are the two conditions of the social contract.

Now there are numerous weaknesses in this view of society and consent. Let us remember that Locke is seeking to justify a revolution and that he does this by showing that certain kinds of government are illegitimate: A government is illegitimate when it does not rest its authority on consent.[35] Because, for Locke, it is the individual that is the basic political unit, consent is understood in the way the individual person gives it—as something given consciously and voluntarily. Yet most of the time we are not actually consenting in this way. Does that mean that we are withholding our consent? Obviously not. To overcome this difficulty, Locke suggests that there is also such a thing as tacit consent. We give our tacit consent to a government merely by being in its territory, even if only as tourists for a day. Of course, the giving of that tacit consent does not make a man an actual member of society any more than mere living among a family makes him a member of it. He becomes a member only by consenting to become one and consenting expressly.

But the *tacit* form of consent is what is problematic, not the express consent. Apparently, Locke believes that men can be tacitly consenting even when they do not know it:[36] Their mere residence in a country involves an implicit acceptance of policies they might not know existed. How do we know, then, when they are *not* consenting? The answer is that, although consent can be tacit, dissent and revolution can only be explicit. The absence of active dissent, therefore, can be taken as consent. Yet Locke has made the concept of tacit consent so broad and so vague as to cover any obligation, so that it leaves the individual with no way of withholding his consent *except* by active resistance. The result can be schizophrenic: I am regarded as consenting as long as I keep my mouth shut; I am told that I agree, even when I inwardly disagree, until no alternative is left me but to cry out.

Another weakness of Locke's theory of consent again grows out of his model of consent as given by individual persons. He implies that because the original contract was *made* by the deliberate consent of individuals the ensuing government ought to continue on that basis, its authority dependent upon the ongoing consent of individuals, who continue to give their consent as long as their rights and goods are protected. The result is Locke's "atomism," whereby society is seen as nothing more than a collection of individuals. They already are individuals in the state of nature and maintain their individuality and interests even in society. And then the powers of government extend no farther than the individual's powers over himself. Thus, the legislature cannot rightfully be arbitrary, because it is nothing more than the assembled wills and powers of individuals. And because no man's power over himself is absolutely arbitrary (for example, he must not commit suicide, because he is God's creature), so the legislature's powers over him cannot be absolutely arbitrary either. Neither can a man alienate his own rights and subject himself to the arbitrary power of another, for no man has, by nature, such arbitrary power over another.[37]

This is all very well, but such atomism ignores the fact that the whole is more than the sum of its parts, that society is a collective reality of a very concrete sort and not a mere assemblage of atomic individuals who remain divided even when together. Future political philosophers, such as Rousseau and Hegel, will seek to account for this reality, where Locke could not.

**The Rights of the Atom**    Locke agrees with Hobbes on two points. First, the social contract is entered into by the consent of the parties. (The point of difference is whether the sovereign is a party to the contract, Locke holding that the sovereign is such a party and is thereby obligated and Hobbes that he is not.) Second, the parties to the contract are individuals who are seeking to fulfill their own selfish purposes in entering into a political arrangement. For Hobbes, that selfish purpose is fulfilled by the attainment of peace. For Locke, however, the selfish purpose that moves men to agree to the contract is the purpose of preserving those natural rights they already enjoy as individuals in the state of nature. Governments therefore have their raison d'être only in that they serve the private purposes of the contracting individuals. As I suggested, this "atomism" becomes an identifiable characteristic of liberalism in general, as late as Mill and after (to the extent that it is combined with the idea of the limiting of state power). It is a view coming under frequent attack by those who believe that the collective, not the individual, is the primary political element and that the individual's "rights" are derived from and are secondary to the primary right of the group.

According to Locke, as we saw, the individual's rights are primary, because the "right" of the collective is reducible to the cumulative rights of the constituent individuals. For the sake of those individual rights, the powers and prerogatives of the government must be critically controlled and limited. This is ensured by a powerful legal structure. The point is not so much whether the government is democratic in structure but whether it operates on the basis of law. The legislative power ought to be the supreme power, to which all the other functions of government must be subordinated. But this legislative power, supreme as it may be, is itself to be subordinated to the will of the people, for it is their right to choose their legislators and to remove them when they fail in fulfilling the trust that has been placed in them. When this happens, the ultimate power returns into the hands of the people, and they may then bestow it where they see fit. As Locke says: "Who shall be judge whether the prince or legislative act contrary to their trust? . . . The people shall be judge."[38]

The people depute their legislators and may therefore discharge them. If the prince or legislators refuse to abide by the will of the people, the people's only recourse lies in an "appeal to heaven"— Locke's euphemism for revolution. In the absence of an earthly judge, there is only this state of war, wherein we appeal to heaven to decide who is right. But the state of war is already initiated by the ruling power itself when it seizes property unlawfully, fails to execute laws, corrupts elections, hinders the legislature, sets up its own law—or generally acts without the consent of the people or against their interest. In such a case all contractual obligations on the part of the people are at an end. As Locke says:

Whosoever uses force without right, as everyone does in society who does it without law, puts himself into a state of war with those against whom he uses it, and in that state all former ties are cancelled, all rights cease, and everyone has a right to defend himself, and to resist the aggressor.[39]

All in all, Locke offers us a very rational picture of the purpose of government: to protect individual rights and to serve individual needs.

The fundamental character of government is that it must be *account-able*. In Hobbes's view, it is never accountable. But in the view of Locke government is assigned a more complex task than Hobbes envisaged—namely, the protection of certain basic rights, account-ability for the general welfare, and responsiveness to the will of the people. Commonplace though all this may seem, it must all be enun-ciated, so that the government's responsibilities and proper limits may be clearly defined.

The characteristic outlook of libertarianism is the emphasis on *limiting* the power of government. Personal rights are defined nega-tively, in terms of what a government may *not* do (for example, it may not deprive me of my freedom without due process of law—that is *my* right and *its* limitation). All this was in the revolutionary air when Locke was writing. Indeed, he had before him a good example of such limitation of state power and of the monarch's self-obligation to a contract. The Bill of Rights, passed by Parliament in 1689 (after James II had fled to France in December of 1688), stipulated that the new king could suspend no law, that he could levy no taxes and maintain no army without the consent of Parliament, and that no person could be arrested and held without due process of law. All these violations had been committed by James. The new terms were accepted by William III upon his accession to the throne, and this meant in effect that the new king had entered into a contractual agreement with the people, whereby he accepted his power with limi-tations and conditions.

Another example Locke had of a contractual agreement was in the compromise reached by the Tories and Whigs in opposing James II. What made the revolution the Glorious Revolution was that sensible men of both sides were able to overcome their considerable differences in a time of great stress and potential danger. It was this good sense, combined with the idea of limiting the power of government, that found its way into the American Bill of Rights in 1789 and into its negative language ("Congress shall make no law . . . abridging the freedom of speech") wherein the individual's rights are defined. It is clear that governments are here being held accountable and being subjected to judgment—with the possibility of further limitation, namely, dissolution by popular will. This popular will is seen by Locke as essentially rational and concerned with its own interests. That rationality is expressed in the fact that when the movers of the American Revolution decided to cut their ties of obligation to their former sovereign they decided to give reasons (in their Declaration of Independence)—and the reasons were those of Locke, down to the language in which the reasons were expressed. And it is significant that there are two headings under which "right" is mentioned: the natural rights of life, liberty, and the pursuit of happiness; and the right to alter or abolish any government that fails to secure these rights for its citizens. In addition, there are the Lockean themes of government by consent and governments formed deliberately by men for their own purposes. "To secure these rights, governments are instituted among men, deriving their just powers from the consent of the governed." As a corollary to the idea of consent and the protection of rights, we have the principle "that whenever any form of government becomes destructive of these ends, it is the right of the people to alter or abolish it, and to institute new government." And underlying all is the idea that these natural rights have been granted to man by God.

The concept of natural rights has had a long and a fascinating history, but it is obvious that there is no longer any basis (today) for the idea of a Creator bestowing rights on man. It is a sad and ironic fact that the doctrine of the individual's "natural" rights had already been attacked by Hume and by Rousseau before the American founders made use of the idea. Although it may linger on today as the official democratic ideology, it nevertheless shows itself to be a strangely outmoded doctrine—already moribund when it was given such vital use by men who ignored the attacks on it or failed to see it as a relic of the revolutionary thinking of a hundred years before.

**New Interpretations**    Like Hobbes, Locke has come in for a great deal of reconsideration in recent years—and all this has led to some intriguing interpretations of what it is that Locke really intended to say. Let us return for a moment to Hobbes and recall what Warrender maintains. He maintains that Hobbes *really* says three things: (1) The laws of nature persist through the state of nature into civil society. (2) They are essentially moral laws that do not apply to man in isolation but rather prescribe duties to man in society and to his fellow man, and these laws are morally obligatory because they are commanded by God. (3) These moral laws are therefore not created by the sovereign but are rather "discovered" by him.

Now I have tried to show why this is *not* the correct interpretation of what Hobbes says. It *is*, however, a pretty good summary of what Locke has to say about natural laws: namely, that they apply to the state of nature as well as to civil society, that they are moral laws commanded by God (and also known by reason), and that the sovereign must govern in accordance with them, so that he discovers them and does not create them by his own dictates.

It would seem, therefore, that Warrender's Hobbes is (by implication) a Lockean. Now, when we come to Locke, we find Strauss saying that Locke is really a Hobbesian. On the other hand, Kendall says that Locke is really a Rousseauian—in fact, one who out-Rousseaus Rousseau! All this is no mere pedantic hairsplitting, no mere question of whether Shakespeare's plays were written by Bacon. Rather, the new interpretations of Hobbes and Locke ought to be seen as a tribute to the strength of their philosophies, in the analytic effort they can continue to evoke in some very fine scholars.

Concerning Locke in particular, the new interpretations revolve around the problems of consent and property—areas in which Locke has quite a lot to say. It is certainly an indication of the complexity of these problems and of Locke's views on them that new interpretations of his views are continually appearing. In addition to Strauss and Kendall, there is Macpherson's work, which has challenged us to look again at Locke and to look as deeply and as carefully as he has. Let us begin with Strauss.

*a.* Leo Strauss maintains that Locke is not a natural law theorist but a Hobbesian and that his Hobbesian egoism is reflected in his treatment of property rights.[40] The reason Strauss gives for the first point is that Locke fails to tell us *how* men can know the law of nature. Now, even if this were true, our not being able to say *how* we know those laws does not preclude the possibility of our knowing or believing them. I can have a belief in God-given natural law without being able to prove that there is a God or that he ordained that law. Locke's mere assertion—that in the state of nature men are free to act and to dispose of their possessions and of their persons as they think fit "within the bounds of the law of nature"[41]—this is enough to classify Locke as a believer in the validity of natural law. In order to be a natural law theorist, a man need merely evince a belief in what he regards as natural law and base certain values upon that belief. It is not incumbent upon him, *qua* natural law theorist, to demonstrate how we can know that there are such laws. This is what I would say to Strauss, if Locke had not given some account of how such laws can be known. The point is, however, that Locke does tell us, both in the *Second Treatise of Government* and in the *Essay concerning Human Understanding* (as I have shown), that these natural laws are available to reason, for any man who will think.

Strauss also says that Locke is a Hobbesian because (following the previous point) Locke recognizes no normative law of nature and regards man as a being who is motivated mainly by egoism and selfishness. Yet, against this interpretation, it should be pointed out that Locke states quite emphatically that every man ought "as much as he can to preserve the rest of mankind" and not endanger the "life, liberty, health, limb or goods of another."[42] This hardly sounds egoistic or selfish. Quite explicitly, Locke states it as a law of nature that men are to be "restrained from invading other's rights, and from doing hurt to one another,"[43] in order that peace and mankind be preserved. Notice that the ultimate interest, here, is not that of the individual but that of mankind at large. Further, in the state of nature, this natural law is already so clear to all that each of us has the right to punish anyone who violates that law. Strauss thinks that, because Locke also says that the observance of such law is conducive to self-preservation, Locke is therefore putting the egoistic aim uppermost. True, Locke does give emphasis to the right of self-preservation—but he by no means regards this in the Hobbesian manner, as leading to a war of all against all. For Locke, the state of nature, let us remember, is one of fairness and cooperation in the best Judeo-Christian sense.

Strauss finds Locke's alleged Hobbesianism in the way he associates the natural right of property with the right of self-preservation. Specifically, Locke approves the unlimited acquisition of property following the invention of money. Before this happens, Locke says that a man may take only as much from nature as will not spoil and only as much as he can use. But with the invention of money we acquire a kind of property that cannot spoil—which means that the spoilage principle is not violated but rather circumvented. Accordingly, Locke cannot be accused of going back on his natural law and of approving unlimited capitalist greed. Further, there is a limitation even upon the acquisition of money for Locke, and that is the obligation to care for the common good and for the preservation of mankind.

The value of the Strauss thesis, however, is in drawing attention to the typically non-Lockean elements in Locke (if such there be), with the result that we are able to avoid giving to Locke's thought the oversimplified view that it is all of a piece. This would lead us, in turn, to look for the true balance in Locke's thinking and to ask ourselves how these atypical elements are to be reconciled with the rest of what he says. The mistake Strauss makes, it seems to me, is to ignore the typically Lockean elements and to elevate the others as Locke's true meaning.

*b.* A more challenging interpretation of Locke is given by Will-moore Kendall, who says that what Locke is really advocating is the obligation of the individual to abide by the will of the majority and that this obligation overrides any rights the individual may have against the majority.[44] It can be said in favor of this view that Locke does place emphasis on serving the common good as one of the major responsibilities of government. Yet it is clear that he does *not* regard the collective interest as the final consideration—simply because his "society" is still a group of individuals, not a collectivity in the Rousseauian sense.

Further, although Locke did not mention the possible dangers in a tyrannous majority and did not warn against such dangers (à la Mill), this does not mean that he would be prepared to accept any and all decrees of the majority, justified by nothing more than a head count. He does say that when a society is unified it is one body and there-fore moves according to the direction of the greater force. But we must not forget that what he sees as the purpose of that unification is the protection of the liberties of individuals. And he sees these pro-tected by means of the limitation of governmental power—even though the government may well be expressing the will of the ma-jority! Thus, when Locke says that a man may not be deprived of his property without his consent (given as an individual), not even the majority has the right to deprive him of it. In other words, for Locke, the will of the majority can never take the place of individual consent.

Rousseau clearly rejects this, for a number of strong reasons (as we shall see in the next chapter), and that rejection is central to Rous-seau's thinking. It follows, therefore, that Locke cannot be the Rousseauian that Kendall makes him out to be. True, Locke says that in joining civil society we obligate ourselves to abide by the will of the majority. But that obligation, he says, lasts only as long as the majority (and its government) observes the rights of the individual and is content to limit itself to that observance. That sort of limita-tion is quite outside Rousseau's spirit, as expressed in his idea of a collective will that cannot be wrong and that cannot be defied.

Ultimately, Locke's basic values are individualistic—and this is what Kendall denies. Not only is Locke's individualism supported by the fact that such atomism is typical of all political theory up to the middle of the eighteenth century; such individualism is reflected also in Locke's writing that "truth and keeping of faith belongs to men as men, and not as members of society."[45] Kendall chooses rather to emphasize Locke's collectivist-sounding utterances.

Thus, for example, upon entering society the individual "has to part with as much of his natural liberty . . . as the good, prosperity, and safety of the society shall require."[46] Now Locke's aim (as we saw) is to justify the 1688 revolution, and toward this end he does not hesitate to invoke the idea of the common good. But this does not mean that he advocates the surrender of the rights of the individual into the hands of society—as Locke repeatedly points out, it is in order to safeguard these personal rights that the individual enters society and gives his consent to it as an individual. Yet it is precisely this absolute sort of surrender Kendall reads into the statement just quoted. As we saw, the natural liberty he is asked to give up is the liberty of being a law unto himself, acting as self-appointed judge over others. It is specifically *this* liberty he gives up, not liberty as such, and the context surrounding the quotation makes that point quite clearly.

Kendall seems to say that according to Locke the individual gives up *all* his rights upon entering civil society and then has certain of these rights granted to him again by society—namely, only those rights that are conducive to the preservation of society or that society finds harmless to its existence. But this reading conflicts with Locke's view that the rights of the individual remain in force and unimpaired from the state of nature through the transition to civil society. If Kendall finds an emphasis on communal rights in Locke, perhaps it is because Locke is aware that society does have certain claims it can legitimately make upon the individual. For Locke, however, these communal claims can never override individual rights. Where Kendall goes wrong is to see a conflict between the individual claims and the social claims *chez* Locke and then to say that what Locke really means is to place the social claims above those of the individual.

Generally, however, Locke sees no such conflict. He believes that the individual's claims and the social claims can be harmonized, that the private and public interests can be made one. Indeed, it can be said that for Locke this is society's main task. And the reason for that view is his atomistic belief that in the final analysis society is the aggregate of individuals who retain their individualities and interests *as* individuals when they join society and that the public good is therefore the sum of the separate goods of individuals. When Locke believes that the private and public interests can be made one, he does not go so far as Plato to say that they are identical or as far as Rousseau, who says that they are identical in essence. Locke merely feels that there is an area of compromise and adjustment shared by the two spheres and that they need not clash as a matter of logical necessity.

Kendall says that Locke, by putting the claims of the collective over the rights of the individual, out-Rousseaus Rousseau.[47] Yet this is so alien to Locke's spirit that he does not even tell us how the will of the majority is determined or expressed. Remember that the majority keep giving their consent as long as they are silent. Such passive acquiescence is expressly rejected by Rousseau, so it cannot be in keeping with the Rousseauian populism Kendall ascribes to Locke. For Locke, the majority is heard from only in revolution. This means that the majority has no active part to play in the normal run of things. Locke would be a populist if he held that the collective will is justified in rebelling whenever it decided to do so.* Then the collective will would always be right. But Locke explicitly says that the community is justified in rebelling only when its rights (as the rights of individuals) have been violated, when the government acts in a way that is contrary to the trust placed in it to maintain peace and property.[48] According to Locke, the people would not be justified in rebelling merely because they did not like their representatives or were dissatisfied with them. That would not be sufficient for an "appeal to heaven." As long as the representatives are safeguarding individual rights there can be no justification for ousting them. More than this, it might even be said to follow from Locke's view that if a government governs in accordance with natural law, which is God's will, then its right to continue in power is, in a way, a kind of divine right![49]

Perhaps the most telling point, however, against the Rousseauizing of Locke is this: What Locke calls the will of the majority is what

* For example, John Milton's pamphlet, "The Tenure of Kings and Magistrates" (1649), says that the people "may either choose or reject him, retain him or depose him . . . merely by the liberty and right of free-born men to be governed as seems to them best." Quoted by J. W. Gough, *The Social Contract* (Oxford: Clarendon, 1963) p. 101.

Rousseau denounces as the mere will of all; it is *not* the general will. It is still a self-interested will of individuals, Rousseau says, and any state based thereon lacks a moral warrant. Locke cannot therefore be said to be out-Rousseauing Rousseau in advocating the individual's submission to the will of the majority (even if, on the contrary, he were advocating this), because Rousseau finds such submission totally unacceptable, and he says so (as we shall see) when he calls Englishmen slaves for doing just that.

The question we may ask is why these new interpretations appear. Undoubtedly it is because they reflect difficulties and possible inconsistencies in Locke's theory itself. Why, for example, does Kendall's interpretation come to light, and what is the reason for its evident appeal? Perhaps it is due to the possible conflict between one's essence as an individual and one's existence as a social being. Thus, the *need* for a new interpretation (Strauss's, Kendall's, or anyone's) stems from the fact that for Locke rights are always rights of individuals, whereas the revolution that is intended to restore such rights is always an event involving a whole society. What Locke must do, therefore, is to show that the social system is justified on the basis of the rights of atomic individuals. This is hard to maintain, because (as has been so often emphasized) a society is more than an aggregate of individuals who stay individuals even when in society. A man does not stay the same man when he makes the transition from the state of nature to civil society: He becomes a member and thus acquires a new status.

The problem of justifying the revolution, therefore, comes down to the problem of equating individual right with the individual's status as a member of a larger entity. Locke does not deal with this problem at all. And it seems not to have occurred, as a problem of political theory, to anyone else in the seventeenth century. Further, it seems not to have occurred to anyone in the seventeenth century that although atomism might be the proper model for man in the state of nature it hardly fits man in the social setting in which he has countless ties of affection, loyalty, responsibility, and obligation to the collective whole. In this light, Locke's attempt to justify the English revolution is faulty. To overcome this weakness, Kendall swings in the opposite direction and says that Locke's justification of revolution is in no way dependent upon individualism but rather is dependent on the idea of collective welfare and collective will—and then, presumably, the problem evaporates. As a result, Kendall may come out

of this with a better justification of revolution, but it is not the one
Locke offers.

c. Perhaps the most exciting new interpretation of Locke is that of
C. B. Macpherson.[50] Far from agreeing with Kendall that Locke is
a "majority-rule democrat," Macpherson says that Locke is not a
democrat at all. Rather, he is one of the apologists of capitalism—a
conservative, representing the views of the propertied class. According
to Macpherson, Locke's attitude to the laborer is characteristic: The
laborer is necessary to the nation, but he cannot have an active part
in civic life or in the political structure; further, the laboring class
cannot be said to live a fully rational life.[51]

The assumption is that if a man is intelligent he takes pains to
make his way in the world, and therefore anyone who is in the laboring class must lack the intelligence to better himself. Thus, the degree
of one's rationality is indicated by one's economic position: The acquisition of property is a rational enterprise, and whoever has failed
in it has thereby failed in his rationality. Further, if rights are somehow dependent upon their being grasped by reason, then there must
be different rights for those who lack that basic rationality. The
laboring class lacks such rationality and thus differs from the upper
class in its political rights. According to Macpherson, then, Locke sees
a difference between the propertied and the nonpropertied human
natures, to the extent of assigning different natural rights to the two
groups.

As we saw, Locke says that it is natural for man in the state of
nature to take only as much as he needs for his subsistence. Anyone
who takes more is unfair (because he invades the rights of another),
is unnatural (because he violates the law of nature), and is irrational
(because he goes against reason). This would hardly provide a justification of capitalist greed. Yet such a justification is precisely what
Locke sets out to provide. According to Macpherson, Locke seeks to
*remove* the limitations of natural law from the property right of the
individual.[52] That is, the invention of money makes it possible (and
permissible) to accumulate far greater property, so that the natural
limits no longer hold. And then, according to Macpherson, Locke
suddenly believes that the desire to accumulate extensive property is
now rational, where it was irrational before. It now becomes reasonable for a man to want to enlarge his holdings. And it is *this* desire to
accumulate property, beyond the needs of immediate subsistence, that
leads the rational man into joining society!

Thus—and all this is according to Macpherson's reading of Locke— Locke is faced with the problem of showing that men are rational enough not to need a Hobbesian overlord yet competitive enough to make them surrender certain of their rights to society for the sake of securing their property.[53] This needed a twofold and conflicting view of human nature. Locke derived his idea of man's rationality from the typical atomism of his era—the atomism that saw all men as essentially the same. But the idea of men's competitiveness held that they are not all the same, that there are two distinct classes, the first being rational and concerned with the accumulation of wealth, the second not rational and concerned only with personal survival.

The individual's unlimited right to acquire property must eventually come into conflict with the rights of others, and it is in order to avoid this conflict that Locke advocates the supremacy of the state over the individual. Therefore, as Macpherson says, "the more thoroughgoing the individualism, the more complete the collectivism."[54] And in this individualism the freedom of the nonowning classes must be denied. We can say, therefore, that the natural right to acquire unlimited property must lead to the limitation of *other's* rights. In this way, presumably—according to Ryan's paraphrase of Macpherson's paraphrase of Locke—Locke argues for the "rightful absolute power of the propertied classes, for a morally justified tyranny of the employers over the employed."[55]

This is quite a long way from the Locke we know, or thought we knew. According to Macpherson, the idea that property is based on labor is *intended* by Locke as a moral foundation for bourgeois appropriation.[56] And, with the overcoming of the limits to appropriation only for one's immediate use, Locke's theory of property is intended by him to establish the natural right to *unequal* property and to unlimited individual acquisition—to the point that this personal right of appropriation overrides any moral claim on the part of society. Locke has presumably overcome, thereby, whatever moral limits capitalism might have been faced with. But that is only a negative accomplishment. Beyond this, Locke also seeks to justify (as being natural) a class difference with regard to man's rights and rationality, thereby giving capitalist society a positive moral basis. The differentiation of rights along the lines of class goes so far that the right to rebel is given only to those who own property: Because a man is justified in rebelling only when his right to property has been violated, it follows that someone without property could never rebel with justification!

Macpherson has drawn some startling implications (that is, if these are indeed implied) from Locke's views. They are startling because, if correct, they reveal an altogether one-sided and materialistic basis for libertarianism and democracy. Yet there remains the twofold question of whether Macpherson is right in saying that these implications can be drawn and whether he is right in saying that Locke himself intended these implications. It is hardly possible to believe with Macpherson that Locke actually believes rationality to belong *only* to the propertied class and that that rationality is displayed only in the acquisition of property.[57] All this is highly dubious, for Locke says that all men can know the laws of nature because all men are rational—even aborigines in Asia and America who never heard of a syllogism. And certainly the Locke of the *Essay* (written the same year as the *Treatise*) would hardly say that rationality is expressed in only one kind of activity and, moreover, an activity of an external sort.

Further, because it is the aim of Locke to justify the revolution on the basis of certain universal principles, there would simply be no sense in his saying that only a *part* of the population (and only a very small part, numerically) was justified in rebelling in 1688 (because they alone had property) and that the rest were not. We must not forget that the basic social conflict, as Locke sees it, is between the king's absolute power and the rights of the people—not between the bourgeoisie and the proletariat.[58] But what is perhaps most damaging to Macpherson's thesis is Locke's continual definition of property as *more* than material possessions—to include life, liberty, health, limbs, and so on. It is obvious, therefore, that when Locke speaks of rights he cannot be speaking *only* of the rights of those who own material property or of the property-owning class alone. And that means that he cannot rightfully be regarded as merely an apologist for capitalist acquisition.

As to Locke's intentions (which the Macpherson thesis rests on, presumably), these are clear: to justify resistance to a particular case of abusive power by directing our attention to the meanings embedded in the universal concepts of "right," "consent," and what is "proper" to man *as* man.

Yet it is equally clear that Locke's lasting contribution goes beyond his immediate intentions. It consists, first, in his taking the discussion out of the realm of contemporary politics and elevating it to the level of philosophy. This already shows us a great deal about the solvency and vitality of political philosophy: It uses both theory and the consideration of immediate political problems as occasions for deeper thinking about man and society. In this respect, Locke's example as thinker *engagé* (and the examples provided by all the other thinkers in our discussion) is of enormous value to political philosophy as a human enterprise.

More specific and of greater importance are his argument for libertarian democracy and the way he connects democracy to human reason. Today, the basis he stood on—that of God-given natural rights—is gone, dead as all metaphysics. Yet there remains the idea that free men, choosing freely, would choose democracy as a system to live by, because it allows for the freest expression and interplay of reason. No finer defense of democracy could be offered.

# ROUSSEAU
## The State as Collective Will

So far, we have seen political theorists bent upon exploiting the difference between description and prescription—that is, pressing the knife-edge of theory into the line that separates how things are from how they ought to be. As far back as Plato's *Republic*, we find political theory projecting a vision of how society ought to be structured in order to achieve some supreme goal not yet at hand: for Plato, the union of power and wisdom; for Machiavelli, a situation of political health; for Hobbes, political tranquillity; for Locke, the securing of individual rights. Accordingly, we may now permit ourselves a generalization: Political theorizing involves criticism (tacit or explicit) of a present political system, with a view of what could take its place. Thus, it would seem that what moves a man to construct a political *theory* is the perceived inadequacy of political *reality*. As a theorist, he attempts to lift the discussion from the level of present politics and to elevate it to philosophy. This is when his thinking begins to interest us and to acquire a relevance to a time other than his own.

We see this pattern of criticism-via-theory to a superlative degree in Rousseau. His is criticism in overdrive, attacking not merely the politics of his time but civilization itself. This is the first time, in the modern world, that we are presented with the idea that civilization is a crime against nature, a fraud of which we must divest ourselves. The criticism is moral: Against the current pride in the advances of the arts and sciences, Rousseau declares that they have fostered merely the *appearance* of virtue, not its actualization. Man has lost an innocuous human nature and has acquired a nature of depravity and enslavement.

In pointing to the remedy, Rousseau is at the same time gesturing in the direction of social forces that are yet to be released, long beyond his own time—forces that would carry implications he could hardly have foreseen. Thus, we find here the first inkling of a distinctly twentieth-century phenomenon: totalitarianism, expressing the will of the mass yet severely restricting its rights. In contrast to Locke's emphasis on the limiting of state power vis-à-vis the rights of the individual, we have Rousseau's doctrine of collective authority. Further—on a broader cultural plane—Rousseau exerts an immense influence in the direction of Romanticism by evoking its characteristic elements in his thinking, using emotionalism to sanctify the contradictions in his personal life. But, more significantly, he used that emotionalism in speaking to forces that would bring men together on the basis of irrationalism and the call to the blood. In this, he foreshadows (again, without foreseeing it) the twentieth century in its return to paleolithic darkness.

Having made our bow to this side of him, we can now go on to examine his discursive argument—in its superb rationality.

**Civilization and Its Discontents**   If we knew nothing more about Rousseau than this one point, that he views civilization as a crime against nature, we might well imagine that it would have led him to look upon nature and natural man as idyllic models to be emulated, restored. But far from it: he describes man in the state of nature as a creature to be pitied, more beast than man. The popular impression of Rousseau, that he advocates a return to nature and to primal man, is mistakenly read into his criticism of modern culture, which he regards as a disaster. Yet, if neither Nature nor Culture provides adequate models for man, what is there left for him?

Rousseau's frontal attack on civilization is felt most powerfully in works such as the *Discourse on the Moral Effects of the Arts and Sciences* (1750), the *Discourse on the Origin of Inequality* (1755), and *Emile* (1762)—although the atmosphere of attack pervades all his political writing. Never before had so strong and sweeping a challenge against civilization been launched; never before had a *political* theory been proposed in response to such a *cultural* challenge. The challenge and the response form a unity. And yet the entire edifice is weakened by a fundamental flaw: Man is seen to emerge out of nature in order to achieve his humanization, but this humanization is itself marred by man's estrangement from nature and the natural, which (far from restoring) he has yet to achieve. There is here a compound ambiguity in the term "nature": In its first occurrence (in the foregoing sentence), it carries a connotation of negativity, in its second that of approbation; moreover, the first use of the term is apparently descriptive, the second prescriptive.

Thus primal man in the state of nature is by no means natural in any positive sense, because he is not yet human. He acquires his humanity only through social experience—and this acquired humanity then becomes his "second nature." On the other hand, society and cultural life amount to a departure from nature: Their function is to "denature" man and make him fit to live with other human beings.

The perceptible difference between how things are and how they ought to be is transformed, by Rousseau, into the difference between how things are and how they were. This gives to the primordial past *something* of the status of an ideal that has now deteriorated. Thus: "Man is born free, and everywhere he is in chains."[1] Or, "Everything is good as it leaves the hands of the Author of things; everything degenerates in the hands of man."[2] Or, "nature has made man happy and good, but society depraves him and makes him miserable."[3] Again, this contributes to the view that Rousseau looks to nature (in the past) as ideal. Yet all this very obviously clashes with his stated views of nature and natural man—thereby leading us to look for some special or technical sense in his use of the term "nature."

In the preface to his *Second Discourse*, Rousseau describes his task as that of separating what is original (natural) from what is artificial (conventional) in the present situation of man. Present man, Rousseau says, is like the statue of Glaucus that was disfigured by time, the sea, and storms until it looked more like a wild beast than a god. So, too, the human soul has undergone a sea change in society until it hardly resembles its own nature, with the result that passion is mistaken for reason and understanding has itself grown delirious. In order to see this, we need a picture of "natural" man to provide a basis for contrast between the artificial present and the "natural" origins of man. And for this, he admits, we must turn to a picture of a condition "which no longer exists, which perhaps never existed, which probably never will exist, and about which it is nevertheless necessary to have precise notions in order to judge our present state correctly."[4]

Let us therefore ask ourselves: What is the cognitive status of this idea—that of "natural man"—and what is the status of the statements made about him? Rousseau declares that we must begin by laying facts aside, "for they do not affect the question," namely, the question of what is natural and what is conventional in man. His investigation, he says, is not historical but is made up rather of "hypothetical and conditional reasonings better suited to clarify the nature of things than to show their true origins."[5] The "natural" man is altogether different from primitive man: The latter actually exists, whereas "natural" man is a theoretical construct, a way of looking at present man with his artificial civilization removed—and then projecting that hypothetical image into the past or the future. (It is in this sense that we are to take his statement that man is "naturally" good: not that the primitive is good but that men as we know them *could* be good if they could overcome what society has done to them, thereby getting "back" to their human nature—and to a "natural" goodness that we might see if we could think away everything men have acquired through civilization.)

We must therefore construct a *hypothetically presocial* stage of human existence. By hypothesis, man at this stage has not yet developed the capacity for language, because this requires social interaction. Lacking language, he lacks reason and therefore all sense of social obligation. We saw how Locke stressed man's linguistic ability in the state of nature: How could man recognize his rights to life, liberty, and property unless he had that linguistic ability? Rousseau's presocial man is capable of no such recognition. The interrelation of these elements is purely formal: Rights depend on their being recognized; their recognition depends upon the ability to reason; the ability to reason depends upon the ability to think in language and to express oneself in language; but the development of linguistic ability, in turn, requires the existence of a social setting wherein communication is carried on. Presocial man, lacking that setting, is thus lacking in linguistic ability and is essentially prerational. *Ex hypothesi*, he cannot be a rational animal. Moreover, he cannot *know* of such a thing as natural law, and he is therefore premoral, sans values, sans everything. He is really prehuman!

Thus, we have hypothetically taken civilized man, stripped him, and thrust him into a hypothetical past; having done this, we can now read "forward" into the present and say (with logical necessity) that everything that is characteristically human about man is acquired through social convention and social experience. But in reading "forward" in this way we are doing nothing more than returning to the assumption with which we began—namely, the assumption that a human being, theoretically stripped down to his "nature," has nothing. Accordingly, I very much suspect that the logical necessity in this chain of statements shows the entire chain to be tautologically empty!

Let us see, however, what content Rousseau attaches to this formal chain. According to the *Second Discourse*, the presocial man is neither sociable nor antagonistic by nature (Locke and Hobbes to the contrary), because these attitudes have meaning only within a social setting. (There is no other person around to receive his sociability or antagonism.) Rather, the presocial man is solitary and uninvolved, concerned only with fulfilling his physical needs. His mental development is severely stunted under such circumstances. If he has enough self-awareness to be concerned for his own preservation, that is as far as he can go in thinking—and even this is not thinking in any real sense, but instinct. Moreover, he lacks the imagination that would go to make him human. As Rousseau says: "His imagination suggests nothing to him; his heart asks nothing of him. His modest needs are so easily found at hand, and he is so far from the degree of knowledge necessary for desiring to acquire greater knowledge, that he can have neither foresight nor curiosity."[6]

In *Emile*, Rousseau talks about a "natural education," one that will enable us to see past the current prejudices of man to his natural dispositions and inclinations.[7] Thus, we are now *educating* a man to naturalness; this theoretically constructed "natural" man *can* see reason, whereas the presocial man (also constructed theoretically) lacks reason and language. Further, whereas the presocial man had nothing, the opposite is true for the man educated to be natural; when we have stripped away the false coat of civilization from Emile himself, we can appeal to his "natural" sentiments (whereas the presocial man is too brutish even for sentiments).

We can summarize all this as follows: Rousseau talks in two different ways about man outside society. The first way is in his *Second Discourse*, in *The Social Contract*, and in *Emile*, where Rousseau "describes" a hypothetical presocial stage that man has passed through: man as prehuman. The second way is also in *Emile*, where Rousseau talks about (what I would call) a postsocial stage: civilized man now having overcome civilization. The first way only seems to be a description, because Rousseau explicitly rejects that view of it and says that his purpose is explanatory, clarificatory, rather than historio-graphic. The second way is not at all descriptive but is clearly a hypothetical model of what a man would be in his true nature with-out the false veneer of civilization—except that he has been placed in the "future" rather than in the "past." Presocial man never had a nature and will never have one; postsocial man is on the way to attaining his nature, as he is having his cultural encrustations re-moved.

Thus, we are dealing with two entirely different creatures: It is only the postsocial man who is "naturally" good and perfectible, be-cause we can appeal to his "nature" and prescribe ways for his self-improvement. The presocial man, on the other hand, is neither good nor bad—and he is so far from being perfectible, Rousseau says, that he never evolves at all. The main contrast, however, is in the different uses to which these two figures are put by Rousseau. The figure of the presocial man demonstrates man's need for society as the collective basis for his humanization. The figure of the postsocial man is the justification for Rousseau's attack on civilization and its corruptive effects. When we put these two hypothetical constructs together, side by side, we can read Rousseau as saying that man acquires his nature by leaving the presocial stage and entering social life; but social life, instead of fulfilling man's nature, inevitably corrupts him. Roger Masters puts this in a way that is paradoxical yet is perfectly in tune with Rousseau: "men are naturally good and become evil only as the consequence of the perfection of the human species."[8]

The one way in which that civilized corruption can be avoided, Rousseau believes, is by establishing a system that is intended to pro-vide for the individual's fulfillment through social life. Man leaves barbarism and approaches a "second nature"—which he cannot achieve if civilization blocks his path. If he can overcome that obstacle, then he can "return" to a condition that is undeniably his (but that he never had). Man has no nature, fixed in advance. The political animal is not political by nature but only becomes so via social experience. Whatever is characteristically human in man is not the gift of nature but the outcome of man's own efforts.

In reading Hobbes, there arose a question of implementation: If Hobbes is correct and man in the state of nature is so belligerent and antisocial, how did he get together with others long enough to form a society? In reading Rousseau, we are led to ask in a similar vein:

If Rousseau is correct and presocial man lacks reason and is concerned to fulfill only his individual physical needs, what is it that leads him to associate with others? He may call upon others in time of need, certainly, but what is it that enables him to form a more substantial relationship if he lacks the most basic of human values?

The answer lies in pity, or empathy, which enables him to identify himself with another's suffering. This is the only capacity that is not excluded by the absence of reason, language, or values (although *we* would certainly attach a value to it). In presocial man there is no emotion in this identification, only a kind of dry imagination, and this becomes the eventual basis of sociability and social values.[9] Further, this act of identification also comes to serve, eventually, as the basis of equality, friendship, love, and patriotism. More important than this, the general will of society consists in a similar identification of oneself with one's fellow citizens—thereby transporting us out of ourselves.[10] Where Rousseau differs from Hobbes, then, is in finding this natural empathy, rather than reason, in presocial man—and in seeing this as the formative impulse that generates all social life and all subsequent values.

This must not, however, be taken as suggesting a continuity between the presocial stage and the subsequent social situation. For Rousseau, the gap between them is almost ontological, as though a gap between Nature and Spirit, between the brute animal level and the human. Should the transition be achieved, however, it allows man to substitute justice for instinct, thereby giving him the morality he lacked. Now he can consult principles and reason, so that he is transformed from "a stupid, limited animal into an intelligent being and a man."[11] With the surrender of his natural condition he loses his natural liberty and the right to take up whatever he wants; but he gains a civil liberty and the right of ownership. He also acquires the self-governance that is moral freedom—a freedom in which he obeys not his appetites but the laws of society. In this obedience he is both moral and free, because these are laws he has prescribed to himself— and only the "obedience to the law one has prescribed for oneself is freedom."[12] Just as it is the function of social life to humanize man in the most elementary sense, so it is the purpose of developed society to "humanize" man in the highest sense—that is, to enable him to become a fully moral and socially responsible individual.

This distinction of mine between presocial and postsocial man (which, I admit, is imposed on writings whose complexity seems to defy such division) is the only way, in my view, to make Rousseau's two figures of man consistent as the thought of one philosopher.* Most English-speaking commentators on Rousseau have overlooked these differences in one way or another, to the detriment of their commentaries. The otherwise astute Roger Masters, for example, writing in the introduction to his excellent edition of *On the Social Contract*, says: "Rousseau's notions of 'natural goodness' and 'freedom' are based on the presumed 'state of nature' which existed before civil society corrupted the human species."[13] But in view of Rousseau's insistence that presocial man has no nature, no values, what is there in him to corrupt? What is there in such a species of man that could degenerate? *Emile* is meant to answer that question—to show in what sense man is "naturally" good.[14] But it answers that question elliptically.

Our human "nature"—that which connects us to all mankind—is revealed in one thing alone: conscience. But because conscience does not exist in presocial man and exists in only a corrupt form in present man, we must point to some hypothetically purified model of man in whom it *could* manifest itself. Thus the idea that man is "naturally good" means that man has the potentiality to *develop* a moral consciousness—and the man with that potentiality is not presocial man (who never evolves) but the corrupted man of the present, the man who (now impeded by society) would *become* "naturally good" if society's pernicious influence were corrected or removed. Thus, it is in his potentiality (as yet unrealized) that we find the voice of "nature" in man, a voice as yet inchoate.

In *Emile*, Rousseau extols a kind of dangerous innocence that follows Pascal's dictum about the heart having its reasons which reason knows not of. Rousseau goes so far as to say: "Let us set down as an incontestable maxim that the first movements of nature are always right. There is no original perversity in the human heart."[15] In the light of his potential "nature," man is a free and sentient animal. Our "natural" inclination is to be happy, to take pity on others, and these feelings exist even in the worst of us: "the most ferocious killer supports a fainting man."[16] If such an inclination is in the killer, then surely it is part of our "nature" as human. It is *this* appeal Rousseau asks us to obey. "There is in the depths of souls, then, an innate principle of justice and virtue according to which, in spite of our own

---

* "There is a great difference between the natural man living in a state of nature and the natural man living in the state of society. Emile is not a savage to be relegated to the desert. He is a savage made to inhabit cities." *Emile*, p. 205.

maxims, we judge our actions and those of others as good or bad. It is to this principle that I give the name *conscience*."[17] This allows us to distinguish between the acquired and the natural and also between thought and feeling. Feeling precedes knowledge. The decrees of conscience are not intellectual judgments but feelings, and it is these alone that tell us of the fitness of things. Above all, to exist is to feel (*sentir*), and if the knowledge of good is not innate in man, certainly the love of it is—the conscience that impels him to love the good, uniting man with man:

Conscience, conscience! Divine instinct, immortal and celestial voice, certain guide of a being that is ignorant and limited but intelligent and free; infallible judge of good and bad which makes man like unto God; it is you who make the excellence of his nature and the morality of his actions. Without you I sense nothing in me that raises me above the beasts, other than the sad privilege of leading myself astray from error to error with the aid of an understanding without rule and a reason without principle.[18]

**Collective Consciousness, Infallible Consensus** It is individual men who cannot feel (and therefore do not really exist). It is individual men who, corrupted by society, fail to achieve a shared life. Individuated in this way, can they somehow be led into a life on an altogether different (namely, communal) plane? We must see this as an ontological problem: Men must go into another order of being, wherein they say "we" instead of "I." The problem is to delineate an altogether different sort of society, one in which honest feelings could be preserved, a society that would *not* lead inevitably to the corruption of individual values but rather preserve them on this higher level of being. For Rousseau, this becomes the methodological problem of delineating a society that is so unified that we can speak of *its* will— yet without denying the wills of its individuals.

This is the essential problem of all social organization as such, and it is the problem that the institution of the Social Contract is intended to resolve: " 'Find a form of association that defends and protects the person and goods of each associate with all the common force, and by means of which each one, uniting with all, nevertheless obeys only himself and remains as free as before.' This is the fundamental problem which is solved by the social contract."*

* "Trouver une forme d'association qui défende et protége de toute la force commune la personne et les biens de chaque associé, et par laquelle chacun, s'unissant à tous, n'obéisse pourtant qu'à lui même, et rest aussi libre qu'auparavant. Tel est

92 THE POLITICAL ANIMAL

The problem, in other words, is to find a form of society in which the freedom of each individual is retained—despite the fact that all association per se involves the surrender of some freedom. (From this point of view, the totalitarian state is not a solution to the problem but a sign of failure.) Thus the problem is to form the kind of association in which the individual is protected yet renders obedience to his own will—and thereby remains as free as he was before.

The solution to the problem, for Rousseau, is that each man gives up all his rights, surrendering them to the community, so that no individual can have claims against the community. If each of us gives up the same rights, Rousseau feels, we gain as much as we lose—and we gain the protection of what we have. Rousseau expresses what he considers the essence of the social contract as follows: "Each of us puts his person and all his power in common under the supreme direction of the general will; and in a body we receive each member as an indivisible part of the whole."[19] He goes on to say that this act of association transforms the contracting individuals into "a moral and collective body," which thereby acquires "its common identity, its life, and its will." The underlying problem is really metaphysical, although Rousseau operates with it on the political plane. The metaphysical problem has to do with the reality of a collective entity: Is it equal to, or more than, the sum of its parts? Rousseau's view is that the act of association makes the contracting individuals into something more than an assemblage of men who think as individuals: Their act of association makes them into a moral entity and a collective self—a sovereign people, whose sovereignty is shared in by its members although it is not divisible among them.

Because the sovereign power is identical with the citizens who compose it, it does not need to give them any guarantees against encroachment upon their personal liberties or against other kinds of harm. Such harm is in any case impossible, because the body *is* its members and cannot injure them. Therefore, the sovereign power can have no legitimate objections raised against it by its members, and it is always what it ought to be!

This identity (of all with each) holds only so long as the citizen is

---

le probléme fondamental dont le Contrat social donne la solution." CEV, II: 32. See SC, I:vi, p. 53. It should be emphasized (as is made clear by Vaughan) that the phrase "le Contrat social" refers not to the book but to the act of agreement in social life. The first draft reads: "dont l'institution de l'Etat donne la solution" (i.e., "which is solved by the institution of the state").

active in political life. If he is passive and takes no part or responsibility in the collective decisions, then he is no longer a citizen but becomes a mere subject. And, as an individual subject, he *can* have interests that conflict with the interests of the whole. Therefore, the social compact must contain the implicit agreement "that whoever refuses to obey the general will shall be constrained to do so by the entire body." This alone gives force to the rest of the compact, Rousseau says, and this means only "that he will be forced to be free."[20] Presumably, he is "free" by being one among equals and thus subject to no man; but he achieves this only by recognizing the rights of the community over him, and only his recognition of the community's superior rights can legitimize social agreements. (Without this priority of the community over the individual, the individual would perhaps be dependent upon the whims of a tyrant—and in this light the citizen's dependence upon and subjection to a community of wills identical to his own is actually a liberating factor.)

On the other hand, if the individual has to be forced, then it *is* actually possible for him to disagree with the collective will. For Rousseau it is the ideal "ought" that is significant here, namely, the ideal situation wherein the individual's interests are identical to those of the collective, so that its interests are his. Only on the basis of such an identity can a social order be achieved that works for the good of all. This amounts to saying that if there is *one* interest shared by all, then a state that *heeds* the unified general will is a state that *serves* that interest. But we might object that this is not necessarily true. A state may *wish* to serve the common interest yet take the wrong means of doing so and thereby do a disservice to that interest. Rousseau goes further and says that unless there is unanimity from the start there can be no state. This, we might want to say, is not true either. Perhaps it is true to say that unless there is unanimity there cannot be a *good* state, but the absence of unanimity does not make a state as such impossible.

In his effort to establish a moral basis for the state, he thus appears to conflate values with factual possibilities. Apparently, he arrives at this through the belief that the bond that ties men together into society is the identity of interests, an identity they feel, and that without such an identity of interests no state can *come into* existence. This would mean that all states *began* with such an identity of interests and have since declined from that initial unity. Yet he nowhere makes that claim. And he would certainly be wrong (from a factual point of view) were he to say that no state can actually continue to exist (regardless of the situation at its origin) *unless* there is an ongoing identity of interests.

I do not believe, however, that he is making such a claim; rather, I believe he is saying that a *true* state, a moral state, cannot exist without such an identity of interests. Yet that says much less than it seems to say: Rousseau is *equating* that ideal state with complete unity in its citizenry and *then* saying that you cannot have the one without the other. Thus, he says this as though the ideal state were the *consequence* of that unity—but all he is entitled to say is that you cannot have the one without the other because they have been equated as co-conditional. Perhaps any effort to introduce value concepts into the notion of society repeats this mistake in one way or another. We simply equate the state's existence with a given moral standard, and then it *seems* that the former depends upon the latter —but the only consequence we are entitled to draw is a trivial tautology, empty of content, to the effect that if the *legitimating* moral standard is not actually fulfilled then no *legitimate* state is possible.

One is tempted to look for other such formal errors in Rousseau. Yet looking for them does not help us to understand his thinking but may lead us into a reductive view of him, whereby we see the totality of what he is saying as depending for its truth on the truth of one or more of its elements. As with other political philosophers, our effort to understand his theory (or theirs) must take us in the direction of seeing its complexity, not in trying to simplify its meaning. Simplification is the method of ideology, not philosophy.

What is of great value is the way Rousseau poses the problem of society in all its complexity: to find a form of association in which we are united as a collective entity yet retain our individuality and personal freedom so that we obey ourselves alone. No one before Rousseau stated it so succinctly—revealing the problematic and even paradoxical character of social life in its highest form, in seeking to promote men's complete individuality together with their complete socialization, a dual fulfillment. Something of this paradoxicality is reflected in the fact that men actually do (to some extent) achieve their individuation through their social involvement and, further, that a proper social structure is achieved only to the extent that men act as socially responsive and responsible individuals.

There is an ironic flaw, however, in the fact that Rousseau does not maintain this sense of paradox: He does not keep up the tension between the two termini by giving equal force to both (so that the rights of the individual would limit society, and the demands of society would restrict the individual). If he could have maintained this tension, he might have managed to rise above it to some sort of synthesis. He does *say* that the terms "individual" and "society" are interdependent and that each can be understood only in the light of the other. But he does not go on to *show* that each term is only partially meaningful in itself and that it gets its full meaning only in this interrelatedness. Instead, the tension breaks down when Rousseau declares that the individual must submit to the general will and must be absorbed in it.

There is a way in which Rousseau does try to achieve a synthesis in the contrast between the individual and the collective. He attempts to do this by *identifying* the private with the public interest. In the ideal society he speaks of, the *moi* is a *moi commun*. As a general truth about all societies, he declares that as soon as a man says about public affairs, "What do I care?" social life is finished and the state may be given up for lost.[21] Of course, the identification of interests is the ideal that ought to be the case; what exists is quite the opposite. Rousseau has not, it seems, actually risen above the implicit conflict between individual and collective interests but only talks *as if* it is in fact impossible for such a conflict to occur, as though nothing but such an identification is possible. We shall see that he is not saying this.

The body cannot hurt its limb, he says. If he is not speaking about factual possibilities, does he mean that it is *logically* impossible for the body to hurt its limb? What we are inquiring about is the logical possibility of the separation of private from public interests: To what extent must we regard such an identification as rational, natural, human? When a man places his own interest against and above the public interest, is he being irrational, unnatural, inhuman?

We heard Rousseau say that it is in man's nature (via his conscience) to choose the good.[22] Socrates had said that it is natural for a man to desire the good and that no man knowingly chooses evil.[23] Critics have argued against this by pointing to the streak of perversity in men, leading them to choose evil over good. It would appear that Socrates is contradicted by empirical evidence. Yet Socrates is not making an empirical observation in the field of psychology: He is not saying that it is a matter of fact about men that they always choose the good. Rather, Socrates is speaking about a *logical* connection

between choice and good—that is, to choose entails (logically) placing one object above another in a scale of values; and, if "good"
means "more preferable than evil," then to choose evil over good
means that the lower is higher than what is higher in the scale.
(When Satan, in *Paradise Lost*, says, "Evil, be thou my good," he is
choosing it *qua* good.) Thus, Socrates is making not the psychological
claim that no man chooses evil knowingly but rather the logical claim
that to choose evil knowing it to be evil is to choose illogically.

Perhaps this sheds some light on Rousseau's problem of the naturalness of the identification of interests. Rousseau says that because a
man's welfare is bound up with the general welfare he must desire the
general welfare as he desires his own; this is the basis for the identification of private with public interests. Now, it is notoriously true
that, as soon as we speak of man's social nature, his antisocial behavior stares us in the face. Is Rousseau saying that, as a matter of
fact, men always desire the common good and find it natural to do
so? He could hardly have meant to say this, for then it would have
been unnecessary for him to write the *Social Contract*, in which he
*urges* us to accept such an identification as natural. Perhaps, then (as
with Socrates), we can say that what Rousseau is asserting is not an
empirical but a logical claim—that is, that the concept "social life"
logically entails the idea of life so bound up in its very essence with
the life of others that to prefer a private good that excludes the
public good is tantamount to preferring what cannot be preferred
without contradiction. To put one's private interest over the general
welfare is to act against that private interest itself (because that private interest is in essence involved in the general welfare). It is like
trying to say: "I am choosing this *for* my benefit although I know it
to be *against* my interest." Perhaps this is what Rousseau means by
saying that a man wills the general good in his own interest[24]—that
any genuine social life involves such an intermingling of interests that
I cannot logically desire my own welfare without desiring the general
welfare at the same time. And, in the light of this *logical* connection
between public and private interests, the mere idea of placing one's
own interests *above* the general interest is logically absurd—just as it
is logically absurd to place one's interest *against* the general interest
when the general interest includes one's own.

All this is of central importance to our understanding of Rousseau:

First, this identification is precisely the challenge he sees as *the*
substantial problem facing all society as such—to find a system

wherein we are united in the fullest sense yet remain individuals and obey ourselves.

Second, it is precisely the absence of such an identification of interests that condemns contemporary political life in his eyes.

Third, perhaps the most important point of all, this conscious and positive identification of interests is what he advocates as the solution to all our political difficulties. Very much like Plato, Rousseau seems to be declaring: Not until private and public interests are one will there be an end to the troubles of this world. In *Emile* he says that the spheres of personal morality and public politics are interdependent, that they cannot be studied separately, and that he who tries to do so will understand neither.[25] Only because the two areas are so closely and essentially related can he condemn civilization on moral grounds!

Thus, this identification of interests is his way of moralizing our political life—in diametric opposition not only to Machiavelli's attempt to separate the two and thus make politics amoral but also to the Christian attitude of resignation, which says, "Render unto Caesar the things that are Caesar's, and render unto God the things that are God's." Such views aim at the bifurcation of man—and with this bifurcation, civilization has failed us most seriously. What Rousseau is after is nothing less than a complete reintegration of man: the natural with the spiritual, the public with the private aspects. It is in this light that we must understand him when he says that the general good is nothing but the identity of interests.[26]

It would seem as though Rousseau bases the moralized political life on conformity alone. Thus: "If you would have the general will accomplished, bring all the particular wills into conformity with it; in other words, as virtue is nothing more than this conformity of the particular wills with the general will, establish the reign of virtue."[27] If this is his way of introducing a moral basis into political life, then he fails, because he has presented a merely superficial criterion of morality: conformity of the private with the public standard. Socrates would have directed his attention to that public standard itself, asking what standard *it* was to be based on—the will of the gods? the will of the ruling majority? or the justification of values through reasoned argument? Without fully explicit knowledge as its basis and justification, the merely formal compliance seems hollow. And then the result is that we do not seek the rational principles of this morality but merely try to give expression to the values we already hold. What this gives us is not reason, not philosophy, but ideology.

Yet in my view Rousseau is not advocating mere conformity, as though he were expecting morality to emerge from conformity alone. If political life needed nothing more than such conformity, then the collective voice would amount to nothing more than the sum of individual voices. What Rousseau wants to show, however, is that the totality is more than the sum of its individual parts, that the difference is a qualitative one, beyond the quantitative element of polls and consensus taking. The collective voice is more than, and other than, the summation of the individual voices—enough to give it a kind of infallibility.

The general will, he says, cannot err.[28] At first glance this seems absurd, to be dismissed out of hand. The challenge to us, however, is to see just how this idea does make sense.*

The question before us is whether the general will is infallible on a quantitative or a qualitative basis. The superficial objection to the idea of its infallibility is that the infallibility of the general will is established on nothing more than a quantitative aspect: unanimity. If Rousseau means that the general will cannot err if it is unanimous, then he is wrong. The mistaken interpretation has Rousseau saying this—as though any act of the general will is justified by its unanimity alone—and then we are not very far from regarding Rousseau as the forerunner of totalitarianism.[29] Further, the quantitative view of infallibility would lead to the criticism that one and the same opinion would be correct if held unanimously but wrong if held by a mere faction, or even a majority—so that what would make an idea right and true is not what it says but who and how many say it.

Yet Rousseau does make a qualitative distinction between the general will (which need *not* be unanimous)[30] and the will of all. The will of all is that of individuals concerned *only* with their own interests as individuals. The general will is concerned with the interest of society as a whole. Thus, it is called general, not because of the

* B. Mayo, "Is There a Case for the General Will?" *Philosophy* Vol. XXV (1950). Mayo points out that whatever objections can be made against the concept of the general will can be made also against the concept of the individual will. Yet if there is no strictly scientific basis for the use of either concept, there is nevertheless a pragmatic basis for both. We need the concept of individual will as a source (not a cause) of action, because we cannot reduce a man's purposes to the "purposes" of his constituent organs and limbs. In the same way, we can use the concept of the general will in the light of certain collective purposes, which cannot be reduced to the purposes of the constituent individuals.

number of persons involved but because of its *concern* for the totality. That concern is the concern of all, even if it is not manifestly there in all.

Yes, the people *can* err as to what is in their interest, Rousseau says. He is not deluded as to their fallibility concerning specific questions on which they might be asked to decide. Rather, he maintains that they are infallible concerning their broadest aim of general self-interest as an end, although they are decidedly fallible as to the means for achieving that end. When ends converge, Rousseau says, then there can be a consensus as to means. But if there is agreement as to means and these are not in the public interest, then it is not the general will that is being expressed but rather the divisive will of all. In other words, a consensus as to means leads to discord as to ends if the means are not objectively conducive to a good end. If the interest of the totality is not being served by a given policy (for example, a tax increase), then this would certainly lead us to question what ends are being served.

Thus, means are to be judged as right only in the light of successful ends and not at all on the basis of unanimity. Yet Rousseau gives support to the idea of the infallible consensus by saying that, even if there is a consensus as to means and the decision turns out to have been a wrong one (objectively), then there really was no consensus after all! This seems to be based on a mechanical relation between means and ends: The only road to the good end is consensus—but it does not follow that every consensus *must* lead to good, so that a bad result signifies that a consensus could not have taken place. Thus, it seems that consensus is a necessary condition but not a sufficient condition of a good outcome.

(An often-heard criticism is that Rousseau's general will involves a confusion of necessary and sufficient conditions: For Rousseau, it seems that the one explanation for things going bad is that men place personal interest over public interest; if things go bad it is only because men act as atomic individuals—even though they might agree as to ends and means. Does this reflect a confusion between necessary and sufficient conditions? Presently I shall try to show that this criticism is not altogether correct.)

The idea of the general will also serves Rousseau as a weapon of attack against the formalistic approach of democracy that bases itself on the belief that a 51 percent majority has, ipso facto, the right on its side. For Rousseau, the general will is not a function of the nu-

merical proportions of voters. Rather, as we saw, it is a function of
the social concern of the citizenry. (And thus we see that the idea
of the general will is fundamentally qualitative, not quantitative.)
Even though the general will is made up of individuals, as is the will
of all, the concerned citizenry places public interest above private
interest—not with a view to enhancing the contrast between them
but rather in such a way that a man's public interest *becomes* his
private interest, as in the Greek polis in the idealized sense. In the
democratic will of all, the citizenry are individuals also, but without
any sense of involvement with one another. Their private and public
interests are and remain distinct worlds, and this distinction results
in a low quality of communal life. For this reason, Rousseau is decidedly against representative democracy: To the extent that representatives represent individual voters (each of whom votes for the
man who will promote the voter's private interest), such democracy
reflects a decay of society and a decay of the general will. The English
are free only in selecting members of Parliament, he says, after which
they revert to slavery.[31]

Once a people begins to act through representatives it is no longer
free, and it ceases to exist as a people. The electorate surrenders its
moral autonomy—and when it does this it surrenders its humanness
and its identity as a people. And then a man's so-called identification
of his private interest with the public interest is meaningless. In such
a condition, a man's personal identity cannot amount to much.

It is *seemingly* paradoxical, then, that I achieve my identity and
fulfillment only by submerging myself in the general will, when I take
society's interest as my personal interest. I say "seemingly," because
it turns out to be not so paradoxical at all: What I thought to be
the road to self-interest does not lead to the service of self-interest;
I serve *my* interest best by involving myself fully in the life of my
fellow citizens and serving *their* interest. There is no paradox in this.
In this way, moreover, I actually retain and augment my individuality.
How?

For Rousseau, this is of the highest importance: The identification
of interests is what makes it possible to say that the individual is
really obeying himself. Not only is this the only way to preserve individuality, it is also a sure way to avoid tyranny. Yet how can we build
a public interest on nothing more than a sharing of private interests?
We can, if those interests are pointed outward, as public goals. He
tells us: "But take away from these same wills [that is, from the

private wills composing the democratic will of all] the pluses and minuses that cancel each other out, and the remaining sum of the differences is the general will."[32]

Apparently, if there is no chance of special-interest groups being formed, then these separate interests balance one another into a general will, and the decision is always good. Thus, we can see that the general will is made of the same basic material as the will of all—namely, private interest. The difference is that in the general will the private interest concerns itself with communal life, whereas in the democratic will of all the private interest is altogether remote from it.

We can see another way, therefore, in which the general will gets its justification on a qualitative basis—namely, in the *kind* of concern on the part of the citizenry in the life of full participation in communal affairs. There are, however, quantitative conditions to Rousseau's idea of the general will as infallible consensus: He rejects unanimity as a *necessary* condition for the general will (that is, the idea that without unanimity there can be no general will); but he does accept unanimity as a *sufficient* condition for the general will and its infallibility (that is, if all men are agreed as to a common end, they cannot be in error about the correctness of that end).

Yet even the idea of infallibility is beset by limitations and qualifications, because he does admit that the people can be deceived when they concern themselves with specific issues rather than broad policy. (Only the prince may decide whether to make peace or war, for example. Now, if the decision whether to have peace or war is not broad enough to be the concern of the general will, then just what political relevance has the general will?) As a result, we would have to conclude that what Rousseau *can* derive from the idea of the general will is not the infallibility of the consensus, in any literal sense, but only the *legitimacy* of that consensus.

This is an important conclusion because it answers the question Rousseau had asked at the outset. He began with a thundering declaration about man's political condition, and that declaration led immediately to the question of legitimacy: "Man is born free; and everywhere he is in chains. . . . How did this change occur? I do not know. What can make it legitimate? I believe I can answer this question."[33]

A little later he says, "one is only obligated to obey legitimate powers."[34] And this takes him back to the question of what can make a political system legitimate. How is political power legitimated? The answer is not only in *consent*, for that can be merely formal and ritualistic. Rather, the answer is in *consensus*, based upon, first, the people's intelligent declaration on the basis of adequate information; second, the absence of factions and cabals, so that each man acts as a free and unbound individual; and third, the fact that each individual takes the public interest as his private interest, so that he shares this with others as his most intensely felt concern.

Need we stress the revolutionary character of all this? The concept of legitimacy gives us a weapon with which to condemn certain governments as illegitimate and thereby to justify rebellion against them. But, more than this, it sets the criterion for legitimacy at the highest conceivable level: Although he says there is no one form of government that is *the* right form or necessarily legitimate,[35] he does maintain that legitimacy can be accorded only to that government that promotes the most complete political and individual fulfillment for man. In this light, what government is legitimate? Outside the Greek polis in its idealized sense of participatory democracy, it is hard to think of any.

The people cannot legitimately divest itself of its sovereign identity or of its responsibility as a deliberative power. Its sovereignty is indivisible—and likewise for the deliberative aspect: It must be a collective will, or it is nothing. With this as the basis of healthy political life, the Lockean stress on the limitation of state power as a safeguard for individual liberty seems small-minded. It all depends on which pole we start with. For Rousseau the main point is the quality of political life. This is why he can say that, if the state is a moral person whose life is in the union of its members, then it can justifiably curtail what Locke would call personal freedom. For Rousseau, however, such freedom (of the individual as juxtaposed to the state) is of value only in the corrupt state that offers nothing else (but freedom) toward the individual's political fulfillment. If a state cannot offer such personal fulfillment itself, as a concrete possibility, then no freedom or anything else it does offer can mean very much; and if it can offer such fulfillment, then its shortcomings pale into insignificance. Let us see why.

When the state has the effect of *socializing* man, it changes his very nature. The lawgiver, Rousseau says, must be brave enough to change the very stuff man is made of. (We shall see, later, the startling use Marx makes of this passage.) If we accept this idea of Rousseau's, that social life changes our very nature, that it transforms an individual (who was self-sufficient and complete in himself) into a being who now is incomplete if he is without other human beings and who thereby becomes a part of something greater than himself and of something moral,[36] then the community cannot warrantably be asked to limit itself with respect to the atomic individual. After all, if we are changing man's nature, what do we owe to his former nature? *Once* he was an atomic individual; now he becomes a Man!

In this way, Rousseau comes to the interesting conclusion that the people are both sovereign *and* subject.[37] It is the government that connects the people with itself (see diagram).

The Sovereign State (the people)

$\downarrow$

Government

$\downarrow$

Subjects (people)

The government is merely a commission to execute the general will, and it exists only so long as the people want it. Above all, each of the three must do only its proper task: the sovereign people to legislate, the government to govern by executing the general will, and the subjects to obey. (Notice how, according to the diagram, the people obey themselves.) Any rearrangement of functions must lead to anarchy, he feels. He has followed Plato in some ways by stressing the differentiation of functions, but he has substituted the infallible general will for the wise philosopher–kings. Can wisdom reside, ultimately, in a people?

Totalitarianism is suggested in Rousseau's observation that the larger the population, the greater the concentration of power needed to control it. The more populous the state, the fewer (!) should be the number of rulers—democracy being best suited to small states and monarchy to the largest. Yet "a true democracy has never existed and never will exist,"[38] because it is against man's nature that the majority should govern and the minority be governed. (Another startling idea, this. I take him to mean that it is against the nature of a man, existing as an individual, to allow himself to be governed by others, even if they are more numerous than his own immediate circle.) Democracy suits only a nation made up of gods, Rousseau says. Such perfection is not for mere men. Although no one form of government is best for all, any more than liberty is suitable for all, we can ask whether a people is governed well or badly. That question *can* be

answered, although we may look to differing criteria, such as security
or freedom.

In the constant opposition between the particular will and the
general will, a tyranny-of-one is inevitable. This is the inherent defect
of the body politic from its very birth, working toward its own death
in the same way that age and death are inevitable for the human
body.[39] "The body politic, like the human body, begins to die at the
moment of its birth, and carries within itself the causes of its destruction."[40]

The one way to avoid tyranny's rise is to hold regular assemblies
of the people on fixed dates, at which time the government is sus-
pended with all its executive power and the people deliberate on
public policy and on whether to continue the government.[41] Other
than such prearranged assemblies, all assemblies are to be illegal because they lead to factions. Because the people are sovereign, because
their voice alone is law, they cannot alienate their sovereignty or be
represented by legislators who will enact laws for them. But they can
be represented by executives who carry out their will.

The setting up of a government, as a body of executors, is *not* a
contract between a people and its leaders.[42] A sovereign people cannot
impose a superior over itself. The government therefore acts as execu-
tor of the general will, and only so long as the people will have it.
The social contract involves only the establishing of a society, as a
sovereign people. Hobbes's sovereign was all-powerful because he remained outside the contract. Locke's sovereign is limited in power
because he has signed the contract and has obligated himself to abide
by certain limitations. But Rousseau's sovereign is the people as a
whole, and the government is nothing but its agent, removable at the
people's will. The Hobbesian contract, as Rousseau sees it, seems to
say to the autocrat, "I will give you all my goods, on condition that
you will give me back whatever [of them] you please." And, in his
view, it is no contract at all. For Rousseau, there is only one social
contract, and that is the original act of association, the act of constituting society in the first place. After this original contract, all
further associations are to be regarded as violations of the original
one—and even as an offense to the cohesion and stability of society.


**Freedom, Equality, and Enslavement**    In commenting on Rousseau,
one is tempted to do it all in a series of questions. Thus, one might
wish to ask:

How can we be *forced* to be *free?* Is such coercion at all possible? Is it to be external or internal? If it is possible, is force compatible with the concept of freedom? Or is being forced to be free a self-contradiction?

How is it possible to have a *society* wherein one obeys only *oneself?* Is not Rousseau here exploiting the paradoxicality of this and thus emphasizing the distance between these two concepts? If so, can that conceptual distance be bridged?

How is it against men's nature for the majority to govern and the minority to be governed? How is such a situation against nature in any special sense if *all* society is conventional (antinatural) in the first place?

It seems that we are constantly engaged in trying to clarify these apparent paradoxes and others, to show them to be not so paradoxical after all. This means that we regard paradox as something to be overcome, done away with. Yet paradox is the very engine of Rousseau's thinking, and we must keep the paradoxicality in full tension if we hope to understand him as someone who thinks deeply, uniquely, dangerously.

In chapter iv of Book II of the *Social Contract,* for example, he speaks in a totalitarian mode (the state as person must have a compulsory force to arrange each member to suit the whole), and he immediately goes over into a libertarian mode (we must consider the private person whose life and freedom are independent of the whole). We find this two-sidedness throughout his political writing. Once again a question enters: Is Rousseau a totalitarian thinker, or is he a libertarian thinker? One well-known book asks that question in its title, and its answer to that question is that Rousseau "is trying to achieve liberal aims by totalitarian means."[43] Another scholar has declared that Rousseau gave rise to totalitarian democracy by marrying the concept of the general will to that of popular sovereignty and popular self-expression.[44] Yet, far from "marrying" the general will to these latter concepts, as though the three were distinct, Rousseau would have said that the general will *is* popular sovereignty and popular self-expression. That is to say, instead of the "is" as copula we have the "is" of identity. Moreover, that identity is such that each individual identifies the general will with his own and the general interest with his own.

This identification is directly connected to the idea of equality: The original compact establishes the equality of all citizens (in that all obligate themselves equally and share equally in rights). Yet it would appear that that equality, taken by itself, is a merely formal aspect, to which a content must be added. (After all, we can all of us be equally enslaved and, as slaves, be treated equally before the law.) The content is provided by Rousseau when he translates the idea of equality into the equality of self-interest (we obligate ourselves because it serves the interest of each to do this). But, if self-interest were the universal spring of action Rousseau here believes it to be, then there would be no question of being *forced* to be free because we would in any case be sufficiently motivated by considerations of self-interest.

In chapter viii of Book I of the *Social Contract*, Rousseau distinguishes between natural freedom (in a state of nature), civil freedom (granted by society), and moral freedom (one's obedience to a law one has prescribed to oneself). We might think that the paradox about being forced to be free has to do with civil freedom, because Rousseau is here talking about obedience being enforced by the entire body of society. Yet there is a view that says that the paradox has to do with moral freedom.* I can see some justification for this view in Rousseau's presentation, in chapter vi of Book I, of the fundamental social problem: to find a form of association such that each one, uniting with all, nevertheless obeys only himself and remains as free as before. The self-obedience would be on the *moral* plane (by Rousseau's own stipulation), although the "solution" to the problem would be on the *civil* plane. What this reveals is that my *social* obligation (as civil) is *self-imposed* (and is therefore moral).

Although this seems to resolve the paradox, I see the paradox as persisting and as merely translated onto another level: How can a socially imposed obligation be a self-imposed obligation, even if it is seen as such by the individual? Certainly, we internalize social standards and make them our own, but then they have become the standards of the individual. On the contrary, the problem Rousseau places before us is this: How can the civil obligation be moralized (held to be such by the individual) and still be a social value? Further, how can society and social life be made moral (as Rousseau

* John Plamenatz, "Ce qui ne signifie autre chose sinon qu'on le forcera d'être libre," in M. Cranston and R. S. Peters, eds., *Hobbes and Rousseau: A Collection of Critical Essays* (New York: Doubleday, 1972), p. 324 f. Plamenatz says: "Evidently, it is moral liberty that Rousseau has in mind when he utters his notorious paradox about a man's being forced to be free." But in my view it is not all that evident that the issue is *moral* liberty, if one considers the civil context of Rousseau's statement.

intends) if moral freedom is the individual's self-obedience and therefore suggests that morality itself is a personal matter? Indeed, does
it not seem that as far as morality is concerned we never get to a
*general will* at all but get no farther than the atomized *will of all?*
The answer, as we saw, comes by way of empathy and conscience—
that is, via one's identification with the interests of others and the
internalizing of that identification. We may presume that, in the
periodic assembly of the sovereign people as a whole, expression would
be given to empathy and conscience—and although these are very
personal indeed, we may expect them to be expressed as *la volonté
générale* rather than *la volonté de tous.* Thus the participants in the
assembly would be obeying themselves in the sense of giving voice to
their individual consciences; and even if there were some individuals
who did not agree with the whole, they would accept the view of the
whole as decisive and give it their consent.

But here further questions arise: If every state is coercive to some
degree, how is it that we *owe* it obedience? In the presence of coercion
there can be submission, certainly, but surely no consent, for in the
moment I give my consent I am not being coerced. (And it is clear
that the obedience Rousseau means is not mere grudging compliance
but consent that is "wholehearted" in the fullest sense.) As we saw,
Rousseau says that we owe obedience only to legitimate government,
and its legitimacy is seen as dependent upon the concurrence of the
general will. But this means nothing more than that we, as individuals, owe obedience only to the general will. To the extent that we
agree with it and participate in it we are citizens; to the extent that
we merely submit to it we are subjects. If we ask how it is that
opponents (to a decision of the general will) can be free although
subject to laws to which they have not consented, Rousseau's answer
is that the citizen consents to *all* the laws, even to those passed against
his will and those that punish him (if he violates them).[45] This is
because of what Rousseau calls "the constant will" (*la volonté con-
stante*)—that is, the ongoing, tacit will that makes us citizens and
free. (Presumably, even the criminal accepts the general structure of
laws by which he is condemned.)

Now our obligation to accept the laws becomes a *moral* obligation
to the extent that our *consent* (tacit or explicit) has been elicited—
for only on the basis of our consent can we be said to be obeying
ourselves.[46] Society, as we now know it, is coercive because it represents the wills of certain powerful individuals who utilize state power
for their own interests and thus against the interests of the whole.

Obviously, it is not ourselves we obey—nor is it our own interests we serve—when we obey the law under such circumstances. In effect, we are not free men when we obey the law under present conditions. Accordingly, the test of our being free and of our being under a *moral* obligation to obey the law is that we have given our consent, that we continue to give our consent through the expression of our general will, and that it thus is ourselves we obey. In an atomistic society, such as Locke visualizes, self-interest is the highest interest and therefore cannot be translated into an expression of the general will. Because it is only the self-interest of *some* individuals that is being served, we are not obeying our own wills (or the general will) when we obey the laws of such a society—and thus such a society cannot be said to be established on a moral basis. Lacking the full participation of all, no state is moral or legitimate.[47]

This is why representative democracy is a failure: Anything less than full participation is less than full freedom (because it is by that much less an obedience to ourselves); and the less of freedom, the more of slavery. This is why Englishmen are deceived when they think of themselves as free. After they elect Parliament, the English are slaves once more. A people cannot rightfully alienate its sovereignty, so it cannot rightfully have representatives do its legislating. The only representatives it can rightfully have are in the executive, which is only the force applied to the law. The Athenians were free because they had slaves to do the necessary work; we, who have no slaves, are slaves ourselves.[48]

This brings us to the problem of equality once more. The *Second Discourse* condemns inequality, as we saw; and when Rousseau attacks contemporary society it is as a rotten structure founded on inequality.[49] In the *Social Contract*, inequality is the main pernicious effect of the existence of special interests: It is corruptive in that it engenders a fallacious concern with status, and it places the poor at the mercy of the rich. Equality, on the other hand, is surely the necessary condition and perhaps even the sufficient condition of the general will.[50] Above all, what is profoundly evident to him is the stark contrast between the equality of presocial men and the inequality created by civil society. On top of this there is the tragic fact that although society has made us dependent upon one another (and this constitutes our humanization) this dependence has led to our mutual enslavement.[51]

Our humanization and socialization have given us but one freedom: the freedom to enslave one another. Thus, our inequality as masters and slaves is the concomitant of our freedom. On one hand, our enslavement is reflected in the *inequality* between rich and poor that is forced upon us by the selfishness of special interests; on the other hand, our enslavement is reflected in our spurious *equality* as political beings, whereby we cast our votes for representatives and then remain silent until the next election, meanwhile having enslaved ourselves to the individual wills of those representatives. The ultimate source (of this complex of enslavement) is our dependence on one another. Realizing that dependence, we seek to overcome it by ambition and by getting the better of another. The "success" of this is therefore the reverse side of that dependence.[52]

Just as a people cannot alienate its sovereignty, so men cannot voluntarily give up their freedom to someone. I would be less than human if I said to you, "Take my freedom, I am your slave. Just tell me what you want me to do with my life." And this holds true no less for the political life of a people than for the personal life of an individual. What Rousseau prescribes is complete self-government, "direct and permanent self-legislation in all aspects of common life."[53] Thus, it is against our nature to be ruled, even if we are ruled by a majority and submit to it voluntarily. What is morally wrong (and against men's nature) in our being governed by a majority is not that it is a majority that governs but that we are being governed at all. What is significant is not by how many we are enslaved but the fact that we are enslaved! To be governed means that there is someone above us to whom we are not equal. To obey ourselves alone, then, is the guarantee of equality—and the only alternative to total equality is total enslavement. (These do not admit of gradations.)

Accordingly, with regard to any political system under discussion, Rousseau asks one question: Does it distinguish between ruler and ruled?[54] If it does, there is slavery, there is war between the parties, even if this is palliated by a show of legality and civility. The acceptance of political authority, as such, is incompatible with human dignity, just as slavery is incompatible with freedom. Wherever there is political authority being exercised, there is inequality—and therefore enslavement. Our situation of inequality and enslavement emerges when seen in contrast to the equality and freedom of presocial men. Yet, although we could not go back to the presocial stage and certainly would not want to (and thus would not hold it up as a standard to be aimed for), the inequality and enslavement in our present situation remain starkly there before us because of that contrast.

There were those in the eighteenth century who saw in history a trend toward increasing liberation. Rousseau, on the contrary, saw only a trend toward enslavement. He saw little or no hope of reversing the trend, because it was entrenching itself further with the help of representative democracy. Against such enslavement, the rule of law was of use only in curtailing the rule of men over men. But in and of itself the rule of law was no permanent substitute for self-rule via the general will. Only then do we obey with no one commanding; only then do we serve although no one is master. These phrases only *sound* like riddles, for they provide their own answers: No one commands if it is ourselves we obey; no man is master if it is ourselves we serve.

**New Interpretations**   There are some typical strategies that have been used in criticizing political philosophers:

1. We can "demonstrate" their "responsibility" for one or more twentieth-century sociopolitical movements—à la J. L. Talmon in regard to Rousseau and totalitarianism. But this approach has fallen into disrepute lately, because of *causal* claims being made that, although illuminating, may be impossible to verify, given the complexity of history.

2. We can ask whether a given philosopher is merely the (say) totalitarian thinker we have taken him to be or whether he has (say) libertarian elements in him as well—à la J. W. Chapman in regard to the question whether Rousseau is a totalitarian or a liberal. This approach, still lingering, has largely played itself out, because it tends to feed off the first approach, no matter how it may try to correct some of its simplistic aspects.

3. We can try to show that the received interpretation of a given philosopher is *altogether* wrong—for example, that Hobbes is, by implication, a Lockean (Warrender), that Locke is a Hobbesian (Strauss), that Locke is a Rousseauian (Kendall), that both Hobbes and Locke are apologists for capitalism (Macpherson). This approach, very much in evidence in the 1960s and 1970s, can take on the character of a game, even an exciting game. But it is serious and consequential nonetheless, because it indirectly reveals (in those philosophers and thus in one or more of their sociopolitical offshoots) implications we may not have seen before. I shall discuss three recent works, each of them looking at Rousseau in a new and exciting way: Andrew Levine interprets Rousseau in Kantian terms; Stephen Ellenburg takes Rousseau to his farthest implications and shows him to be

an anarchist; and John Charvet tries to show just what it is that civilization corrupts in the natureless presocial man.

a. Andrew Levine gives us "a Kantian reading" of the *Social Contract*.[55] The Kantian approach had already been sketched by Ernst Cassirer in *The Question of Jean-Jacques Rousseau* and in *Rousseau, Kant, and Goethe*.[56] In Levine's book the Kantian aspects in Rousseau are made explicit, and the Kantian ethic is shown to provide the key to Rousseau's political thinking. At issue is the *moral legitimacy* of the state—that is, the state considered de jure, not de facto. And because it is conceivable that the state, as such, lacks moral legitimacy, we are faced with the possibility of having to accept a philosophy of anarchism. (It is interesting that in two books appearing in the same year and in apparent ignorance of one another—Levine's and Ellenburg's—the one confronts that possibility by overcoming it, the other by affirming it.)

What Kant derived from Rousseau are the concepts (among others) of self-legislation and the moral autonomy of the agent. These are now being read back into Rousseau as central themes. What this shows is that these "typically" Kantian elements render the Kantian reading of Rousseau a Rousseauian reading. It also shows that Kant was astute enough to derive from Rousseau those core ideas absolutely essential to morality as such, whether it be Rousseau's, Kant's, or anyone else's. This is not to suggest that Rousseau is not Rousseau until fulfilled by Kant but rather to say that the Kantian edifice restores to Rousseau's thinking (more accurately, to our picture of Rousseau's thinking) the dimension of moral necessity that Kant had derived from him in the first place.

What Levine shows us is that Rousseau adopts the social contract in form only, not in substance; he is thinking new thoughts by means of old concepts. The "Kantian" substance, introduced by Rousseau, is that any political system in which there is a distinction between ruler and ruled amounts to a denial of the moral autonomy of those who are ruled. And because no act whose principle denies the moral autonomy of the agent or recipient can be a moral act, any claim to moral legitimacy that such a political system might presume to make is thereby nullified. (We ought to savor the shock value of this. To deny the moral legitimacy of *all* government is one thing, and that stance might even be waved aside by those who regard Rousseau— superficially, of course—as a doctrinaire ideologue and a proto-Jacobin. But when the denial of legitimacy comes, by implication, from Kant's

ethics we must treat it very seriously indeed—even though Kant may
not have subscribed to it.)

The crucial point is that Rousseau sees in political life, as such,
the self-alienation on the part of the individual. That is to say, membership in a state—any state—entails the individual's renunciation of
his freedom, not partially but totally. And this is deplorable on two
counts: It is against man's nature, and it deprives his actions of all
moral justification.[57] We can see now that the "fundamental problem" (namely, to find a form of association in which we obey ourselves, etc.) is a problem that reveals a new dimension when put in
Kantian terms: that is, to find a form of government in which we *do*
retain our status as self-legislating moral agents. As Levine puts it,
the problem is to reconcile authority with autonomy. But the problem is loaded with difficulties because, for one thing, the authority
is social, whereas the autonomy (Kantian) is individual. Can these
two planes be made to coalesce? But, beside this, we cannot even
be certain that states operate on a plane that is even susceptible of
moral action and moral judgment, let alone demand (as Rousseau
does) that they be made to do so through the unified moral actions
of individuals. Where Machiavelli and Hobbes see the state as morally innocuous and Locke sees it as continuous with the morality of
men in nature, Rousseau wants the state itself to be moral *ab ovo*
and in a way that, though *dis*continuous with nature and thoroughly
artificial, fulfills criteria suited to the moral capacities of individual
man. (The problem proliferates: Can these planes even be conceived
as coalescing? If so, can they be made to? And, if they can be made
to, ought they to be made to?) We could say that Rousseau saw all
this as an ideal, but as an ideal whose realization is impossible—which
would explain his rather extreme suggestions to the Poles and the
Corsicans. That is, his view was that where state and individual inter-
act the effect is always coercive and therefore immoral.

What Levine has done, therefore, in his very insightful reading of
Rousseau, is to show us that Rousseau posed the problem of the state
entirely in terms of individual morality; that the state's legitimacy is
a direct extension of that individual-moral foundation, and that in
the light of such a criterion the state as such can make no *moral*
claim to legitimacy.

In Rousseau's view, the trouble with existing states is that they *are*
continuous with nature in the sense that the natural situation of
men's alienation is not overcome in civil life. The way to overcome

this is to require the total alienation of every member (with all his rights) to the community.[58] Thus we alienate our rights to ourselves *as a totality*—and this means that, by virtue of my membership and full participation, I alienate my rights *to myself.* This sounds altogether impossible (as we saw in our previous discussion), even self-contradictory; yet it is no more self-contradictory than any self-relation (as when Kierkegaard speaks of the self as the relation to the self). This provides us with an important clue to the solution of the puzzle: In alienating my rights to myself, I am doing nothing more than asserting my selfhood, my identity as a moral agent. It is a step inward but also a step outward, for in this way alone do we regain the freedom we were born with and lost.

All this has the vivid effect of recasting Rousseau's problem in a new light. It now is clear that his problem *emanates* from the fact that he has placed the individual and the sovereign state in the disparate roles of contracting parties that preexist the contract (the way any "contracting" parties do). Yet this model does not hold up in this case, because the state does not exist prior to the contract but is constituted by the contract. When free men constitute a state, the state is not another entity but they themselves—themselves constituting themselves as a state—and this is how Rousseau overcomes the difficulties in the interaction of the two (supposedly disparate) planes. Thus, the *language* Rousseau uses is the Lockean language of "contracting parties" who "give up" rights and gain others, and so on. Yet the *meaning* he loads onto that language is the Kantian meaning of the assertion of the moral autonomy of a self that legislates for itself and thus is self-mirroring, self-related. It is the concept of the individual *self* but disguised in the language of multiple and separable *selves.*

Perhaps we can now see that the supposed paradoxicality is a function of a built-in linguistic ambiguity. That is, it merely *sounds* paradoxical to say that to give up one's liberty is to gain it; yet it is not all that paradoxical when we see that there are not two opposed parties involved but only one party contracting with itself—as two personae.

Does this reading, brilliant as it is, dissolve the paradox? I believe it melts the surface a bit but does not dissolve it entirely, because Rousseau insists on confronting the private interest (*l'intérêt particulière*) with the will that is *general*—as though this were nothing less than an ontological confrontation between particulars and universals.

Here is where the Kantian connection falters, for Kant speaks of a Kingdom of Ends (*Reich der Zwecke*)—and, as I see it, this is not at all Rousseauian, for it gets us no farther than an aggregation of autonomous individuals *qua* individuals; and so we are back with *la volonté de tous*, which we were to have left behind us, according to Rousseau. If anything, therefore, the Kantian reading strengthens the tension between the particularity of the moral agent and the social morality of the will made general—and perhaps that is just as Rousseau would have it. It is not enough to say that the private interest is *replaced* by the general interest, as though this were a simple matter of replacing (say) tokens. The "replacement" *does* necessitate an ontological shift from particular to universal, *even* if the two are one and the same!

    *b.* Stephen Ellenburg takes Rousseau's purpose to be that of showing the ultimate aim of politics as the achieving of absolute liberty (that is, establishing the form of association in which no man governs another).[59] This involves what Ellenburg calls a "radical egalitarian imperative," which he identifies with anarchism. He explains Rousseau's "anarchistic imperative" as signifying that every exercise of political authority by *some* men over others is incompatible with liberty and that it constitutes the enslavement of the many to those few. No one, I think, would argue with this characterization of Rousseau. What is unique in Ellenburg are the conclusions he draws— as conclusions to which Rousseau is implicitly committed. This is what we have to evaluate.

    It would certainly seem that Ellenburg is going far out on a limb, especially as he admits that Rousseau rejects the term "anarchism" for his own point of view. Ellenburg is here making that term do far more work than it usually does. Thus, he also uses that term in order to detach his interpretation from any Kantian interpretation of Rousseau—namely, from any interpretation that attempts to establish state legitimacy on the basis of standards derived from personal morality. In connection with Ellenburg's view there are at least three clusters of questions that might be raised:

    First, in view of the fact that Ellenburg associates the term "anarchism" with a vision of "a united and disciplined citizenry obedient to rules but not to rulers," could we not ask whether this rule obedience introduces the Kantian element he is seeking to avoid? According to Ellenburg, however, what the Kantian interpretation obscures is the radical egalitarianism that betokens a degree of political involvement (on the part of said citizenry) irreducible to the aggregation of personal wills and personal moralities (no matter how these might or might not be universalized). Yet, may we not challenge this by objecting that the *degree* of involvement does not of itself guarantee the presence of the collective consensus, that the quantitative element does not of itself produce the qualitative effect?

Second, with the so-called obedience to rules, could there not be a danger of enslavement to rules, just as there can be an enslavement to rulers? Does the obedience to rules automatically render enslavement impossible, even if the rules are self-given? Can we not imagine a people alienating its freedom to a legal apparatus that is no longer directly responsive to its wishes and no longer susceptible to change? I think we can readily imagine a reign of pure law as being impersonal and even heartless, and as far less attentive to the popular voice than any man or men might be.

Of course, Rousseau speaks of such rule obedience in the context of the general will, where the popular voice *is* heard directly. Yet the whole idea of a rule or law is that it binds us through its formal aspect; and that means that with every law, as such, something of the contextual aspect must be ignored. Now it is in this way and for this reason (that is, due to the formal character of *all* law as such) that a law can become tyrannical, if a people has undertaken a "moral" obligation to uphold it and it constrains their will. It certainly seems, moreover, that *any* restriction to the collective voice (whether by rule or by ruler) would have to be unacceptable to Rousseau, because we can say (consistently with his line of thinking) that it matters little what it is that rules and that even if a rule is what rules a people then that people does not rule iself.

Third, is rule obedience to be regarded as equivalent to "anarchism" (even in Ellenburg's rather special use of that term)? Even if a people has set a rule above itself and therefore can be said to be obeying itself when it obeys the rule it has set up—even here can we not point to something like the incriminating distinction between the ruled and the ruler (as the ruling force of the rule)? The question we are asking—and it seems to have eluded Rousseau as well as Ellenburg—is whether it is not possible *for a people to rule itself despotically?*

Literally, "anarchy" is absence of rule, and a people would be anarchic (in a positive sense) if it listened to its own voice from moment to moment and had no need of a rule. Thus, its setting up of a rule is a people's way of stilling its present voice, because the rule is yesterday's voice. But if a people were to obey itself from day to day, then perhaps no rules would be needed (and that would be positive anarchism); and if it does not obey itself, then no amount of rule obedience can mitigate its enslavement to whatever it does obey. It would appear, therefore, that rule obedience is neither the necessary nor the sufficient condition for the instantiation of the general will.

As Ellenburg shows, Rousseau speaks in favor of constitutionalism but also in ways that are inconsistent with it. Thus, he speaks of law as "the salutary and gentle yoke" but also as the chains securing an illusory freedom and as the instrument of the powerful for their protection against the multitudes. Yet, despite this diversity in his views, Rousseau was emphatic on one point: The fundamental purpose of law is that it take the place of political authority. Its purpose is not merely to limit such authority but to eliminate it—to overcome the distinction and confrontation between ruler and ruled by substituting the law for the ruler. Thus, by eliminating that distinction, the law has made us equal because there is no one over us. It is therefore the universal subjection to law (in a totally free society) that actually *produces* equality—because (as Rousseau says in the *Second Discourse*) if there is but one man who is not subject to the law then all others are necessarily at his discretion.

Another answer, therefore, to the riddle we posed earlier (as to how it can be that all obey and no one commands) is that if *all* obey the laws they themselves have made, then *no one* person commands (and the ruler/ruled distinction collapses). Thus, the law (when it serves as the immediate expression of the general will) is not only the producer of equality and the medium of equality but also the connecting medium between the morality of the individual and his complete social involvement; and the involvement is such that we now see our state as moralized without being dependent for this on the aggregation of individual moralities! The voice of fundamental law is not the voice of particular men, as Rousseau says (and as Ellenburg reminds us). Accordingly, *anarchism* is to be seen as *rule* (not as the absence of rule)—but as the rule of the collective will through its own law, such that that self-rule becomes a rule of law, not of men. In this way alone do we overcome the social dependence that is a necessary condition for mutual enslavement.

As we may gather from this and the foregoing discussion, Rousseau's most profound challenge is to provide a moral basis to political life without resorting to personal morality—in any of its forms, elements, or implications. Ellenburg's analysis has gone a long way to meeting this challenge. He shows that there *are* some purely political values—radical equality, absolute liberty, full political participation, and direct expression of the general will—and that these are moral values. If this view could be brought to its farthest point, moreover, then positive anarchism would be the successful answer to the challenge.

As valuable as his contribution is, however, I do not believe that Ellenburg has succeeded altogether, not because of any failing on his part but because the challenge cannot be fulfilled totally. These "purely" political values feed on the concept of person and of personal autonomy, and these are derived from an individualistic ethic. It would appear, therefore, that this reflects on Rousseau and that he must be judged to have failed in his attempt to moralize collective life in other than the terms of individual morality.

c. The popular view of Rousseau as a thinker riddled with paradox was fostered (and exaggerated) by Rousseau himself. Yet there are enough contradictions in him to keep us irritated and alert and to keep any reading of him from being a smooth ride. One seeming paradox lies at the very basis of his view of nature and society: On one hand, he stresses the difference between nature and society; on the other hand, he wants us to reestablish society on the natural basis. Now I believe I have helped to resolve this supposed paradox by showing that Rousseau speaks in terms of two "natures": a post-social as well as a presocial nature. With these two "natures," the inconsistency is dissolved, for the "nature" we leave behind us is not the "nature" we are to aim for. John Charvet, however, sees the paradox as the source of "Rousseau's ultimate incoherence."[60] On one hand, man is denatured by society; on the other hand, the good society is founded on man's nature. We are to believe that the dissolution of this paradox "involves the dissolution of Rousseau's whole enterprise."

Now I believe that Charvet is setting up a straw man (or a straw Noble Savage) and that he is needlessly polarizing certain contrasts into paradoxicality. In order for man to have been corrupted by society, it seems (to Charvet) that he has to have a nature, that there must be a goodness to his nature, and that he has to be human—before entering society. Yet (as we have seen) all this conflicts with Rousseau's own statements, especially in Book I, chapter viii of the

*Social Contract,* when he speaks of man's transition "d'un animal stupide et borné" to "un être intelligent et un homme." As Rousseau suggests in *Emile,* this natural creature is morally neutral (and is therefore without a natural goodness); he is prehuman and (if left to himself) will not evolve. Contrary to what Charvet characterizes as Rousseau's view, it is more to the point (and closer to what Rousseau says) to admit that the corruption enters with man's humanization itself!

Charvet tries to get around all this by saying that the aboriginal natural goodness is nothing distinctively human and that whatever Rousseau says about natural man can be said about animals as well. But that is true only because neither of them is morally good. Thus, there is not a "good" human/animal nature being corrupted; rather, a morally innocuous creature *becomes* human and becomes corrupted at the same time as its life takes on a moral dimension. There is nothing that is theoretically problematic about this—if we see that it is a corrupt humanity that we are acquiring with our humanization.

Our humanization involves our mutual interdependence in society, and this is concomitant with the basic evil whereby we seek to compare ourselves competitively and to acquire status. If there has been anything "good" about our presocial existence it is in the fact that we lived entirely for ourselves, needing to impress no one; only in society do we think of our image in the eyes of the other, of our comparative superiority and inequality. The ills of present society— the distinction between rich and poor, between ruler and ruled, the exploitation of man by man—all this is describable in terms of such inequality and the potentiality for status seeking; and the fact that this is engendered at the very onset of social life does nothing to mitigate the evil. We are humanized by needing others; yet the need of others (especially of their opinion of us) is what corrupts us.

Status and dependence go hand in hand. (I am dependent upon the person whose opinion I seek. Further, my superiority requires me to make others inferior and thus dependent upon me.) Obviously, Rousseau is urging us to overcome such dependence, but if this is inherent in social life itself, this means we must aim for a society based on the overcoming of society; and this implication is what Charvet points to as the ultimate incoherence in Rousseau. Thus, status and dependence may well be the social sources of man's corruption, but their elimination would deprive him of the *social* framework needed for a social solution to the problem! Charvet also restates this in terms of the previous paradox: namely, that the desired social reform must preserve nature yet destroy it. As I have indicated, this is neither paradoxical nor problematic. What is so is the paradox of having to overcome society in order to reform society.

Yet, in order to see the point of this—and the point of what Charvet is saying—we must *preserve* the element of paradox in Rousseau and give value to it. And therefore, to the extent that we seek to condemn the paradox and to accept the cogency of what Charvet is saying, we must dismiss the importance, the cogency, and the value of the philosophy he is criticizing—and that would redound negatively on Charvet's contribution itself.

To sum up, we can say that Rousseau's contribution consists, first, in his unwavering challenge to the modern state to meet his stringent criteria of absolute freedom or give up all claim to legitimacy; second, in establishing the narrow criteria for such freedom on the basis of reason; third, in showing that no substitute for such freedom is in any way warrantable. He shows us that we are like Aesop's domesticated dog, who is unaware that in being collared he has lost everything. Further, Rousseau has shown us the correlation between freedom and equality: When men are unfree, it is in the fact that one of them rules the other, and their freedom is assured when the equality is restored so that the ruler/ruled situation no longer obtains. Those of us who may have thought that it is somehow in the nature of things for there to be rulers now are made to realize that this is unnatural and are told the reasons why. Above all, we are shown that participatory democracy—and only such democracy in its fullest expression—can ensure freedom and equality and thus achieve that moral legitimacy governments have never enjoyed.

The political animal, then, is to be fully free and fully active, and he is this by "nature." By contrast, modern democracies have made our lives very "unpolitical" indeed: Our governments see themselves as functioning best when least encumbered by the voice of the electorate. In this century, our once loosely structured "governments" have evolved into state systems, centralizing their power and acknowledging only the slimmest of procedural restraints. For the purposes of such state systems, democracy is nothing other than a useful myth; its genuine exercise would interfere with effective state functioning.*

If Rousseau has thus set up criteria we cannot hope to meet, he

---

* Some of these latter points are powerfully made in Sheldon S. Wolin's article in the *New York Review of Books*, Dec. 18, 1980—perhaps made all the more effectively for not invoking their Rousseauian counterparts.

has at least shown us how far from morally legitimate political life we actually are. It is at least this disturbing realization that must remain with us—and this is the closest we have come to genuine humanization.

# HEGEL

## The State as World Reason

**Nature and Spirit**    Some philosophers of the past can be of interest to us because their thinking is so close to our own in manner or outlook. Hegel is of interest precisely because his thinking differs so greatly from ours, thereby revealing something of the vast range of human creativity. Contemporary Anglo-American philosophy reflects the current scientific outlook by being analytic and reductive—approaching its problems by splitting them into ever smaller fragments. Hegel's approach, by contrast, is synthesizing and comprehensive—seeking to include the entire world within the scope of one unifying vision. The world's complexity and its paradoxes are always in sight, so that his vision could never be taken as a simplification; yet it is broad enough to include the opposed worlds of nature and culture, of matter and spirit.

The worlds of nature and culture, although so opposed to one another in essence, compose one complete system for Hegel. This is because there is one motivating force that impels it all and one goal to which everything is tending—and impulse and goal are one. All existence—from inanimate matter all the way up the scale to human civilization—forms a continuum. Its purpose, from start to finish, is the development of self-conscious rationality in the world. This is the goal toward which everything aims. What impels the entire process is an inchoate rationality that seeks to emerge and to become actual. The lump of molten matter that first formed the earth, the early differentiation of the elements, the growing complexity that led to life—all this seems to be pressing toward the goal of consciousness.

And, finally, animal consciousness leads to human self-consciousness and spirit. The drive toward such emergence impels the whole process from the beginning, and the goal of a fully manifest rationality draws the process toward its fulfillment.

Thus, it is the principle of rationality that gives Hegel's system its unity. If we approach the world with our own rationality, he says, the world will respond by presenting itself to us in a rational light. This is not merely a matter of our subjective way of looking at it. For Hegel, there is no doubt that the world can present itself in this way because it is, in the deepest sense, a rational whole. To regard a thing rationally means not to impose reason upon it externally but rather to find that the thing is rational on its own account.[1] Hegel's task, therefore, is to find the rationality of the world as its objective characteristic. Once this unifying vision is put forward, it then becomes his task, as far as his political philosophy is concerned, to show us what part in this vast continuum is played by social and political life. The overall vision is metaphysical. He will attempt to show just where political life fits into the broad process from nature to self-conscious spirit. This will have a direct bearing on his interpretation of law, authority, and the state.

All this might well seem remote from the immediacy of political life. Yet even the very concrete concept of "political animal" contains two parts, a spiritual and a natural, showing us that the problem of continuity is not all that remote. We could even go so far as to say that all previous political philosophy has concerned itself, in one way or another, with the relation between man and what is "natural." Does human society emerge out of nature and leave it behind (as for Hobbes)? Does human society preserve what man has already acquired in nature (as for Locke)? Or does human society repress man's original nature, so that he may go on to fulfill a "second" nature (as for Rousseau)? Hegel's answer stresses the metaphysical relation between nature and spirit—in the way they reflect the same emerging reality—and then goes on to show how human society is the connecting link between them. It is man's status as the link between nature and spirit that enables him to transcend human society itself! "Political animal" is therefore not the final definition of man. Indeed, Hegel lets us see the paradoxicality of that definition (as a definition) in the way it attempts to combine the two opposed worlds.

Is there an unbridgeable duality in this? The world of culture/spirit appears fundamentally opposed to (and irreducible to) the world of matter/nature. Yet Hegels' vision would not constitute a unified system unless it could see these two "worlds" as two aspects of one reality. Hegel finds the connection in the way time and space are interdependent, as though they were interchangeable terms to describe one world. He devotes a single sentence to this profound equation: "History in general is therefore the development of Spirit in time, as Nature is the development of the Idea in space." The two are connected by the idea of development, or emergence, toward self-consciousness. The difference between them is that a material object is moved by forces outside it, whereas anything having spirit is self-moving, self-directing.[2]

Of course there are various levels of spirituality, just as there are levels of consciousness. All human beings might be capable of self-consciousness, yet not all of them have achieved a *social* self-consciousness. This is something that exists in time rather than in space. It involves men's identification of themselves as members of a cultural and historical continuum known as a people. Human beings begin to have a history when they share an awareness of their collective identity as persisting through time. Time is its essential dimension: That identity, as spiritual, can be expressed only in time.

According to Hegel, the primitive man has no such awareness, or if he has there is not enough of it to make him *record* his experience so that others may know it and surpass it. He does not see himself as spiritually autonomous. It is only with the development of a higher self-consciousness that we begin to see ourselves as self-moving, as free, and as bound to transcend the past. (This is where we can see the status of man as a link in the process from outer-directed matter to self-directed spirit.)

Thus, the oldest civilization, the Oriental world, believes that only *one* man is free (the king) but not man as such.[3] And because these men do not believe themselves to be free, *qua* human, they are not free. In that world, a man has very little self-consciousness as a being who is responsible to himself for his own code of values; and there is no attempt to apply rationality to the conscious shaping of social and political life.*

* It should be pointed out that Hegel is not offering a factual description, as he includes under the heading of "Oriental World" certain cultures and eras that had neither a spatial nor a temporal connection with one another. Rather, he takes the various headings to refer to *essential* stages in man's development, irrespective of time and place.

The Greek world believes that only *some* men are free—and this belief accounts for certain cultural limitations, such as their scant grasp of history and their view of individual and collective destinies as controlled by capricious deities. Not until the development of the European world and its special consciousness, with its deliberate reflection of the Judeo-Christian heritage, do we come to realize that *all* men, as men, are free. And with this realization we become sufficiently concerned with our political life that we have a sense of our existence as part of a nation or people, as well as a sense of that nation's place in history.

But this is not the end; we can go farther still. At the highest level of such awareness, we come to understand this history, of which we are a part, as a progress in man's awareness of his own freedom. In other words, we come to see that this awareness of ourselves as free is what history itself is all about. Hegel says this in so many words: "The history of the world is none other than the progress of the consciousness of freedom."[4] Of course, he is speaking here not of personal or political freedom but rather of metaphysical freedom—that is, as spirit is distinct from matter in its capacity for self-movement, so freedom is itself a self-consciousness of that capacity, a realization of one's rationality as inhering *in* one's capacity for self-direction and spiritual autonomy.

For the purpose of our understanding of his political theory, we can see that his aim in all this is to show that the state (not this or that one but the state in essence) is a rational apparatus making possible a life of freedom and spiritual autonomy—and that the state is therefore a part of the general rationality emerging through time, as the world's history. "Society and the state are the very conditions in which freedom is realized."[5] That is why it is only states, not primitive cultures, that can have a history in the true sense. The state is the one and only vehicle of history. This is because the state is the outer embodiment of the deeper world spirit that drives the whole evolution of human consciousness through time.

In this way, Hegel ascribes to the state (in essence) a rationality and a metaphysical importance such as no other philosopher ascribed to it. He often rises to a pitch of exaltation about this. And it is perhaps this tone that accounts for the stream of adverse criticism his philosophy has aroused. His tone is oracular in places, making it easy for critics to focus on isolated sentences—and thereby to misread his philosophy as nothing more than the blind worship of state power.

Here are some of his statements, receiving an altogether un-Hegelian meaning when taken out of their contexts and strung together in this way:

The state is the divine idea as it exists on earth.*

The state is the divine will, in the sense that it is mind present on earth, unfolding itself to be the actual shape and organization of a world.[6]

The state is the actuality of the ethical idea. It is the ethical mind *qua* the substantial will manifest and revealed in itself, knowing and thinking itself, accomplishing what it knows and insofar as it knows it.[7]

The march of God in the world, that is what the state is. The basis of the state is the power of reason actualizing itself as will.†

We ought not to take these statements at face value; rather, we must go far deeper to find out what Hegel actually meant by them. He is not merely saying that the state is more important than the individual. It will be recalled that Rousseau had spoken of the general will as the source of all decision. This does not do for Hegel, for whom Rousseau's idea sounds much too contingent, too dependent upon the particular situation in a given culture. What Hegel shows is how Rousseau's idea can be given a cosmic scope and can be re-expressed so as to reveal something about the essential structure of the world:

The world is a continuum from nature to culture, as we said, and the complete world view must embrace them both. The point of connection between nature and culture, between matter and spirit, is in man. It is man who makes the continuum possible. He is part of nature yet becomes something more, something entirely different from nature, through his participation in the state and in political life. If man is a political animal, this is only because the term "political" connects him to all that is *not* animal. The gap between nature and culture is qualitative, even metaphysical (as we saw). It is the difference between the inertness of matter and the self-movement of spirit. One could also say that it is the difference between the strict causality governing material things in three-dimensional space and the

---

* *Philosophy of History*, p. 39. The context lends another meaning to this passage: "Truth is the unity of the universal and subjective will; and the universal is to be found in the State, in its laws, its universal and rational arrangements. The State is the divine idea as it exists on earth." See *Werke*, XII pp. 56–57.

† *Philosophy of Right*, p. 279, addition to par. 258. This is a rather egregious mistranslation. See my discussion of it in the section, "Recent Commentary," below.

freedom in which thoughts follow one another in unidimensional time.

But, above all, the gap is a moral one: between a value-neutral nature and the value-laden life of spirit. It is up to man to span that gap and transcend it. But how? Only when the individual unites his subjective will with the rational will of the state is there formed a higher moral whole; and it is in this context alone that he acquires self-directedness (that is, freedom and self-conscious spirituality). It is here alone that he attains his freedom—"but on the condition of his recognizing, believing in, and willing that which is common to the whole."[8] In effect, this is Rousseau Hegelianized—but with a difference. We saw that Rousseau gives *logical* reasons why man achieves his humanness only in a social setting (that is, the logic implicitly connecting humanization with morality, morality with reason, reason with language, and language with society). We now see that Hegel gives *metaphysical* reasons for the same idea. That is, when Hegel says that the individual gains his freedom only by willing that which is common to the whole, we must bear in mind that this is no mere point of local politics as far as Hegel is concerned. Rather, the idea reflects for him the metaphysical difference between inert matter and the fully realized human spirit.

Man is in process, and thus he occupies a position somewhere between these two poles. For Hegel, Rousseau's presocial man is part of the world of matter, of things in space, of objects moved by forces outside themselves. Man in society is moving *toward* his fulfillment in the world of spirit, in the world of time and experience, in which he achieves self-consciousness and the power to direct his destiny in a fully rational manner.

If we take the phrase just quoted at literal face value, then it is impossible to agree that we are free only to the extent that we submerge ourselves in the collective will. If society is composed of individuals, and social morality is therefore continuous with individual morality, then society cannot make its claim upon us and say that it is part of some higher morality. What Hegel must do, therefore (in Hegelianizing Rousseau), is to find a moral standard that is suitable to the state alone and that is not derivative of a personal ethic. For Hegel, the state cannot be judged by the standard of a personal morality, because it is not that sort of entity. It is the bearer of cosmic spirit, as the individual is not. The state is always something more than the individual or than a number of individuals; it is a collective moral whole. As such, it is *metaphysically* different from an aggregation of individuals, no matter how united their consensus might be. As a state they have risen to another level:

the state is the actually existing, realized moral life. For it is the unity of the universal, essential will, with that of the individual; and this is "Morality." The individual living in this unity has a moral life; possesses a value that consists in this substantiality alone.[9]

What all this shows us is that there is at least more than one frame of reference for speaking about the state. The metaphysical and the historical are already considerable departures from the ordinary ways of looking at the political animal. There is yet another way, which is the phenomenological and is perhaps the strangest of all (as a departure from the ordinary). To this approach we now turn.

**Alienation**   Hegel's first major published book, and perhaps his greatest, is his *Phenomenology of Spirit*.[10] Here he takes us through a series of hypothetical world outlooks—the variegated ways in which it is possible for human consciousness to relate itself to the world, to other selves, and to itself. He begins with our everyday grasp of ordinary objects, then shows us how that grasp is problematic, forcing our consciousness to question itself and thus to turn inward upon itself. From this, he shows how consciousness is forced (logically) to turn outward again, coming into conflict with other consciousnesses. Out of this conflict, certain characteristic world views emerge. Hegel's approach is neither empirical nor metaphysical here but phenomenological. That is, he is not discussing the ways men have behaved, nor is he talking here about the world reason that makes the world evolve. Rather, he shows how certain ways of looking at the world follow logically from certain others and from the ways men confront one another.

Thus, phenomenology is "the science of the *experience* which consciousness goes through." Once the human spirit has turned outward again, Hegel displays the formal possibilities of human interaction. And, after an incredibly intricate course, we find how the human spirit is led to create society, art, religion, and philosophy. We thereby go through the essential phases available to human consciousness in its broad generic development. Its final truth emerges only when the entire process is completed. "The True is the whole."[11] In other words, we are not "true" to ourselves until all potentialities have been fulfilled. Just as the human embryo recapitulates each of the stages through which our genetic evolution has passed, it would be "false" to itself if it stopped short of the end, at anything less than the entirety of the process.

The *Phenomenology* therefore gives us what one scholar has called a "universalized biography" of the human spirit.[12] Yet it differs from an ordinary biography in that the *Phenomenology* is an account not of actual events but of the various ways it is possible to relate to the world. Suppose, for example, that I believed that all things are moved by ghosts. I would have to ignore a considerable part of the real material world in order to make that belief work out and lend it the appearance of cogency. As a world view, then, that belief could be only partially true (because it accounts for only part of the world); eventually I would have to go beyond it, to a more complete truth. Our beliefs develop because each is merely a one-sided view. If the truth is the whole, then each part-truth contains a part-falsehood; these will eventually clash with one another, forcing us to overcome the piecemeal outlook and replace it with a better one. For Hegel, this process of conflict and resolution is the key to all spiritual development. Let us see how:

There are three broad sections in the *Phenomenology*: "Consciousness," "Self-Consciousness," and a very extended portion that an earlier translation labeled "Free Concrete Mind." In the first section, "Consciousness," Hegel is concerned with the relation between consciousness and its immediate object, its world. Man relates himself to "this thing," which he regards as "there," as though there were nothing problematic in that relation. Yet the very concepts of "this" and "thing" are radically ambiguous (for example, "this" refers to anything pointed to; "thing" is the name of no one thing, because it refers to everything). Moreover, the object itself is fundamentally different from the consciousness that grasps it (that is, the object *in itself* is not what it is *for us*). Yet the explanation of all this rests not in the object but in consciousness! Accordingly, consciousness must turn back to itself, questioning *itself* in order that it may understand the *world*. In this way, consciousness gets a new object: itself. In ordinary consciousness, the object is different from, other than, consciousness. But, in self-consciousness, consciousness has itself as object, so that the knowing subject and the object known are one and the same.[13]

Yet, although we have turned inward, we are led outward again. This is because, in considering our own consciousness, we are led to consider what it is that characterizes all consciousness as such. In this way, our self-consciousness leads us to an awareness of other selves who are like ourselves. The self-consciousness saying "I" inevitably says "we," so that the self-consciousness on the part of the individual requires the background of a community of minds. Further, the idea of "self" leads to its counterpart in the idea of the "other." I arrive at an idea of my "self" only in distinction from some other self. For this reason, self-consciousness is inevitably conflicted: It is an awareness of oneself as well as an awareness of the other person who is not oneself yet who is a precondition of one's own self-awareness.

This nascent conflict is reflected in a primitive hostility toward *any* other person, simply because he is there. The most basic relation between two people—with nothing else going for them—is that of enmity. The other person is therefore a threat: Being hostile, he can kill me or dominate me; so I must kill or dominate him. It is Hobbes's state of nature all over again, with its war of all against all—except that Hobbes's account is psychological, whereas Hegel's is phenomenological, showing that the attitude of hostility is *logically* implicit in this stage of experience. Thus, the Hobbesian war is produced by human greed and the will to power. For Hegel, this primeval war is a logical stage in the evolution of consciousness: (a) the recognition of oneself involves the recognition of others, (b) the recognition of others involves the recognition of difference, (c) the recognition of difference leads to the question of who is superior, who will dominate, and (d) this leads to a test by open conflict.

At this primitive stage of self-awareness, I achieve my sense of selfhood only at the expense of the other. That is, my idea of self requires a contrast with its foil. Even if there is no hostility to begin with, the sense of one's selfhood (at this minimal stage) depends upon recognition by another. But in that dependence the self loses something of its selfhood: It, too, becomes an "other," an "object" for the other person. It must in some way overcome the other, in order to overcome its dependence and gain its real sense of self.

It is the basic problem of creating one's identity—whether as off-spring vis-à-vis parent, lover vis-à-vis beloved, individual vis-à-vis group, or whatever. The relation between the self and its "other" is recipro-cal, because the other finds himself in the same relation to you. It can be a fatal ambiguity, for each must do something to break the deadlock, yet each can act independently only if the other does so too—and this is a relation of dependence, not independence. It can also be a fatal ambiguity because, although the other stands in the same relation to you, he does not know it or accept it. Each one, in taking the other as object, fails to see that the other is just as much a self as he himself is. In this failure, we can see that the idea of "person" has not yet emerged. Although each knows his own self, he cannot attribute a similar selfhood to the other. Each is still enclosed, lacking any universal idea of Man. I want you to recognize me, but you are not a full "you" in my eyes. (All this is discussed in the famous subsection called "Lordship and Bondage.")[14]

To the extent that each one's sense of self depends upon the other, each is in the power of the other—and each aims at the "death" of the other, to eliminate that dependence. Each must therefore risk his life in order to assert his freedom from the other. Yet neither one can kill the other, for that would deprive the victor of the recognition he needs.

Eventually, two positions are polarized in this struggle—the master and the slave. This is not a complete resolution of the problem, however. Both are alive in order to receive and give recognition as superior and inferior, respectively, so neither the victory nor the defeat is final. The master wants recognition from another *person*, a man like himself. But, if being a person means being a master, then the slave is not a person and cannot grant the master the recognition he desires. Thus, recognition from an equal is impossible, because such an equal (being himself a master) would start another fight to the death. And, in the first place, the master fought because he preferred risking death to having a superior. So recognition from an inferior will not do, and recognition from an equal he cannot have. Thus, the master has not achieved that for which he risked his life, and he remains in an existential impasse.[15]

Although neither the victory nor the defeat is final, there has been a significant change in both parties. Before this polarization into master and slave, each had recognized the other as a mere thing. Now each does recognize the other—if not as a person, then at least as a source of recognition (inadequate) or as someone to be recognized.

And with this, the relation to *things* has become polarized as well. This is the significant change that has taken place in both parties, that is, in their respective attitudes to objects. The master appropriates the things made by the slave. The slave does not possess the thing, yet he cannot ignore its existence because he is forced to work on it. His labor is therefore an incomplete negation of the thing. The master, too, has an incomplete relation to the thing, because he owns it but does not produce it. (There is, then, a vital sense in which it is not "his"; it is not an expression of himself.) He merely enjoys it, through the labor of the slave.

The master has interposed the slave between himself and the thing, between himself and meaningful production, between himself and the natural world. Thus, the master knows the thing from one aspect only: its dependence on man. Only the slave knows the thing from the aspect of its independence: in the way it resists him as he works over it and never possesses it. And yet it is the slave who achieves, who fulfills, who thinks about the world because he works in it, who modifies the world and thereby promotes progress and actuates history.[16]

In recognizing the possibilities of history, the slave is made aware of his slavery all the more. Because he sees freedom as an unrealized ideal, he has a higher understanding of the meaning of Man. Thus, the humanizing process, the historical process whereby we become what we potentially can be, is the achievement of the slave/worker, not of the master/warrior.[17] It proceeds (as we said) by way of an enlarged understanding of what it means to be human. The master can have no such understanding, because he has not been enslaved and thus been driven inward into himself. The master thinks he is more human, more an individual, but it is the slave who knows what humanness means.

The slave's humanness is recognized by no one but himself. Yet, in doing so, he also recognizes the human dignity and the role of the master. The slave thereby negates himself, so that he does to himself precisely what the master does to him. On the other hand, the master must, for the sake of the slave's (inadequate) recognition, grant some measure of importance to the slave's consciousness, even though the master would like to minimize his importance. In this light, the slave's consciousness is the only independent one! The master therefore fails on two counts: to establish his superiority as though it were something objective, and to subordinate the slave into nothingness. The slave, on the other hand, being repressed within himself, has achieved a kind of psychological autonomy, "a mind of his own."

All this has certain consequences (logical, not historical ones) for culture in general. The master–slave relation drives each party back upon himself, toward a greater recognition of self-consciousness. Each one internalizes his state, *each* one becomes *both* his own master and his own slave, and the struggle between master and slave goes on within the self-consciousness of each. Hegel discusses three such internalizations—world views in which the aim is to have one part of oneself master the other part. These are Stoicism, Skepticism, and what he calls the Unhappy Consciousness (namely, medieval Christianity).[18]

Stoicism believes that it is all the same whether a man is an emperor or a slave, because the real mastery and enslavement go on within: The emperor can be a slave to his passions; the slave can be free in his spirit. This is an inadequate kind of freedom and therefore leads to Skepticism, which rejects all values of society as illusory (and again there is no significant difference between master and slave, and no reality to any social conventions). This, too, is inadequate, because the skeptic continues to live in society while he keeps negating its values. In the Unhappy Consciousness, therefore, we reject the world altogether. We thereby experience even more powerfully the master–slave relation within ourselves. This is a consciousness divided against itself. We see the world as transitory; we connect ourselves to a world beyond, although the connection is extremely uncertain. One rejects the changing world for union with an unchanging God. But we reject ourselves in this, so each victory is a defeat, and the desired union is put farther and farther out of reach. Eventually we are forced to pass from this unsatisfying self-consciousness to a more radical and unifying Reason.

This leads to a new and still higher level of awareness. Reason thereby passes from what it was implicitly to what it is explicitly. We now leave the stage of Self-Consciousness and enter the stage of Free Concrete Spirit. Here we find reason manifesting itself in certain concrete forms such as the state, law, culture, and religion. Reason's potentialities are gradually being realized, that is, made real. Reason also "realizes" itself in coming to an awareness of itself, so that it *is* what it *ought* to be. This is not a simple linear process but rather a series of complex struggles. At one point, reason will try to make the social world conform to reason's demands, through a conscious reconstruction of that world. This is the polar opposite to accepting the world passively (as in Stoicism) and to rejecting it entirely (as in Skepticism). Reason now seeks to satisfy itself that the world, too, is as it ought to be. In this way, the mind's own process is externalized, projected outward onto the world, whereas the previous stage was one of increasing internalization, leading to a complete retreat from the world.[19]

In social life, there is generally a complacent and unreflective acceptance of social values, as society demands. Socrates knew that society feels itself threatened as soon as we begin to think. Once we begin to question inherited values, there is no knowing where we will come out—perhaps with a total rejection of what was once accepted. At some point, reason *will* come to oppose the blind compliance that society asks of us. As a result, the questioning spirit will find itself estranged from society. In Hegel's view, society is characteristically unthinking, which means that it is at an inferior stage of self-conscious rationality, the stage at which certain values and social forms are maintained but are not submitted to philosophic scrutiny.[20]

Accordingly, Socrates was right to characterize the state as a lazy (though noble) horse and himself as the gadfly that must sting it to taking thought for itself. Governmental forms are the product of culture operating darkly, not yet consciously or deliberately. Culture does not set out to satisfy reason's demands. The state is therefore not yet fully rational, not a full realization of reason. Hegel was very deeply involved in the work and dream of social reconstruction. When he says, therefore, in the preface to *The Philosophy of Right*, "What is rational is real, and what is real is rational," the implication is that, as the state is not yet a full realization of reason, it does not yet comprise the full reality of man.[21] (This is why I said, earlier, that for Hegel "political animal" is not the final definition of man.) And, if this is so, then his task in this work is to show how the state *can* be made rational and satisfy reason's requirements.

All this is shown by another treatment Hegel gives to the master–slave relation. The *Phenomenology* had shown how this relation leads to certain cultural attitudes such as Stoicism, Skepticism, and other-worldly Christianity. In his *Encyclopaedia*, Hegel makes the master–slave relation do another job: He shows how it leads to the political state itself.[22] As I suggested, he is going over Hobbes's ground, except that Hegel is more basic by showing that the state is the outcome of the struggle for selfhood, individuation, identity.

The master–slave relation hints at a social outcome; the relation itself is a rudimentary political arrangement of ruler and ruled. The element of force is a necessary but not sufficient condition for the existence of the state. Force is not the state's justification. It must rise above force and get its justification in reason. It emerges out of a struggle for personal identity (not in fact but in essence), which is the struggle for humanness itself. Animals fight, and the victor eats the vanquished or takes his food or mate. Men fight, and the result is that ethereal thing called recognition. Without their being aware of it, these battling men are serving the advance of humanness and reason. The state, then, is continuous with that implicitly rational goal, no matter how unthinking and irrational it may happen to be at the moment. From the earliest, Hegel expresses the conviction that despite all the irrationality that has gone before man does stand at the threshold of a rational rebuilding of society.[23]

We have seen how, according to Hegel, thought leads to the thinker's "estrangement" from his world: He is no longer immersed in it, nor is he accepting its values uncritically; he now steps out of it and sees it in a new light. Yet there is another sort of estrangement, at a deeper level: the estrangement of the products of culture from their source within culture. If culture creates law and government, it must at the same time remove the traces of the creative process in order to bestow upon law and government their authority and their semblance of universal validity. Thus, in order for us to be able to regard the law as something absolute and universal, we must somehow forget that it was actually made by human beings; then we can come to consider it as "natural" or as "divine" in origin.

Culture performs this amnesiac service for us, in such a way that we do not generally regard its products as products at all (for example, who devised our language? who chose our customs?) but as things that are "there" and are "right" in and for themselves. Thus, the human spirit projects its creations into the world and at the same time "estranges" itself from them, "alienates" them from their source in the creativity of the human spirit. In this way, self-consciousness externalizes itself, as Hegel says, and preserves itself.[24]

Hegel uses two terms for this process: *Entäusserung*, the externalization whereby the human spirit projects its creations into the outer (-*ausser*) world; and *Entfremdung*, the process whereby the product is alienated, is made strange (-*fremd*) to its source. This is a necessary and essential part of all culture and all creativity. And yet, if the ultimate goal of history is a fully realized self-consciousness, then we must somehow overcome this alienation. Necessary though the process of alienation may be to ongoing social life, we must ultimately see through that process itself and come to realize that the human spirit is behind it all. In this way, we overcome unconscious alienation by means of self-consciousness.

The way Hegel expresses this is to say that in this creativity the human spirit creates not merely one world but a twofold world, divided against itself. And this is the essential character of the creative spirit: its outwardness, the way it points beyond itself and beyond its own inner creative processes:

Nothing has a spirit self-established and indwelling within it; rather, each is outside itself in what is alien to it. The equilibrium of the whole is not the unity which abides by itself, nor its inwardly secured tranquility, but rests on the estrangement of its opposite. The whole is, therefore, like each single moment, a self-estranged reality.[25]

To the extent that the reality is estranged from itself, it is opposed to itself, so that the created world is opposed to the spirit that created it. The created social world ignores the fact that it too was created by men, and it is thereby separated from its source.

Presumably, the overcoming of that separation would consist in recognizing the original creative spirit *in* the product, seeing the product as the outcome of spirit. And then, in consciously reshaping our world, in deliberately making it conform to reason, we gain a new sense of our individualities as creators and shapers. In this light, both mind and world are evolving in one process, and at the end of the process the world is no longer alien to us. The creating mind and the created world converge as each grows more rational. The identity of each and their identification with one another are realized in that cryptic and most challenging of Hegel's statements: "What is rational is real, and what is real is rational."[26] This is the goal toward which all philosophic vision is to strive (namely, to grasp this as true), but it is also the goal of the concrete world itself.

What Hegel's theory of alienation gives us, then, is a sweeping vision of the world as it originates in undifferentiated unity, then becomes divided against itself in its creation of itself, and finally achieves unity once more as it grasps its own creativity so that it sees this very unity as the pinnacle of creativity itself. This latter unity amounts to man's understanding of himself, together with his self-awareness in the fact that his spirit (the human spirit) is the source of everything. In man's self-estranged creativity, the political state is merely one of the intermediary stages—a stage wherein man's spirit has not yet come to itself, so that it may see the state as its own production. It is therefore a stage that must be overcome by man in his progress to the higher vision and the higher realms of spirit.

This view of Hegel's may or may not balance his more exuberant pronouncements about the state, quoted earlier. The state is still of great metaphysical importance for him: It is the vehicle of history, and thus it is the only bearer of the cosmic spirit in its human dimension.

**Metaphysics and the Person**   The master–slave relation is Hegel's version of the problematic "state of nature"—it is the problem to which the political state is the solution. What distinguishes Hegel's solution is that it is dialectical; that is, it does not eliminate all traces of the problem but incorporates its one-sided elements into an all-inclusive synthesis. Thus, the need for recognition is not altogether overcome when the struggle is over, nor is it replaced by something entirely different. Rather, it is taken out of its restricted and obsessive framework and is made part of a broader arrangement. The recognition that both master and slave had sought and had failed in achieving is now freely given by the citizens of the state in recognizing one another as fellow citizens. And the unsatisfying relation to actual things on the part of both master and slave is now overcome in the social reciprocity whereby we work to fulfill one another's needs. But, most important, the one-sided relation of ruler to ruled is now enlarged, diversified, and elevated to a moral (or universal) level in the rule of law, custom, and reason.

This last sentence leads us back to the problem of alienation: Once we regard the political animal as *homo faber*, man the maker, we become aware of the relativity of his creation. We see that he creates varying political arrangements to serve a thousand and one purposes and needs. And yet when he creates his political values he projects them as absolutes. Now if *we*, as observers of the human scene, take a relativist position, we obviously fail to understand his creativity from the inside; that is, we fail to grasp the absolutist "sense" in which those values are issued—and in that way we fail as observers. On the other hand, man the maker allows himself his absolutism by virtue of his self-alienation, and in that way he fails as creator; that is, he loses sight of his own role as creator, of his freedom to alter his situation as he creates it, and therefore of his responsibility for his situation. His is therefore a failure of reason, because his self-alienation prevents him from reshaping his political environment in a more rational manner (when he tells himself that what is *must* be, that it is "natural" for things to be that way, etc.). In addition, his is a failure of insight; he overlooks the inescapable contingency of his political reality, the reality in which all things must pass, change, and die.

Can these attitudes be reconciled? When we deal with mathematical truths, we ignore the question of who "created" them; we focus our attention on their "objective" absoluteness, as though these truths were not created but "discovered." In political creativity, however, we are never far removed from the active human will. Perhaps the only way to overcome the particularity and relativity of that will, together with the illusion of its absoluteness, is to try to raise it to the level of genuine universality and reason, so that the values and systems created might be seen *by us* as approximating some sort of "objectivity." Hegel's resolution of the problem is to say that, although a value may be the expression of an individual will, it can be raised to universality in a political state when that value is promulgated as law. Then the personal "I wish" becomes the universal form, "All men shall . . ." Does this solve the problem? I think not, because the so-called universality can be illusory. Raising an illusion to the form of "All men shall . . ."—or even to "Thou shalt . . ."—does not make it any the less an illusion. The universality can turn out to be merely formal.

There is in Hegel enough of the influence of Rousseau and Kant for him to identify universality with rationality. When Kant speaks of the categorical imperative, it is obvious that a broadly human rationality is the precondition for the universalization of a moral judgment. When Rousseau speaks of the infallibility of the general will, it is obvious that social "universality" is the precondition for the rightness (and rationality) of a judgment. For Hegel, however, rationality is itself identified with universality (but the term "universality" includes, for him, both the Kantian and the Rousseauian meanings: the broadly human and the social).

It is this outlook that leads Hegel to identify rationality with reality, and reality with rationality, in the statement that what is rational is real and what is real is rational.* The state is a "real" state

* *Philosophy of Right*, p. 10; see Knox's n. 27, p. 302. The German text reads: "Was vernünftig ist, das ist wirklich; und was wirklich ist, das ist vernünftig." *Werke*, VII: 24. Although the translator renders "wirklich" as "actual," he admits

to the extent that world reason is manifested through it. But only the most acute philosophic vision can grasp this in connection with the "actual" world. The challenge is "to apprehend in the show of the temporal and transient the substance which is immanent and the eternal which is present."[27]

We can now see what part the concept of the state plays in Hegel's broader system. That system—as put forward in Hegel's *Encyclopaedia*—is meant to encompass all reality: the world of nature, the world of human spirit, and the realm of pure, logical concepts. Spirit is given three main divisions: the subjective, the objective, and the absolute. Subjective spirit is concerned with the internal realm, and with epistemological issues such as the nature of the soul, mind, and consciousness. Objective spirit is concerned with the external realm, and this takes up the social and political issues that comprise the subject matter of *The Philosophy of Right*. Absolute spirit is concerned with the realm of art, religion, and philosophy.

If we take our clue from the nature of the triangular structure that dominates the system as a whole, then it is clear that, for Hegel, the subjective and objective realms are not complete in themselves. Rather, they comprise part-truths, which therefore engender conflicts with one another such that these conflicts are resolved only in the next higher level: absolute spirit. (On the same basis, the parts within absolute spirit are conflicted, and the conflicts resolved. Thus, art and religion are not complete in themselves and resolve their conflicts only in philosophy.) In any of the triads, each of the first two members has only a part of the whole truth, which is why they stand opposed to one another. If subjective spirit stands opposed to objective spirit, this means that the interior life is not all there is, and psychology cannot be the ultimate science of man. The same holds true for the exterior life, and so sociology cannot give us the final understanding of man.

These realms must therefore be absorbed in a more inclusive vision wherein the one-sidedness of each is overcome. This suggests that for Hegel the theory of politics is systematically incomplete; the political sphere cannot of itself provide its own intellectual foundation. If this

---

that "real" expresses the proper meaning. The word "real" involves the synthesis of essence and existence, the fulfillment of an essence by something that exists. The "real" statesman fulfills the essence of statesmanship; the corrupt statesman does not, although he is just as "actual" as the "real" one.

means that our political concepts must, in the end, come to philosophy for their justification, this is nothing less than what *all* political philosophy has been saying.

Objective spirit (the realm covered in *The Philosophy of Right*) is itself divided into three parts: "Abstract Right," "Morality," and "Ethical Life" (called, elsewhere, "Social Ethics"). Once again, the first two areas will be regarded as inadequate in themselves because they are abstract and relatively unreal. Social ethics, therefore, will provide the fulfillment of these first two areas as "the unity and truth of both these abstract moments."[28] Abstract right deals with the concepts of property, contract, and wrong. These are abstract because of their remoteness from all considerations of actual social setting and actual political effect. Hegel is thereby criticizing earlier political philosophies for basing their views of society on prior concepts of property and contract; these get their meaning only within a social setting.

His criticism of past philosophers is to show that they never get beyond their basic presuppositions. Politics and social life belong to the sphere of the will. Hobbes, Locke, and Rousseau take this as basic and deal with the will on either an individual or a collective basis. The problem is to make the will concrete in the social world, so that it becomes "the realm of freedom made actual, the world of mind brought forth out of itself like a second nature."[29] The proper study of politics, therefore, is the will as actualized in its social effects rather than the will in itself. Although abstract concepts such as "property" and "contract" can be shown to be expressions of this will (as an abstraction), it is obvious for Hegel that one cannot deduce the concept of society from the concept of *individual* will, as Hobbes and Locke tried to do. The emphasis on individual interests does not explain the state. It is right, therefore, that Rousseau sees it as his main problem to show how the individual will can become identical with the collective will. Here the problem reached the point at which it was begging for a synthesis, and that synthesis was not forthcoming.

For Hegel, the individual is incapable (as individual) of reaching that stage of idealism whereby his social interest becomes his most pressing private concern. His particular will lacks such universality—because it is a *particular* will. His individuality does not permit him to submerge himself in the general will (if, that is, we define man *abstractly* as nothing but an individual, the way Hobbes and Locke do). By saying this, Hegel rejects any idea of a social contract founded on an individualistic basis.[30] As long as the individual is motivated by his private interests (and acquires property as the extension of his individuality, by excluding others from its use), he cannot overcome that privacy of interest. For this reason, no contract between individuals can transcend their individualism. Thus, if we consider the realm of political right abstractly, we find nothing but the paradox of the universal, which is somehow expected to emerge out of the particular but which it cannot do.

The problem before us is really that of political solipsism. Descartes asked how he could be sure that there really was a world existing outside his mind. The problem facing Hobbes, Locke, and Rousseau (and only Rousseau faces it explicitly) is how the individual, by nature separated from others and interested only in himself, can overcome his isolation to create a social world. (It is no use reading a social element *into* the state of nature, as Locke does, because that is precisely what we want to come out with.)

Hegel poses the problem of political solipsism in terms of a metaphysics of the ego: "The ego determines itself in so far as it is the relating of negativity to itself." (This is the source, apparently, of Kierkegaard's remark, to which I alluded earlier, when he says that the self is the relation to itself.)[31] As is clear from Hegel's context, this negativity is the ego's freedom: Its self-relatedness makes all things possible for it, because it thereby becomes independent of anything external to itself. What I am, as a person, as an ego-and-nothing-else, is a self-relation. And, although I am a finite and particular individual in this self-relation, "I know myself as something infinite, universal, and free."[32] It is precisely here that we are led to ask: How, in its independence and isolation, can the ego bestow reality upon a world external to it and relate itself to it?

The answer given by Hobbes, Locke, and Hegel is that the individual does this by appropriating things from the world around him, thereby giving that world an importance and relating himself to it. This means that the political animal is first an acquisitive animal. For Hobbes, this appropriation of things leads the individual into conflict with others (a conflict whose resolution requires the formation of society). For Locke, this appropriation leads to the individual's cooperation with others (and so society exists even before a political state is formed). For Hegel, this Lockean appropriation of property (prior to the existence of the state) is altogether unreal and abstract, and not only because of the valid empirical objection that property relations exist only within society and cannot therefore be the basis upon which society is formed. There is also the metaphysical objection that the self-enclosed individual is a contradiction in terms. Just as a man cannot be a property-owner-and-nothing-else (which is the empirical objection), so a man cannot be an ego-and-nothing-else (which is the metaphysical objection).

That is why all traditional political philosophy comes under the heading of Abstract Right, as far as Hegel is concerned. Hobbes and Locke never resolved the problem of the abstract ego, never extricated their "man" from his isolation. Hegel attempts to arrive at some sort of solution in the master–slave relation: here the ego does get beyond itself by requiring recognition from another ego, but this leads to a life-and-death struggle in which neither party wins and even the "winner" loses.

In *The Philosophy of Right*, Hegel makes a new attempt to let man emerge from the solipsism of the abstract ego. He tells us: "Personality essentially involves the capacity for rights."[33] We cannot derive, from this statement, a full concept of society. Yet, because rights involve obligations, we can see how this concept of personality does lead to certain obligations of others toward us and vice versa. The obligations are still abstract, almost empty of content, and lacking all applicability. But that is as it should be, because we are still within the area of Abstract Right. What it all comes down to is a principle that Hegel calls "the imperative of right," namely, "Be a person and respect others as persons." How can we give flesh to this bare skeleton of a statement? It is easy enough to imagine the different, and opposed, kinds of actions that could come under the heading of "Respect for Persons." Perhaps this is why Hegel places so little importance on the amplification of the statement and says, "Thus abstract right is nothing but a bare possibility and, at least in contrast with the whole range of situations, something formal."[34]

The challenge, then, is to find the means for a transition from the abstract to the concrete. A few pages back, I pointed out that, according to Hegel, one cannot deduce the concept of "society" from the concept of "individual will"—and this is because the individual is *ex hypothesi* involved in nothing but his own concerns. But what about the more general concept of "person"? It is, one would think, sufficiently empty of content to allow almost anything to be deduced from it. (In ordinary talk, we use that concept to mean almost anything at all.) Perhaps, then, its very looseness could make possible a transition from the abstract world of theory to the concrete world of society. I suggest, therefore, that a transition could be found if both the following conditions were met: (a) if the concept of "person" could be shown to contain the concept of "property" analytically— that is, if every sentence using the concept "person" would necessarily be a sentence about "property," directly or indirectly; and (b) if it could be shown that the state is an instrument that, in its essence and of necessity, is designed to secure the right to property. We could then lay a straight path from the abstract concept of "person" to the concrete concept of the state. Let us discuss each of these steps.

a. In my opinion, Hegel does not at all succeed in his attempt to deduce "property" from "person." He merely declares that property is an extension of personality. Thus, he says that a person must extend his will beyond himself, into the world; that a person, by nature, has a part of himself within himself and another part in the external world; that a person has the right to express his will over things in such a way as to appropriate them for his purposes; and so on.[35] Property thereby gets its justification not merely as a way of satisfying a person's needs but also as a way of externalizing his personality so that he overcomes his inwardness. Property is therefore also an extension of a person's freedom—even if it is a false freedom, because it is material rather than spiritual.

I would say, therefore, that Hegel has not shown that the connection between "person" and "property" is necessary or analytic. And it is obvious that there is no such analytic connection, because we can think of a propertyless person. Further, Hegel has spoken in two opposed ways about freedom: as one's relation to an external thing, and also as a relation to oneself. But, if the ego involves a relation that the person has to himself and not to an outward object, then the concepts of "person" and "property" are altogether unconnected and distinct.

b. Despite all this, the concept of "property" is extremely useful to Hegel in distinguishing the state from other kinds of political organization. This is one of Hegel's most important and fruitful distinctions, that is, between the state and civil society (and presently I shall be discussing that in greater depth). For now, we can say that the state serves the collective social life in history, whereas civil society serves individual interests. Whatever form of organization is designed to secure the right of property, the state is *not* that form but is intended for higher purposes.

Earlier political philosophy disagrees with this and therefore makes no such distinction. For Locke (as we saw) the concept of property plays a central role in the theory of government: The right to property is the paradigm of all rights in general (my life is my property); and it is the main purpose of government to safeguard my property (including my right to life). This shows that the government is there to serve the individual and his interests. Hegel agrees (as we saw) that property is an extension of the individual, and he agrees that there *is* a kind of political apparatus for protecting the individual's right to property. But this apparatus is *not* the state. It is civil society that serves the individual's interests and performs other mundane functions (for example, delivering the mail). By contrast, the state has a spiritual or metaphysical purpose, as the expression of a national identity and as the vehicle of world reason in history. Its true purpose is therefore higher than the utilitarian one of providing personal protection or satisfaction. Hegel's distinction provides him with a basis for criticizing all earlier political theory and is meant by him to constitute an advance over individualistic theories.[36]

I would say, therefore, that Hegel has not satisfied condition *a*, although he has tried to do so; and that he has emphatically rejected condition *b* by showing that the state is not there to serve private interests. This means that he has not established a theoretical transition from the abstract to the concrete, even though, as we have seen, he is intensely concerned with both and with providing that connection. Yet this absence of a connection does not prevent him from discussing the state in the most concrete and immediate way.

We have seen how Hegel criticizes the abstract concepts of property and the social contract. His criticism rests on the idea that the "individual" who figures in earlier political philosophy is nothing but an abstraction. This comes out in the short passage called "Morality," which is the second part of *The Philosophy of Right*. Some commentators have felt that Hegel has no moral theory.[37] Yet one important contribution he makes to it is to accuse the tradition of ethics of treating the subject matter too theoretically. Once again, the nub is the problematic status of the individual. Ethics has concerned itself with the decisions of a self-enclosed will ever since Socrates, for whom the inner psychic state is our most important concern. Kant says that the good will is the only thing that is good in itself—as though the will can somehow *be* (in and of itself, as a *Ding-an-sich*) without content, without an external expression, and without a connection to other men. But there is no such thing as an isolated will with no connection to anything else, and this outlook is what brands abstract morality as useless for Hegel. The categorical imperative, for example, gives us nothing more than a formal criterion, but not the content, of morality. And this is what is wrong with ethics as a whole.[38]

The personal will is not the place to look. For Hegel, all values find their justification in the rationality of the concrete social world. Both abstract right (directed outward) and abstract morality (directed inward) are inadequate, theoretical, and cannot give us a set of values to live by. They therefore stand against one another as thesis and antithesis. Only social ethics can provide the synthesis to resolve their contradictions. And this is as much as to say that the concept of "person" does not begin to find its whole "truth" until it is seen in the wider context of social life.

**Civil Society–Bourgeois Society** Due to the limitations built into theoretical morality, it cannot provide us with a realistic basis for talking about values. We must therefore turn to concrete social life for such a basis. The fullest realization of values is not to be found in the private world. As one commentator puts it, "Morality is individualistic; the ethical life must be social."[39] Individual morality is subjective, "capricious and indeterminate," whereas the full ethical life has its social base and is therefore something objective.

No doubt this view comes by way of Rousseau, although it has its roots in Plato. In Hegel's time this view had wide currency: Consider *Fidelio* or the chorus of the Ninth Symphony. Consider Faust, who goes through two distinct lifetimes devoted to individualistic pursuits —power, honors, sensual experience—only to find, when he is old and blind, that his one true moment of happiness has come now in what he hears (mistakenly) as the sound of a free people working together to reclaim their land from the sea. Personal redemption is mirrored in social fulfillment. Faust says, "Auf freiem Grund mit freiem Volke stehn"—to stand upon a free soil amongst a free people—this is the highest moment for him. No better words could be found, I feel, to express Hegel's political ideals.

One of Hegel's most important points is that the idea of the isolated individual is not real. To make that idea the basis of social relations is to reverse the order of things, to ignore the role of society in first forming the individual's personality as well as providing the framework for his wider experience. As the same commentator says, "Self-conscious individuality is not a datum but a result."[40] The genuine individual is a union (paradox!) of the particular with the universal, Hegel says, in such a way that he is shaped by the universal element (in the form of codes, values, customs), whereas the universal exists only in the practices of individuals. For Hegel, the most elementary datum of social life, however, is not the individual but rather something already social: the family.

The major portion of *The Philosophy of Right*, the part called "Ethical Life" (better, "Social Ethics"), is itself divided into three parts: the family, civil society, and the state. It is in the family that certain social values first appear: love, loyalty, continuity, stability, and so on. Hegel gives us an interesting discussion of marriage, revealing certain ideas that will appear in his views on the state. We could, for example, take it as a cliché that, although marriage serves natural purposes such as sex and security, this is not really what marriage is all about. (The state, too, has its "natural" purposes but must rise above them.) Nor is marriage merely a contractual relation. (Here we see the nub of Hegel's critique of the social contract.) Kant had visualized marriage as just such a contractual relation, as though it were an arrangement for the exchange of goods and services. For Hegel, on the contrary, "Marriage is in essence an ethical tie."* Although marriage begins in the service of nature, therefore, its true aim is human spiritual fulfillment.

Another way in which marriage reflects the concept of the state is that, although the partners are individuals, their marriage gives them a higher unity; it is they *plus* their marriage. This seems paradoxical, because their individuality is actually completed by their "surrender" of individuality. I put the word "surrender" in quotation marks because nothing is really being surrendered in marriage (or in the state, as such). Only a superficial individuality is given up in marriage. Only a superficial person regards marriage as, *in essence*, a giving up of freedom—the sort of person holding a neurotic and unrealistic view of what is to be given and what is to be got. It is significant that such people speak of marriage in ironic terms of the master–slave relation. Actually, the problem of identity and recognition (which the master–

---

* *Philosophy of Right*, addition to par. 161; see also par. 163. Hegel also criticizes Kant on this matter in the 1805–6 Jena lectures on the Philosophy of Spirit, section on "The Coercive Law." The source in Kant is the 1797 *Philosophy of Law*, pars. 24–27.

slave relation failed to resolve in the *Phenomenology*) is given a successful resolution in the marriage relation.

We saw, earlier, that it seemed paradoxical that we should become individuals only in a social setting. Does it seem so paradoxical in marriage? We become more ourselves as we overcome the isolation of our individual existences. As Hegel says, "I . . . win my self-consciousness only as the renunciation of my independence and through knowing myself as the unity of myself with another and of another with me."[41] (He is speaking of marriage, but he could just as well be speaking of one's membership in society.) Surely every newlywed has had, consciously, to replace the word "I" with "we" in conversation. Eventually, the replacement becomes automatic, reflecting a change in one's very being. In the state, too (for example, the polis), the political "we" reflects the completion of individuality; the self is universalized, so that the person achieves his freedom only to the extent that he can grasp it as an idea applicable to all human beings. This idea—that all men, as men, are free and are individuals—is a value to which only the state and the fullest social life can give substance. Otherwise it is merely theoretical and abstract.

Family and civil society stand opposed to one another, as the private versus the public spheres; and there are certain points where they make conflicting claims upon the individual.* The family structure cannot satisfy all the interests of the private individual; he needs civil society to maintain order, protect rights, and so on. Yet the family and civil society have this in common: Both serve only the limited interests of the individual. His involvement with others is only on the basis of utility, a private happiness. The members of a civil society never rise to the universal level, never transcend themselves, never see themselves as sharers in mankind.

As we saw, Hegel's criticism of individualistic theories such as those of Hobbes and Locke is that they reach this stage and go no farther: The highest entity they are speaking of is the civil society, not what Hegel would call the state. They speak of the functions of maintaining peace and safeguarding property; and it is true that no state could exist for long without such functions being performed. Yet we do not

---

* One sort of resolution, albeit an imperfect one, would be an organization such as the Mafia, which is familial in structure yet stands opposed to the immediate family because it (the Mafia) can make demands of its members such as no family can. In addition, it stands opposed to the wider civil society (which protects the public's property), yet it functions as a civil society of its own, satisfying certain vocational interests, etc.

need a state for these things. They are the functions of civil society, with its system for satisfying mutual needs through capitalist enterprise, its mechanism for administrating justice, its apparatus for the performance of services such as sanitation, post, and water supply.

Notice that we use here terms such as "function," "system," "mechanism," "apparatus," and the like. All this is entirely remote from the state's role as the universalizing and rationalizing vehicle for a collective entity known as a people. If we limit our picture of political life to that of civil society, then state power might be regarded as something of a necessary evil,[42] and this is the attitude that is characteristic of atomistic liberalism. Yet what is lacking in civil society is the metaphysical component that connects social life to a broader historical and spiritual basis. We might not wish to accept such metaphysical underpinning, nor would we want to hold any political theory in abeyance until such a metaphysical "basis" could be *fully* justified on theoretical grounds. Yet, even without a cosmic or metaphysical foundation, it is still possible to see in the state a purpose higher than the utilitarian one served by the Hobbesian and Lockean contracts. Edmund Burke, for example, makes no attempt to provide a metaphysical "basis" for the state, and yet he can speak of it in rather exalted terms as a partnership between the past, the present, and the future, thereby acknowledging its uniquely spiritual dimension.*

What all this leads to is the vexing problem of what it means to say that the individual must submerge himself in the state, that the individual shall be forced to be free, and so on. Statements such as

* E. Burke, *Reflections on the Revolution in France* (1790), in *Works* (London: Bohn, 1861) II: 368. He says: "Society is indeed a contract. Subordinate contracts for objects of mere occasional interest may be dissolved at pleasure—but the state ought not to be considered as nothing better than a partnership agreement in a trade of pepper and coffee, calico or tobacco, or some other such low concern, to be taken up for a little temporary interest, and to be dissolved by the fancy of the parties. It is to be looked on with other reverence, because it is not a partnership in things subservient only to the gross animal existence of a temporary and perishable nature. It is a partnership in all science; a partnership in all art; a partnership in every virtue, and in all perfection. As the ends of such a partnership cannot be obtained in many generations, it becomes a partnership not only between those who are living, but between those who are living, those who are dead, and those who are to be born. Each contract of each particular state is but a clause in the great primeval contract of eternal society, linking the lower with the higher natures, connecting the visible and the invisible world, according to a fixed compact sanctioned by the inviolable oath which holds all physical and all moral natures, each in their appointed place."

these seem to be the hallmark of crypto-totalitarianism, with Rousseau and Hegel seen as the chief offenders. Rousseau and Hegel have mild as well as extreme ways of stating such claims. Rousseau presents the problem in mild form by saying that the public interest must become the individual's most intense private interest. The paradoxicality of this becomes more evident when Hegel distinguishes civil society from the state (and here we see his mild way of stating the problem). As long as we regard society as having nothing more than the private interest to serve, then we cannot arrive at the concept of the state in its broader, spiritual function. Herbert Marcuse put it thus: "Hegel had seen that private property relations militate against a truly free social order. The anarchy of self-seeking property owners could not produce from its mechanism an integrated, rational, and universal social scheme."[43]

This gives us a better idea of what Hegel means by saying that the individual must submerge himself in the state. The state must transcend the service of private interest, and in that case private interests can make no claim upon the state—even when those private interests include such things as personal rights! In other words, we are not to *begin* our considerations with the presupposition that personal rights are there to be served by the state and then fashion a state to serve them. Rather, we are to begin with the idea of the state as such. And then what is at issue is not the right or rights to which the individual may lay claim *in abstracto* but the integrity of the idea of the state itself, in its independence from all other considerations.

Only then, having reversed the order of thought, can we see that, if the end of the state is what is to be highest and absolute, then "this final end has supreme right against the individual, whose supreme duty is to be a member of the state."[44] (This seems to be the extreme form of the idea of the individual's submersion.) Accordingly, when Marcuse characterizes Hegel as saying that it is a matter of indifference to the state "whether the individual exists or not," it ought to be pointed out that Hegel is definitely *not* saying this about the state. Rather, he is saying this about what he calls the "ethical order"[45]—which is the unreflective political arrangement where no consideration is given to the individual, the situation Hegel deplores. After all, Hegel's mild version of his problem is how to devise a system that would rise above private interests *and yet* would preserve individual freedom.[46] If individual freedom is what he wants to preserve and the state is to rise to an ethical, universal, rational level, then it is certainly *not* indifferent to the existence of the individual.

It then becomes clear that the submersion of the individual is not what the Hegelian state is all about. The fulfillment of the individual—the identification of the particular with the universal—is possible *only* in the state; and that is why the state has absolute authority.[47] For decades, this view has come under attack as being totalitarian. But is it? It is close enough to the *words* in which totalitarianism expresses its claims upon the individual. Yet Hegel's own view of the state is quite opposed to such ideology. He tells us explicitly that in the state

personal individuality and its particular interests not only achieve their complete development and *gain explicit recognition*. . . but they also pass over of their own accord into the interest of the universal, and . . . they know and will the universal; they even recognize it as their own substantive mind; they take it as their end and are active in its pursuit.[48]

Thus, it is not in the state, as such, but rather in the unreflective way of life so characteristic of modern society that we find the individual being submerged. On the other hand, where the individual's rights and prerogatives are made explicit and are kept before our consciousness—this is where (on the basis of that consciousness) the individual can play an active part in shaping his social existence. So much, then, for the view that Hegel advocates the submergence of the individual in the state.

An interesting result emerges from all this. Hegel shows that the idea that society is built to serve the individual, the idea that is the heart and soul of the liberal outlook, is antiliberal (and even totalitarian) in the way it works out. Internally, such a society becomes the instrument of blind economic forces, leading to the polarization of classes. It is a society that is the effect of determinism, not of freedom: Wealth inevitably becomes concentrated in fewer hands while the poor become poorer and more numerous. Externally, such a society must be forever expanding into new markets, and this leads to imperialist adventures![49] The conclusion we may draw, therefore, is that as long as society is intended to fulfill only its banausic utilitarian purposes—and this is the way it is seen in classical liberalism— the result is a society that is totalitarian and imperialistic. These are precisely the weaknesses that Hegel intends the state to overcome.*

---

* An interesting result. The language is close enough to the language of Marx to allow our drawing parallels. Where Marx regards totalitarianism and imperialism as the outcome of capitalism, Hegel sees them, in a wider context, as the products of civil society and liberal ideals!

The differences between civil society and the state show us what the state is not. We can now express these differences negatively, in concentrated form (after which we can go on to a positive characterization of Hegel's state in the next section). The differences can be discussed under at least five headings: (*a*) as a difference in ways of life, (*b*) as a difference between nature and spirit, (*c*) as a difference between understanding and reason, (*d*) as a difference between timeless abstraction and the historical approach, and finally (*e*) as a difference between the bourgeois outlook and the philosophic.

*a*. Fundamentally, we have seen that civil society and the state reflect a difference in ways of life—the self-interested life as against the socially involved life, or the service of private interest as against the service of public interest. If, as we saw, the main problem for political theory, since Rousseau, has been that of relating the personal will to public institutions, then we must say that Hegel has widened the gap between the self-interested individual and the general will. Rousseau looked for a synthesis in the kind of society wherein individual self-interest would be reconciled with the general will and yet remain self-interest. Hegel foresees no such synthesis as long as the terms "private" and "public" retain their opposed meanings. These opposed meanings are bestowed by a limited understanding. A synthesis can be forthcoming only from all-inclusive reason (see paragraph *c*).

*b*. A further difference between civil society and the state is to be seen in the metaphysics of nature and spirit. Civil society is the plaything of natural laws and natural forces. Its operation is deterministic and mechanical. The state, on the other hand, transcends nature. Its realm is spirit, mind, culture—the plane of freedom, self-consciousness, self-determination.[50] This is the freedom that transcends deterministic necessity: Men become sufficiently aware of their collective identity to adapt their political life to the conscious purpose of realizing their freedom. In contrast to the day-to-day adjustment to external natural pressures, there is the long-range aim of giving shape to our spiritual and political life in the light of full rationality.

*c*. The idea of transcending nature is familiar enough. In Christianity, man transcends nature by the aid of grace; in the Enlightenment, by means of reason. When Hegel says that the civil society is the product of Understanding, he thereby indicates that he has a higher way of thinking about political life, and this is Reason.[51] For Kant, the understanding is the highest acceptable level of thinking, because it is still based on experience. That is, the attempt to transcend the understanding must fail; it leads to pure reason, which is detached from experience and is therefore self-contradictory and abstract. For Hegel, on the other hand, it is the understanding that is abstract and self-contradictory, because its view is never complete but is always limited to one-sided and conflicting aspects of experience. Man *must* transcend this understanding; pure reason can provide a synthesis of these contradictions, because of its all-inclusive perspective. Now the civil society is a system for satisfying needs, a reciprocal arrangement for promoting personal happiness. It is therefore limited to the interests of individual persons; and because these persons necessarily have limited views these must come into conflict, as must their interests as individual. (Thus, the commercial mind never goes beyond the Understanding.) These conflicts of interest can be reconciled only in a higher Reason—of which the state is the expression and embodiment.

   *d.* The philosophies of Hobbes and Locke visualize political life in terms of certain eternal patterns, as though human nature never grows. They speak of the theoretical individual who never undergoes change, never arrives at a higher insight. Their civil society is composed of such timeless and isolated individuals, engaged in nothing better than the give-and-take that serves their selfish purposes. It is a social life reduced by theory to the level of "business." What it lacks is the element of the historical, the dynamism that only the state is capable of achieving, the consciousness of national identity that eludes the "business" mind—the awareness of there being a higher historical purpose to be served.

   *e.* As a way of summarizing all this, we can say that the classical individual and the classical conception of civil society are products of the bourgeois outlook, whereas the Hegelian idea of the state is philosophic.[52] Indeed, the phrase *bürgerliche Gesellschaft* means both "civil society" and "bourgeois society" (and Marx thoroughly exploits this double meaning). The bourgeois consciousness, enmeshed in its small aims and limited by its small view of social life, lacks all metaphysical perspective. Bourgeois individualism has always been seeking to devise a structure that will automatically and naturally harmonize conflicting interests. Yet there is no automatic or natural way to make men come to a genuine social awareness or higher historical consciousness. This must be the work of reason, of philosophic vision.

**The State as Higher Reason**   One approach to Hegel's view on any issue is to decide just what problem he is trying to solve. With him, the question "What is the problem?" can be just as complex an issue as "What is the solution?" As I suggested earlier, the fundamental aim in Hegel's political theory is to give the idea of political life the broadest, most sweeping, even cosmic perspective. He makes a beginning toward that aim by widening the perspective in which he regards the individual. As we saw, the individual is fully comprehensible only within the collective social framework, never in terms of his isolated self. A further step toward the broadening of perspective is to distinguish civil society from the state: Civil society is undoubtedly indispensable to political life, but its emphasis is utilitarian and individualistic, whereas the true state is to be regarded as the embodiment of universal reason, a part of the rational fabric of the cosmos itself. Just as individuals must be seen in the framework of the state, so the state itself must be seen in the broader movement of universal history.

Now it is easy enough to put forward such a view, if it is stated as an abstract metaphysical doctrine. It is quite another matter to show just how that idea is to work out in reality—to show what its essential structure must be and how its parts fit together. Hegel is more than ready for this challenge. Over and over, he attacks "abstract" philosophy for its failure to emerge into the concrete world of men and their social reality. That social reality must be lifted above its particular concerns, so that it is seen in its universal light and yet retains its concreteness—that is the challenge.

Because the state is in essence rational (in serving an ultimately rational end, despite its irrational means), the political structure that Hegel builds up must be shown to be rational as well. The next problem, then, is to construct a political framework that is the embodiment of cosmic reason—and that can be shown to be such in a rational manner. To "show" this, he presents a theoretical model and then applies it to political philosophy, thereby extending it beyond its literal meaning. Such use of a model has characterized a great deal of political philosophy, most notably in Plato and Hobbes. The model may lack strict deductive rigor, yet it enables us to think of the state in new and imaginative ways, so that we reach a deeper insight into man's political possibilities.

Hobbes's model is that of the mechanical man (as the first few sentences in the introduction to *Leviathan* show). There is no strict reason, however, why the mechanical model (of individual man) must eventuate in the Hobbesian idea of the state, because it is possible to begin with the same "premises" and arrive at a totally different system. Plato's model is that of the human mind: Its tripartite structure gives him the clue for the tripartite state. The psyche is made up of reason, will, and the senses; from this we get a state made up of philosopher–kings, executives, and the passive citizenry. But, again, there is no compelling reason why we should accept the assumption on which all this is based: that the state is the soul "writ large."

All such presentations suffer the weaknesses attached to any argument by analogy: If two things resemble one another in some respects, it does not strictly mean that they must resemble one another in any further respect. Thus, even if we accept Plato's "premise" that the state is the soul writ large, it does not at all follow that if reason ought to rule in the soul it ought also to rule in the state. Fortunately for ourselves, we need not take these arguments in the strictest sense—and if we do not take them strictly, then the associated concepts become all the more fruitful and suggestive.

Let us suppose that we are neo-Pythagoreans. We might then say that the point, line, plane, and solid are the most basic concepts for describing the world—and that the ideal state must therefore correspond to those concepts if it is to be a genuine state and a true part of the world. Then the king would be the point, the line would be the executive branch, the plane the legislature, and the solid would be the supportive ("solid") citizenry. It would then be an easy matter to draw some "conclusions" from these "premises." We might conclude, for example, that the king ought to be supreme because all circles ("social circles") revolve around a point or because the point is the most basic datum in geometry. On the other hand, perhaps the king ought to be powerless, because a point has position but no dimension. Further, it could be "concluded" that it is the proper task of the executive branch to establish foreign policy, because the straight line is the shortest distance between two points. Yet if we reverse all this and adopt a democratic geometry wherein the citizens are the points, then we could make some use of the idea that any line, whatever its length, is composed of an infinite number of points. (God must have loved the common people, because he made so many of them, as Lincoln said.) Just as we have social "circles," we might also have distinct social classes represented by different shapes—and have appropriate "conclusions" drawn from that analogy as well.[53]

All such models have their suggestive power. Yet any question as to whether the king *really* is or is not a "point" is otiose and irrelevant. One cannot question an analogy, or an explanatory model. Now I would like to suggest (but not to take the time to prove) that in the field of political philosophy a great deal of what passes for criticism amounts to little more than subjecting such analogies to needless torture. Does Hobbes, or does he not, "imply" that the natural laws are promulgated by God? This is the sort of question that is asked, in a kind of Pathetic Fallacy.

Let us return to Hegel. If the state is the vehicle of cosmic reason, it ought to be modeled after reason itself. Hegel therefore offers his own peculiar model for presenting the state, a model that (in his view) reflects cosmic reason in its deepest significance. The model he adopts is that of the three abstract categories of reason: the universal, the particular, and the individual. These terms are the names of quantitative categories in logic: Every categorical proposition must be either *universal* in scope ("All men are mortal") or *particular* ("Some men are mortal") or *individual* ("Socrates is mortal"). These three categories exhaust all the quantitative possibilities of declarative sentences. We can see, therefore, that we have hit upon something very basic indeed—about as basic as the point, line, plane, and solid. Not only do the three categories comprise all the fundamental ways we can talk about the world, they also constitute the basic division of the actual world itself.

When Hegel applies this model, the "universal" stands for the legislature, the "particular" stands for the administrative or executive function, and the "individual" is the king.[54] This, then, is Hegel's metaphysical model for a constitutional monarchy. Let us see how he establishes this idea and what "conclusions" he draws from it.

We must counter the possible impression that Hegel is speaking of the state as a rigid structure or that he is speaking in purely formal terms. On the contrary, the first point he tries to make, in his discussion of the state, is that it is not a structure but a *process*—a process wherein the ethical Idea is being actualized. It is a process wherein the political mind is being revealed to itself as the creative source of its own values. Of course, the state can be regarded as an immanent system still lacking self-awareness. Yet for the individual it provides the possibilities of "self-consciousness, knowledge and activity," so that he comes to see the state as the goal of his activity, and in this realization he achieves his substantive freedom.[55]

Thus, it becomes possible to say that at some point the state *is* not rational but is in the process of *becoming* rational. It achieves its rationality in the rationality of its members—when the particular self-consciousness ("particular" in the logical sense of "Some men . . .") has been raised to the awareness of its own universality (in that it speaks for "All men . . ."). Here we have an application of two of the three categories of our model.[56] Although we grasp our freedom in this way, it is a freedom that sees its duties to the state (in a sense that we shall discuss presently). The full realization of self-consciousness involves the recognition that the state has a higher right, a right over the individual, because his own self-consciousness is limited and partial and is not the totality. This duty is implicit in individuality itself, because the individual is the union of the particular and the universal, as we shall see.

The idea of the individual, considered formally, is the last part of this Hegelian triad. It is therefore the synthesis of the first two elements: the universal and the particular. But that very fact gives the formal idea its content. It is, in other words, "This man, Socrates . . ." It is therefore the most concrete part of the triad—the actualization as well as the existential import of the first two elements. Now the state, too, is a union of the universal with the particular. Rousseau, as we saw, tried to demonstrate this in his own way, by bringing the public interest down to the level of the private. Hegel reverses this: The particular is raised to the level of the universal, so that the actions and decisions of particular persons receive a universal ethical dimension. Thus, I act not as an Athenian shoemaker but as an Athenian. Here we can see *how* the individual is a synthesis of the universal and the particular (and notice that in a typical synthesis the first two elements are included as well as negated in the third): The individual achieves the fulfillment of his individuality by overcoming the abstractness of universal law (when he *acts* as Athenian) as well as overcoming the particularity of his private concerns (when he acts as *Athenian*, not as shoemaker).

Another way, then, of stating the difference between Rousseau and Hegel is to say that, although both agree that the individual becomes an individual only in a social setting, Hegel maintains that this individuality is gained by one's self-identification with the universal value, not merely with the collective being of society. So, when Karl Popper calls Hegel's view "tribalism," it should be pointed out (in rebuttal) that Hegel's constant emphasis is on rationality and self-consciousness—that is, on a level of awareness far removed from the tribal.[57] Thus, the universal cannot be achieved in the mere submersion of oneself in the static collective. Rather, it must be achieved entirely as a conscious process, whereby we see ourselves as individuals who owe our being as individuals to the higher entity unifying all.

Moreover, the process is such that the rights of individuals are maintained (as we saw).[58] In this way, the universal is never cut off from the individual element of subjectivity. As Hegel says, "It is only when both these moments subsist in their strength that the state can be regarded as articulated and genuinely organized."[59]

This is hardly tribalism. And it is a long way from the totalitarianism of which Hegel has been accused by Karl Popper and others. When Hegel says that the state is "higher" than the individual, it is because the state directs itself to the universal, the right, the true— and above all to the rational. Arbitrary dictatorship is opposed by Hegel's emphasis on law, on constitutionality, and on the rights of the individual within the state. Although the state can be spoken of as "higher," it must never be something imposed from above. Not only would such an imposition go against the idea of the state as a freely developing process; it could never prosper, Hegel says, for by being imposed upon a people, such a state would be alien to the free expression of their cultural spirit.

The not very surprising result is that we find Hegel opposed to totalitarianism as well as to libertarian democracy. He makes this clear in his discussion of duties and rights. In a nutshell, we might say that totalitarianism lays stress on the individual's duties *to* the state, whereas libertarianism stresses his rights *against* the state (although we ought to regard such simple generalizations with caution). According to Hegel, each of these standpoints is one-sided. He maintains, rather, that duties and rights are reciprocal conceptions, dependent upon one another for their meaning. Thus, "individuals have duties to the state in proportion as they have rights against it." "A slave can have no duties; only a free man has them."[60] Obviously, he means duties that are given to oneself, in Rousseau's sense. A slave is compelled and therefore has no inner obligations, as he has no rights. A free man has duties *because* he has rights. To separate duties from rights, therefore, is to dissolve the meaning of each. As free men, we have the duty to vote because we have the right to vote; we have the duty to serve on a jury because we have the right; and so on. And to achieve this reciprocity is precisely the task of the state. In their one-sided emphases, both totalitarianism and democracy fail at the task.

Such reciprocity is the inner strength of the state.[61] What it amounts to is (once more) the coalescence of the universal with the particular. By contrast, the separation of duties from rights leads to the isolation of the individual from the state. In totalitarianism as well as in democracy, the individual and the state are opposed to one another: Under totalitarianism, the individual is suppressed by state-imposed "duties" to the extent of limiting the freedom he needs as a rational and spiritual being. In democracy, the individual's "rights" are expressed in terms of what the state may not do to him, thereby creating the impression that the state is his natural enemy and that it would trample him underfoot if it got the chance.

The challenge, then, is to see just how it is that "what the state demands of us as a duty is *eo ipso* our right as individuals."[62] It is the connective phrase, *eo ipso*, that contains the problem: namely, to show how a duty is, *in virtue of itself*, a right. Find that connection, and you have found how the state can be identical to its members and how the universal can be brought into unity with the particular. This is an identity of interests to a degree not even Rousseau could envisage. According to Hegel, neither totalitarianism nor democracy can approach it.

This identity (of the state with its members) is expressed by Hegel in still another way—in the idea of organism. In his effort to avoid part-truth and to give the idea of the state a metaphysical base, Hegel is led to combine concepts that do not ordinarily go together. He can speak of the state as nascent rationality, for example, and he can speak of it as an organism. Now, if he had spoken in these different terms in two distinct places, we could suspect an oversight. But he speaks in these two opposed ways in the same place, thereby indicating that he is aware of the contrast and intends it to be absorbed in a higher view.

One thinks of the organic as belonging to the realm of nature, whereas rationality belongs to the realm of spirit. This is just the sort of contrast that Hegel is fond of posing and then resolving. The state is organic in the sense that all its parts are vital to its functioning, and it is in the nature of the state for it to be articulated in this way.[63] And the state is rational in that it sets universal goals for itself and pursues them rationally. In terms of the first metaphor (organism), the state's means are unconscious, inchoate. In terms of the second metaphor (rationality), the state's means are conscious; it is in full awareness of what it is doing. To combine both ways of speaking, it might be said that the state is the world's reason unfolding itself as a unified organism. Or, we might say that the metaphor of organism befits the idea of the state in process of emerging; and what it emerges *to*, as its goal, is an ultimate rationality.

Hegel sees in this the general task of civilization—the transition from the potential to the actual, from the implicit to the explicit. Or, as he puts it: "the prodigious transfer of the inner to the outer, the building of reason into the real world." So when he says, in his preface, that what is rational is real and what is real is rational, he is not extolling an existing state, Prussian or other. Rather, he is speaking of the ultimate goal of the civilizing process; and this is aided by the state when it consciously knows its aims and knows them as ethical principles. Were we to need any further evidence of Hegel's opposition to totalitarian dictatorship, there is his statement that "an oriental despotism is not a state, or at any rate not the self-conscious form of state which is alone worthy of mind, the form which is organically developed and where there are rights and a free ethical life."[64] The reader ought to observe, here, the connection between rationality and the organic—and the connection of both with freedom.

In a sense, the idea of the organic completes the idea of rationality. What characterizes rationality is differentiation and structure. A rock can be a piece of uniform matter. Whatever is rational, however, has parts that must be harmonized. The rational state cannot, therefore, be monolithic. But does its rationality run the opposite risk, that of being divisive? We have already seen that rationality has its "parts": the universal, the particular, and the individual. In applying this to the state, we seem to get another divisive picture in the familiar doctrine of the separation of powers. The trouble with that doctrine, however, is that in its democratic application each element is forced into opposition to the others (as in the idea of checks and balances). If we remain with this sort of opposition, then we are still at the level of what Hegel calls Understanding, with its typical distinctions and one-sidednesses. We have not yet arrived at Reason, which overcomes distinctions (even those of rationality) and achieves a synthesis.[65] This is why Hegel urges that the various parts of government ought not to be self-subsistent, that each ought to contain elements of the others, so that the whole structure is organically interrelated.

Let us see what problems Hegel faces in attempting to reach such an organic interrelation. In applying his model of rationality,[66] the "universal" corresponds to the legislative function in the state, because that function establishes standards of action in universal terms, as laws. The "particular" corresponds to the executive function, which applies the universal to particular cases in executing the law. So far, so good. It is when we come to the category of the "individual" that the difficulty begins. Offhand, one might be inclined to say that the "individual" is the state as a totality, combining the legislative and executive functions—that is, the state in its actuality, in its independence and sovereignty. (The last element in a triad is always a combination or synthesis of the other two.)

Hegel does speak of the state in this way. Yet, in addition, he identifies individuality with the subjective will, as expressed in decision making. *Therefore* (*sic*) the "individual" is the king. Thus, when Hegel says that the category of "individual" is the synthesis of "universal" and "particular," he gives this idea two distinct interpretations: The "individual" is the state as a whole, containing the legislative and executive functions; the "individual" is the crown, and it too contains the legislative and executive functions as elements. This is difficult to see. Why must the "subjective" power be a king? Why could not the function of decision making be performed by a president or even a dictator?[67] Yet, as Hegel says, "In the crown, the different powers are bound into an individual unity which is thus at once the apex and basis of the whole, i.e. of constitutional monarchy."[68] He feels, apparently, that because a dictator would be despotic his system would not be a true state ("an oriental despotism is not a state"); and a president would be too close to the "particular" aspect of executive functioning to be able to unify the state into a whole.

There are a number of profound reasons why Hegel advocates a constitutional monarchy, and one of these reasons becomes clear in the emphasis on the state as organic. He tells us that the modern state ought not to be viewed as the creation of men working at a specific moment in time. Rather, it ought to be seen as the organic outgrowth of history itself, in the sense that history is the expression of world reason. This is the process of alienation in its positive aspect: that is, world reason giving itself an outward expression in culture. This is another part of his attempt to give to political life a broad metaphysical perspective. Yet I think he goes wrong here. On one hand, he speaks of self-consciousness as the basis of freedom in the state—let us call this his rationalistic emphasis. On the other hand, he asks us to deny all this and to regard the state as emerging out of its own mysterious roots—let us call this his organicist emphasis.

Now the question to be asked here is whether Hegel really succeeds in combining the conceptions of the state-as-rational and the state-as-organic. These can be combined as metaphor, but can they be harmonized as literal concepts, literally intended? This is no mere point of pedantry. I shall try to show that his entire project falls asunder over just this issue. If we ask men to close their eyes, deliberately, to the idea that the modern state is their own creation and ask them rather to regard it as something transcendent or divine or something that has grown by a power of its own (organically), then self-conscious reason must deny its own self-consciousness—and this it never can do. What this involves is the schizoid situation of dealienated reason realienating itself; or a being who is a being "for itself" consenting to return to being a self-enclosed being "in itself"; or the liberated consciousness reenslaving itself.

Along similar lines, Hegel urges that the constitution ought not to be regarded as something made—presumably because it could then as easily be unmade. "It must be treated rather as something simply existent in and by itself, as divine therefore, and constant, and so as exalted above the sphere of things that are made."[69]

Must we, therefore, close one eye—knowing that these things are made but ignoring the fact? Must we thereby deny some part of our self-consciousness and self-determination in order to give to our own creation a semblance of divine authority, as though we had not made these things? Hegel seems to be saying just this. It can, however, be said in his favor that he does not only stress the self-alienating aspect in the idea of organicism. That is to say, he also takes the idea of organicism to be more than an "as if," to be literally true. As the state is the expression of the consciousness reached by a people's cultural spirit, its Volksgeist, so each culture gets the kind of state that is proper to it, the state it is ready for (or, more cynically said, the state it deserves). And so, in a very real sense, no constitution is merely the creation of men, as though they were capable of choosing from among innumerable possibilities.[70] Rather, they can choose only from among the possibilities they themselves are capable of envisaging and are culturally prepared for.

Now, just as the cultural spirit dominates every aspect of the cultural life, so the state (as the expression of a culture) ought also to "permeate all relationships" as well as the "manners and consciousness of its citizens."[71] This takes us back to the question of constitutional monarchy. Is Hegel correct in saying that only a constitutional monarchy can provide this sense of unity and all-pervasive meaningfulness to political life?

His argument for this view is that the crown alone contains all three elements: the universality of the lawgiver, the particularity of the executive in applying laws to specific situations, and the individuality of the act of decision making that is the king's.[72] A president could not make law as something transcendent and universal (or in Hegel's sense of "divine"), because he was elected by us and elected for a limited term (and we cannot allow ourselves to forget that). And, in the divisive system of checks and balances, a president would be in great trouble with his electorate if he tried to overstep himself in this way. (Because we know that we have *made* him president, he cannot presume to *make* a law that would have "divine" authority, as though no one had "made" it.) A dictator's decrees are not laws either, because they never rise above his own subjectivity to reach universality. Only a king has the requisite *authority*—as is evidenced by the fact that the state, too, is an individual and contains the three elements just mentioned. That is, if both he and the state qualify as such "individuals," then he is the state. Thus, the king is identical to the state and is the personification of its sovereignty.[73] ("L'état, c'est moi," as Louis XIV is to have said.)

The analogy of the state-as-organic leads to the "conclusion" that the concept of the state must include a diversity of functions and that the separate parts are dead without the whole. And if Hegel is right in saying that a group of people without a state is a "formless mass," so that only a state can give them an identity as a people, then if the king is the personification of the state, it is he who gives them that national identity. But this is a two-way street: as much as the people are bound to their monarch, so is he bound to them. He must not act capriciously but be led by his counselors. And in stable situations he merely signs his name to their decisions. As Hegel puts it, "he has only to say 'yes' and dot the 'i' "—although this is important because there is no higher authority (and therefore no higher responsibility, we might add).[74]

Yet it is difficult to see how such rubber-stamping expresses the sovereignty of the state or the "individuality" of the king. In answer to such doubts, Hegel urges that the institution of monarchy ought in no way to depend upon the personal character of the king. Does this mean that it is not the king himself but the institution that is dotting the i's? Hegel says that "the monarch is . . . essentially characterized as *this* individual, in abstraction from all his other characteristics."[75] Yet I find it hard to grasp his "thisness" without referring to specific qualities such as "wise" or "unwise," "just" or "unjust," and so on.

Hegel is trying here to combine the concepts of "monarch" and "monarchy." Now what characterizes monarchy (for him) is its immediacy, its "objective" status, its unquestioned thereness, solidity, and presence. Hegel therefore tries to bestow a naturalness on the institution of the crown, and this is part of the organic analogy. It must be so natural that it depends upon the accident of birth; monarchy must therefore be hereditary. When we elect a president, on the other hand, we know it is we who made him president, and so his decisions lack the superhuman status consistent with the exaltation of the state. The monarchy gets something of this exalted status if we regard it as a phenomenon of nature beyond the control of human choices (although Hegel rejects the notion of the divine right of kings).[76] The question remains, however: How could a "natural" phenomenon—which is in essence a limited event—include universality, particularity, and individuality?

Part of the problem stems from the fact that, for Hegel, *both* the state and the monarch are sovereign and "individual." Yet in one sense they are *not* identical: Although the monarch himself might be a natural phenomenon, the state is a nonnatural institution designed to serve higher-than-natural (that is, spiritual) purposes. As an accident of nature, the fact that it is *this* person who is monarch is somehow unessential and even contrary to the rationality of the state. (Thus, the concept of "state" cannot include analytically the identity of, say, Louis XIV, for then *every* state would have to have *him* as king, or it would not be a state!) So the naturalness of the monarch is contrary to the spirituality of the state—the spirituality that transcends nature and utility.[77]

*a.* What all this shows us is that Hegel is speaking simultaneously on conflicting levels—the natural versus the spiritual, the organic versus the rational. And this means that the organic and the rational *cannot* be harmonized—and, ultimately, that his system of constitutional monarchy cannot be given a fully rational foundation!

In the opening section, we saw that Hegel's metaphysics attempts to resolve and synthesize such conflicting concepts. We now see that

that attempt breaks down in his political theory. As Hegel realizes,[78] what it all comes down to is the question of whether reason can accept the idea that ultimate right can have a natural basis. From what we have seen, Hegel does not succeed in showing that that connection is essential or well-founded.

This leads me to two further objections:

*b.* Hegel's main fault is in trying to associate the concept of monarchy with the concept of the state. Now, if the state is already the "individual" and thus includes the universal and the particular, then it is logically complete. And, in that case, there is no point in adding yet another individual (the king) to the already complete individual that is the state. If the idea of "state" is completely explicit, it has no need of the concept of the king to complete it or to shed additional light on it. If the state *is* sovereign, it has no need of *a* sovereign.

*c.* Hegel is torn between enlarging the individuality of the king in his decision making and limiting it to mere approving of the decisions of his counselors. Further, the constitution sets limits to all decision making and thus to *all* individuality (even that of the state). If we are to regard the constitution as not made by men, then even the king cannot change it.[79] To the extent that he is limited by counselors or a constitution, he is not a *ruling* monarch (but only a reigning one), nor is he a fully free, decision-making individual. On the other hand, to the extent that he rules in full sovereignty, he does not rule constitutionally. This suggests such possibilities of conflict as to render the idea of "constitutional monarchy" a contradiction in terms.

Despite this negative criticism, there is much to be said on the positive side. Obviously, our political life is immensely important. We can express that sense of its importance in emotional terms. But we all know the danger of that course: Once we take the path of emotionality, the greater the "importance" we bestow upon the state, the more we blind ourselves to it—and even enslave ourselves to it. Hegel has put that importance in *rational* terms, and here, the increased sense of that importance reaches metaphysics. The state, in its rationality, is given a cosmic meaning to bear—it is a part of the very reason for there being a world at all, life at all, self-consciousness at all. If these are mysteries (and why should they not be?), then the state is a part of the mystery. The point, however, is that Hegel demystifies the state. It *is* a human product, although we its creators may seek to give it a higher-than-human significance. We are asked to forget our part in creating it, therefore, and we cannot do this. What we can do is to see, in that day-to-day shaping of our political life, a rationality that (in the best of states, the only kind worth having) takes on a dimension that is higher than human. It is a healthy and a productive schizophrenia: We know the superb rationality of Bach's *Well-Tempered Clavier*; we know it as a human invention; yet is it so strange to consider it divine?


**Recent Commentary** International Hegel criticism has become something of an industry. Yet there are aspects unique to Hegel criticism (as distinct from, say, the *Kantindustrie*): The earliest of its products, for example, those of Kierkegaard and Marx, are important in their own right. (Indeed, Hegel is unique in that entire philosophies have been built upon criticism of him.) Twentieth-century criticism of Hegel has ranged from the brilliance and originality of Georg Lukács to the obtuseness and abusiveness of Karl Popper. Hegel has exerted a direct influence on modern philosophers such as Croce and Bradley, as well as on philosophers not acknowledging a connection to him, such as Heidegger and Sartre. In addition, there has been a recent revival of interest in Hegel among Anglo-American philosophers, leading to many fine books and to translations of the works of the Jena period. From the wealth of this material, I shall discuss only two items. The first is the "recent" discovery of the early lectures of Hegel's Jena period. The second is the "recent" controversy (raging for more than three decades) over the connection between Hegel and fascism.

*a.* Hegel taught at the University of Jena from 1801 to 1806, until Napoleon invaded the city and the university closed down. Hegel's lectures of that period were first published in 1923, 1931, and 1932, in three volumes. It is the latter two volumes that are of especial interest to political philosophy. They go under the title of *Jenaer Realphilosophie*, volumes I and II (1803–4 and 1805–6, respectively).[80] Because they are only now being translated into English, their full impact has not yet been felt amongst English-speaking scholars—which is why these works can be regarded as being of "recent" vintage. Thus, Stace's book makes no mention of the Jena philosophy, even though that book went into a new edition in 1955. Findlay's excellent book, written in 1957 and reissued in 1962 in paperback, devotes no discussion whatever to Hegel's Jena philosophy, beyond a single mention of it. Plamenatz has a 140-page treatment of Hegel's political philosophy; that treatment is often profound and must make a significant contribution to anyone's understanding of Hegel, yet there is no mention of the Jena philosophy. Continental philosophers have of course taken account of it from the beginning. In English translation, a short but good discussion is given by Löwith; there is a short and superficial discussion by Hyppolite. Of works originally written in English, the ones that provide the best discussion of the Jena philosophy, within a discussion of Hegel's political philosophy as a whole, are those of Marcuse and, more recently, Avineri.[81]

There are a number of good reasons for regarding the Jena philosophy as important. It enables us to round out our picture of Hegel's political thinking. It enables us to appreciate the objectivity of his social and economic interests, thereby allowing us to discard the image of Hegel as "purely abstract and theoretical." The Jena philosophy also shifts the weight of the interpretation of *The Philosophy of Right,* showing that his emphasis on constitutionalism has its beginning at the very start of his intellectual productivity.

Above all, there is the uncanny way in which his discussion of modern industrial labor anticipates Marx. Obviously, Marx could not have known these works. He knew only Hegel's view of alienation as a positive and creative factor—the self-alienation of the world spirit in culture. Marx felt he was providing the emphasis Hegel had overlooked—the emphasis on the negative and destructive aspects of alienation, the worker's alienation that is part of the system of capitalist production. Marx says that Hegel grasps the idea of work as the essence of man but that it is only as an intellectual and abstract work. We see now that this is not so.

The intriguing question is why Hegel never developed these ideas into a full-dress social criticism. Marcuse suggests that it is as though Hegel were terrified by what his analyses had disclosed and that he therefore turned away from the concrete view of society toward a more abstract mode of philosophic speculation. Yet the Jena philosophy remains a challenge to commentators: Had Hegel incorporated these views of negative alienation into his published work, would he eventually have come out closer to what was to become the Hegelian Left?

From Marcuse's discussion we can readily see that the Jena philosophy anticipates both the *Phenomenology* and *The Philosophy of Right*. Here, too, there is an evolution through stages: First, there is the level of ordinary consciousness, grasping concepts through the medium of language; next, there are individuals or groups coping with nature through the medium of labor; and finally, there is the community, arriving at a sense of nationhood through the connecting medium of property.

The initial consciousness is not, to begin with, that of an individual; rather, it is a collective consciousness, and only later does it turn subjective and become individualistic. Eventually the individual comes into conflict with others, as the result of his individuality and his consciousness of it. This clash of subjectivities is overcome only in the nation. The nation has a self-awareness of its own, and in that self-awareness the nation is a subject that has itself as object and thus develops a sense of history. What is important in the whole evolutionary process is the role of the media: language, labor, and property. We can see the connection between them in the fact that language is already a kind of community, even though it is also the means of a person's individuation (because it allows the individual to "appropriate" concepts as well as property and make these his own).

The conflicts that may arise between individuals are variously resolved through the medium of labor. Labor also is the mediator between man and world,[82] enabling man, as subject, to overcome his estrangement from the world of objects. By working upon the natural world, man makes it his own and thereby develops his sense of selfhood. At the same time, his labor leads him to overcome his isolation and to join others. Compare this to the Hobbesian reasons for the establishing of the community: Hobbes's reasons are psychological, whereas Hegel's (even in this early work) are already metaphysical. As Marcuse put it: "The individual, by virtue of his labor, turns into a universal; for labor is of its very nature a universal activity: its product is exchangeable among all individuals."[83] Thus, the concept of labor is already a rich and many-sided one for Hegel (despite Marx's estimate). That is, it universalizes man, leads him into community, connects him to the world of nature by enabling him to overcome it; but labor also alienates man from the world because of labor's universal and abstract character. Even in his earliest thinking, then, Hegel stresses the dialectical and ambivalent character of all social activity.

The medium of labor leads to the grouping of individuals into families and to the development of family property. The struggles between these groups of property owners become the eventual material of history. Property becomes the medium of a struggle for recognition, which struggle can be resolved only if individuals can rise above themselves and become a nation. The problem in rising to a national consciousness is that we must first rise above the family (and this is by no means easy, as we see when Lorenzo de' Medici tells us that Florentine politics is the politics of families). Only a national consciousness can harmonize conflicts between the separate interests of individuals.

When Hegel turns to describing modern labor he becomes especially fascinating: first, because he is so deadly right in his description; second, because he comes so close to the views of Marx; third, because his entire subsequent view of culture seems to emerge from this. As Marcuse pointed out, the concept of labor is central to the way Hegel conceives of the development of society. Above all, Hegel grasps the fact that modern labor is self-alienated, and he is the first to express this:

The individual does not work toward the direct fulfillment of his needs. Rather, he works indirectly, on a commodity that he does not produce in its entirety and that he never gets to own through his labor. (By contrast, let us think of the simplest and least alienated model of labor: I chop some wood, it then is mine, and I use it to cook my food, and so on. Modern self-alienated labor is the polar opposite to this.) Modern man does not "appropriate" the product of his labor; and his effort is not valued for its worth to him but for its general (or "universal") value to all. His labor is therefore abstract, even inhuman. The "labor-saving" machine enslaves him and also reduces the importance of his individual contribution. The value of his actual activity declines as the machine makes his productivity grow. The machine is a self-sufficient tool, a perfect mediator of work; but it puts a distance between man and nature, and it reduces man to a "thing."[84] In using the machine, man deceives nature into working for him. Yet nature avenges itself: As man "conquers" nature, he sinks lower and lower into it. His work becomes more mechanical, more remote from his spiritual life, less an expression of himself— and less valuable. The machine increases his output but not his creativity or fulfillment (because what he does has become so simplified that anyone can duplicate it). The man himself is reduced to apathy, to dullness and stupefaction. Men are more and more in control of nature, yet more and more dependent upon it.

We have seen that because the laborer produces only a small part of a commodity he can never satisfy his needs by himself. The system of exchange is blind to his needs as an individual. It is vicious in its workings. Men come to depend more and more upon one another, but instead of a genuine community there is nothing but "a moving life of the dead." Marx will carry this theme much farther, of course. Hegel stops at this point—as though (again, according to Marcuse's suggestion) he is terrified by what his analysis has disclosed. Commodity-producing society is a wild animal, and only a strong state can curb it. Industrial capitalism is a sort of state-of-nature for Hegel. But, where Hobbes's answer would be authoritarian repression, Hegel's answer is the rational state under the rule of law.[85] The blind mechanism of civil society, concerned only with the exchange of goods and services, must give way to conscious regulation by the state. The alternative to this is continuous impoverishment and dehumanization of the laborer, who is at the mercy of the workings of civil society. Hegel even foresees a social polarization into extremes of wealth and poverty, resulting in "the utmost dismemberment of will, inner rebellion and hatred."[86]

Because we cannot here go into an extended discussion of this work, we shall have to content ourselves with touching only on a few points. One of these is Hegel's picture of the social destructiveness of civil society (thereby showing us to what extent he was attuned to the realities of his time). Another point is his strong emphasis on democracy and the rule of law. I have tried to show how much this emphasis dominates his *Philosophy of Right*, even though the "standard" criticism has fostered the myth that Hegel is a Machiavellian monster opposed to democracy in its egalitarian and libertarian aspects. In the Jena philosophy, he is still very much under the influence of Rousseau, to the extent of regarding democracy as the identity of the individual and the collectivity. Hegel's individual is the self-interested bourgeois—but he is also the *citoyen*.[87]

For Rousseau, as for Marx, bourgeois and citoyen are two different sorts of man. For Hegel, it is one and the same person, considered from two different viewpoints. As Avineri points out, this is Marx's basic quarrel wtih Hegel.[88] For Marx, the split between bourgeois and citoyen is a measure of modern man's alienation. For Hegel, it is a dialectical stage in the process of man's self-recognition—and it is not an antithesis so radical that it requires a whole new synthesis to overcome it. For Marx, the distinction is socially destructive, and it is to be overcome together with the overcoming of the class distinctions resulting from the division of labor. For Hegel, the distinction is a legitimate historical differentiation, as legitimate as class distinction itself.

A more fundamental difference between Hegel and Marx, however, is that Hegel's social analysis leads to no call to revolutionary action. As Avineri puts it (applying one of Marx's most famous sentences), Hegel believes that philosophy can only interpret the world, not change it. We may well ask why Hegel—by the time he gets to *The Philosophy of Right*—drops the discussion of alienated labor. Perhaps he feels that even if one cannot change society, it is nevertheless possible to *point* to a solution; and if he does not discuss the problem later on, perhaps this is because he is more concerned with an exposition of the solution. This is Avineri's answer,[89] and it strikes me as too pat, just as Marcuse's answer (about Hegel being terrified) strikes me as too extreme and altogether out of character.

The philosophical meaning of this discussion of labor (following Avineri)[90] is in the idea that labor is the externalization of man's capacities but that it also engenders the conditions that stand in the way of man's integration into his world. This reveals the dialectical, antinomic character of human progress—the fact that progress enlarges life but makes life more problematic. But to express an idea as a cliché is never Hegel's manner. He would never put things so simply, because simplification is never the whole truth.

Here is another indication of this: Hegel's well-tempered society has its class distinctions (which, by the way, are never rigid or hereditary but are always mobile). There are the various estates: the peasantry, the commercial class, and the universal class (that is, the civil service, whose concerns are "universal," not private). Yet the worker, whose plight Hegel recognizes and describes, takes no part in any of this. As Avineri points out, this is a serious flaw, both in the *Realphilosophie* and in *The Philosophy of Right*.[91] If Hegel has failed to solve this problem, we can say at least that he is frank enough not to ignore it and wise enough not to suggest any easy solution.

There cannot be an easy solution when the viewpoint is cosmic, because such a view must of necessity include every existing contradiction. We can say, however, that what Hegel is driving at is unity (in the bourgeois and citoyen; in the individual whose rights the state must safeguard as though he were above the state although he is a part of the state). The best way to promote such unity is, according to Hegel, by means of a state that is composed of estates and that is based on constitutional monarchy. Whatever the solution, this is the problem that began as Rousseau's, and it remains Hegel's. There is small comfort in the fact that no philosophy (or ideology) has yet found a satisfactory solution to it.

b. The controversy continues regarding Hegel and Prussianism/ nationalism/fascism/totalitarianism/nazism. And there seems to be no end in sight. What has been happening, however, is that over the years the pro-Hegel arguments have been growing more and more expert, better grounded in Hegel's philosophy and modern European history; the anti-Hegel arguments, on the other hand, have always been a mixed bag of red-eyed abuse and bizarre misinterpretation.* The best-known anti-Hegel critic is Karl Popper. His treatment is so violent and is based on such bad scholarship that one is at a loss to explain how he ever was taken seriously. Walter Kaufmann did a great deal to expose Popper's shoddy work and to bring the controversy back to common sense. (In English, the two most knowledgeable and sophisticated commentators on the controversy are Marcuse and Avineri.) Popper is quite blunt in stating his thesis: "I have tried to show the identity of Hegelian historicism with the philosophy of modern totalitarianism." (The word "identity" alone ought to be enough, here, to condemn his thesis.) He also says that Hegel "became the first official philosopher of Prussianism."[92]

Now there simply is no space in these few pages to deal with these charges in any detail. Kaufmann has shown the fragmentary sort of reading Popper must have done in order to make his assertions, as is revealed in his use of patched "quilt quotations" (the phrase is Kaufmann's). Marcuse has discussed the rejection of Hegel by the Nazis and has shown that Hegel opposed ethnic nationalism and favored the rule of law. But the evidence against Popper can come from anyone with a full knowledge of Hegel's views (his *Philosophy of Right*,

* See the debate about Hegel and Prussianism between T. M. Knox and E. F. Carritt, in *Philosophy* (1940); reprinted in Walter Kaufmann, ed., *Hegel's Political Philosophy* (New York: Atherton, 1970). Reprinted in the same anthology is the well-known interchange of Hook, Avineri, and Pelczynski, which appeared in *Encounter* (1965–66). Karl Popper's book is *The Open Society and Its Enemies* (London: Routledge & Kegan Paul, 1963), Vol. II. For Kaufmann's exposé of Popper, see "The Hegel Myth and Its Method," in A. MacIntyre, ed., *Hegel: A Collection of Critical Essays* (New York: Doubleday Anchor, 1972). See also Avineri's article, "Hegel and Nationalism," *Review of Politics*, Vol. XXIV (1962), reprinted in the Kaufmann anthology, and Avineri's "Hegel Revisited," *Journal of Contemporary History*, Vol. III (1968), reprinted in the MacIntyre anthology.

his *Political Writings*, and his *Realphilosophie*), as well as from the perspective of European history from 1789 to the present. In the light of all this, Popper's contribution can be regarded as lightweight and dismissible.

Shlomo Avineri turns to a detailed consideration of Hegel's early essay, "The German Constitution" (1802), as well as to a later essay, "The Württemberg Estates" (1815–16),[93] and these go a long way toward clearing up the matter. Sidney Hook, in his articles in *Encounter*, regards Hegel as a nationalist on the basis of the earlier essay. Yet Avineri shows (as Marcuse did) that Hegel rejects any sort of nationalism, whether it be ethnic, linguistic, or cultural. Hegel calls for a modernization of the defunct political system in Germany—and not for nationalism or unification. He even endorsed the 1814 decision of the Congress of Vienna not to set up a unified Germany. Further, Avineri gives us a condensed list of the criteria Hegel considers irrelevant and immaterial to statehood. Of the nine criteria, at least two are cultural and nationalistic—and Hegel rejects these (in "The German Constitution"). There need not be a common language, for example, in order for a state to consider itself a state. Ties such as these, among others, are the things nationalists emphasize. Yet Hegel says: "The dissimilarity in culture and manners is a necessary product as well as a necessary condition of the stability of modern states."[94]

Hegel's support of monarchy in "The Württemberg Estates" is sometimes taken as evidence of antiliberal bias. As Avineri explains, however, the historical reality was such that it was precisely the conservative and reactionary elements that opposed the monarchy. The king rather represented the liberalizing effects of the French influence.

The allegation that Hegel is a nationalist has its own peculiar history. In his Württemberg essay, Hegel applauds the well-deserved demise of "the nonsensical arrangement called the German Empire." Rudolf Haym, writing in 1857, points to this passage as indicating that Hegel is devoid of national feeling. And it is on the basis of the supposed *absence* of such feelings that Haym is the first to accuse Hegel of Prussianism—because Prussia was, at the time, the enemy of German unification.[95] Only when, a decade and a half later, Prussia did emerge as the champion of unification was this new position fathered on Hegel, who (forty years after his death) was now seen as the advocate of German nationalism—on the basis of the allegedly pro-Prussian sympathies. As Avineri points out, such allegations rest, to a great extent, on a backward projection of what is meant by the terms "Prussia" and "Prussianism." We now read into those words the militant nationalism of 1870, 1914, and 1939—and then Hegel becomes responsible for nazism as well. Yet the Prussia of 1818 is not the Prussia of Haym's 1848, let alone the Prussia of 1914 or the Third Reich of 1939.

Hegel's experience was of the reforming and modernizing influence that Prussia exerted as one of the most enlightened states in post-1815 Europe. The goal of modernization was realized between the years 1806 and 1815 in Bavaria, Württemberg, and Prussia—which is why Hegel did not call for unification. Because the idea of the modern political state had already taken root, Hegel felt that any further unification would be only on the basis of ethnic nationalism, and to this he was utterly opposed. He actually fears the Prussianization of Germany—"the dullness, spiritlessness and sterility" that would follow upon a unification of Germany under Prussian aegis.[96] It would be bourgeois civil society at its worst. If Hegel does exalt the state, therefore, it is never the Prussian state that he exalts.

The fallacy of backward projection is most plainly in evidence when critics come to consider Hegel's supposed remark that the state is "the march of God in the world" (*der Gang Gottes in der Welt*). Now this is a very serious mistranslation, on a number of counts.[97] For one thing, the German word "Gang" does not at all mean "march" but rather "course" or "way" or "process." Once we remove the militaristic association of the word "march," we come closer to the rational metaphysics that is Hegel's genuine concern. Much of the violent criticism of Hegel has focused on this one phrase, with the word "march" evoking visions of the goose-stepping hordes. No one knows why Knox mistranslated the word or why he decided on the construction which reads: "The march of God in the world, that is what the state is." Kaufmann is right to treat this as a boner, along with the mistake of taking the word "dass" (the conjunction, "that") as though it were "das" (the pronoun, "that"). Kaufmann therefore corrects the translation as follows: "It is the way of God with [literally, in] the world that there should be [literally, is] the state." Kaufmann's explanation is worth quoting: "The point is that the existence of states is no mindless accident but, metaphorically speaking, God's plan or providence, and it is the philosopher's task when discussing this institution to discover its *raison d'être*."[98]

This most "incriminating" of Hegel's passages actually exonerates him as far as any identification with German nationalism or Prussianism is concerned. We see this in the very same sentence, which continues by giving the whole statement a metaphysical sense, rather than referring to any particular political entities. And if this is not sufficiently clear, Hegel makes just that point in the sentence that follows. Here, then, is the full passage. I have taken the liberty of inserting Kaufmann's correction into Knox's translation:

It is the way of God with the world that there should be the state. The basis of the state is the power of reason actualizing itself as will. In considering the Idea of the state, we must not have our eyes on particular states or on particular institutions. Instead we must consider the Idea, this actual God, by itself.[99]

This ought to dispel the idea that Hegel was an apologist, or that he set out to defend any and every state in general or the Prussian state in particular. The defects of *all* existing states are all too clear to him—namely, they are not real states but civil societies. Hegel's critics have accused him of regarding the state, any state, as an ideally working structure. Yet Hegel refuses to see the state as something ideal, and he says so, in the same paragraph as the above:

The state is no ideal work of art; it stands on earth and so in the sphere of caprice, chance, and error, and bad behavior may disfigure it in many respects. But the ugliest of men, or a criminal, or an invalid, or a cripple, is still always a living man. The affirmative, life, subsists despite his defects, and it is this affirmative factor which is our theme here.

To sum up, we can say that Hegel is concerned with the idea of the state as such and with how that idea may participate in the rationality of the world as a whole. What exists—amid caprice, chance, and error—is not *the* state; what Hegel exalts, therefore, is nothing in this world. Perhaps he exalts that ideal in order to show us how far from it we really are.

In the daily life of the political animal, so much is unplanned, is a muddled modification and facticity, that only the perspective of universal reason can point to what a state should be: instead of modification and muddling through, a sound and stable reality; instead of caprice and chance, a grasp of the cosmic dimension and the noble purposiveness we have lost (and therefore find it easy to deride); instead of facticity and error, a logic and necessity in the existence of that tragic animal.

# MARX

## The Restoration of Political Man

**The End of Philosophy**  At the University of Berlin in 1830, a year before he died, Hegel concluded his lectures on the history of philosophy with the view that philosophy had at last reached its goal and conclusion.[1] Yet could this view be taken seriously by the philosophers of the new generation? Could they actually believe that philosophy had come to its end? Looking back from the standpoint of our own time, we can see that this view of Hegel's had to be set aside, if only for the sake of the future of philosophy in general.

To Hegel's immediate successors, however, the challenge was felt as most pressing in regard to political philosophy. Although Hegel's influence was broad and deep, his *Philosophy of Right* could not stand as the last word. The French Revolution, the Napoleonic Wars, the Industrial Revolution, all demanded philosophic rethinking about the nature of society and the state. And, although Hegel himself had initiated that rethinking in his Jena lectures of 1803–6, subsequent social changes had become so acute as to force the new generation to rethink Hegel and go beyond him.

Around 1836, at the University of Berlin, Karl Marx joined a group of serious enthusiasts calling themselves the Young Hegelians. The group cherished two mottoes—"Atheism!" and "Realization of Philosophy!"—and held these mottoes as essentially Hegelian. The problem facing the new generation of philosophers was that it felt the need to liberate itself from his powerful influence yet could not turn its back to him entirely.

The process of liberation could take various paths: (*a*) reinter-

preting Hegel in ways that would allow philosophers to regard themselves as Hegelians but in new ways; (b) attempting to criticize
Hegel from the Hegelian standpoint itself; (c) seeking a way of
overcoming philosophy altogether and thus actually achieving its
proper "end" or realization. The first approach was embodied in
Ludwig Feuerbach's humanistic/materialistic Hegelianism, in what we
might call a Hegelianism of disenchantment. The last approach (not
at all remote from the first and eventually very much influenced by
it) was taken by Marx; this, too, was a humanistic and materialistic
Hegelianism—yet, with its emphasis on the possibilities of political
action, we might call it a Hegelianism of hope.

What Feuerbach presented was a technique for reinterpreting
Hegel and with it a new view of culture. The new approach was offered in his *Essence of Christianity* (1841) and *Preliminary Theses
on the Reform of Philosophy* (1842).[2] In the *Theses*, Feuerbach
suggested a new way of reading Hegel's philosophy: Instead of regarding the world spirit as the source of culture and man as the
product of spirit, we ought to reverse the order. Man is to be seen as
the source and the producer, and the so-called realm of spirit (man's
thought and culture) is *man's* product. Thus, when we read Hegel,
we are to take every subject as a predicate, every predicate as a subject. Man can then be seen as the true subject, his thought entirely
dependent upon him alone, without reference to a *Weltgeist*. With
this transformative method, Feuerbach suggests that we can understand the Hegelian vision correctly. (And in this we find the roots of
the subsequent Marxian "inversion" of Hegel.)

Thus, in *The Essence of Christianity* it is man himself who creates
culture and religion, a view that must have shocked those who believed that the source of Christianity was God himself, just as it must
have irritated those others who believed its source to be the world
spirit. Yet Feuerbach is enough of a Hegelian to retain some of
Hegel's most vital concepts. The concept of "alienation" is the prime
example: It is as essential a part of Feuerbach's vision as it is of
Hegel's. The difference is that, according to Hegel, culture is the
world spirit projecting and manifesting itself but alienating and externalizing that culture from its spiritual sources, whereas in Feuerbach's view it is man himself who is the alienator. Man gives an
"alienated" expression to his self-concern through the media of culture and religion, by projecting an image of himself as God without
realizing that it is only himself he sees.

The new challenge, therefore, was to find the hand of man (rather than that of the world spirit) in all cultural creativity. Hegel had stripped religion of its godly origin by seeing it as the work of the world spirit. The task that remained was to strip this away also and to show religion to be altogether human in its source and purpose. If religion could be successfully criticized in this way, then all the other illusory human productions (political as well as cultural) would be exposed as well. To explain religion correctly, then, would be to explain it away. We would then recognize our responsibility in creating whatever we had, as well as our freedom to re-create it anew. We would no longer think of the political, economic, or social systems as "natural"—that is, as created by nature or God and as therefore immune to change. If we can see that even God is man-made, then surely we can see that society is man-made and that it does not operate automatically on the basis of superhuman laws. We must therefore begin by taking religion as the prime example of man's self-alienated creativity. This is the point in the motto "Atheism!"—and it explains why Marx says that the premise or basis of all social criticism is the criticism of religion.

For Feuerbach, then, religion is a projection by man of man's own essence. Religion is not the story of man's relation to God but rather the expression of man's relation to himself. Man inevitably alienates this self-relation and projects his own image as "God," so that God is nothing but human nature elevated, rarefied, and made "other." What characterizes the human creation of God is its peculiar dialectic: "To enrich God, man must become poor; that God may be all, man must be nothing." In this way, man takes back by reflection those human qualities he projected as those of God. Man's consciousness of God is nothing but man's consciousness of himself—although it is not a direct self-consciousness, for then the self-alienation would be at an end. As Marx says, if such consciousness could be "turned" into a direct self-consciousness, then man would recognize his own self in the things he creates and would cease to create "God."

Man's great life-problem is his relation to nature and his effort to control it. Therefore, the prevailing view of God is not a stage in the process of the world spirit striving toward self-awareness. Rather, the prevailing view of God reflects the current stage of man's ability to exploit and explain nature—that is, the present stage of his technological development. That technological stage represents the relative success or failure of his efforts. It is his success or failure that must give man his world outlook, as it must give him his religion, general culture, and social structure. (Agrarian societies have corn gods. Ought we to wonder at this?) From this view of Feuerbach's, we can easily foresee Marx's economic explanation of society, as embodied in statements such as: "The mode of production of material life determines the social, political, and intellectual life processes in general,"[3] and "The handmill gives you society with the feudal lord; the steam mill, society with the industrial capitalist."[4] But above and beyond this mode of explanation there is this indictment: If the main problem confronting mankind is that of living in the natural world and controlling it, we may well ask what part or parts of man's culture have aided or impeded that effort. All in all, man's attempts to dominate material nature have failed. Rather, through man's own efforts, nature dominates *him*. Moreover, he has suppressed his own material nature, so that it has become warped and he has not conquered it. Religion is a false conquest of man's material nature because religion posits a false, nonhuman spirit that governs the world. Only when man acknowledges his own sensuous and material nature can he recapture his true *spirit*. Only by acknowledging no otherworldly ties can he achieve true freedom.

Not only is the criticism of religion the basis of the criticism of society; it is also the basis of the criticism of Hegel. The Hegelian system, as a whole, is seen by Marx as a piece of self-alienation in its own right. In positing a world spirit, the Hegelian system commits the same error as religion does in positing a God. History is nothing more than man: It is not theodicy, nor is it the cunning of divine reason. These Hegelian elements have to be rooted out and rejected.

Yet, although Marx might have wished to reject the content of Hegel's philosophy, he certainly retained Hegel's style of thinking, expressed in a convoluted language that is more obscure than it need be. This is in part due to its paradoxicality. We might well expect the dialectical *style* to flourish at the hands of such avowed anti-Hegelians as Kierkegaard and Marx. After all, the dialectical approach does regard things as generated by their opposites, then producing opposites of their own in turn. From Marx's earliest philosophical writings to his last, the tone of his thinking is Hegelian through and through. His anti-Hegelianism is in the content of his thinking, not in its form.

Yet, it is also true that in the content of his thought, Marx remains Hegelian even in his anti-Hegelianism. From the earliest to the last period there are certain Hegelian problems and conceptions that continue to concern Marx. One of these is the problem of the end of philosophy (which problem Hegel presented not only in his lectures on the history of philosophy but also in *The Phenomenology of Spirit* and *The Philosophy of Right*). For Marx, this "end"—in both senses, termination and fulfillment—is to be found in the concept of "praxis." As early as the notes to his doctoral dissertation (1839–41),[5] Marx is concerned with the problem of philosophy's relation to praxis. It is a problem that is to intrigue him for the rest of his days. Granted that theory and practice are as opposed to one another as the universal is opposed to the particular, is there some way for this division to be overcome?

For Marx, this division can be overcome only if praxis can be made to be the fulfillment of philosophy itself. This is why he can so boldly proclaim, as the last of his *Theses on Feuerbach* (1845),[6] that although the task of philosophy has been to *interpret* the world its task as of now is to *change* the world. That is to say, philosophy has itself come to the point where changing the world is the next specifically philosophical task. To show that philosophy has indeed come to this point, he uses as argument not the observations of the social critic but rather the most abstract arguments of philosophy itself. This he does in the doctoral notes. We ought to pay special attention here to the way in which the dialectical style of thinking already manifests itself, especially in the way he turns the *form* of Hegelian thinking against its own *content*. What he says is this:

To the extent that a philosophical system purports to be a complete totality, it must include an account of both nature and spirit (as Hegel's system does). But then the so-called totality is not a unity. The world it describes is split in its very essence: One part, spirit, comes to stand for the whole (because the synthesis is, after all, intellectual). As a result, *philosophy* perhaps may be regarded as unified, yet the *world* it describes remains divided against itself. As a further result, therefore, the world and philosophy stand opposed to one another, as division stands against unity. Because philosophy is thus set off from the world, the objectivity of philosophy itself is as fragmented as the world it encounters. And as philosophy is fragmented, so is its praxis, its way of working in the world. Thus, such philosophy is itself not truly unified; its "parts" (nature and spirit, matter and mind, or whatever) contradict one another. For this reason, the manifestation of such philosophy—its realization in the world—is itself contradictory. Because it fails to connect itself to the fragmented world, philosophy turns back on itself: Its objective universality reverts to a concern with subjective consciousness, to the subjectivity that created that philosophy in the first place.

Thus, we come to a false "end" of philosophy, an end that is not a fulfillment. If it were a fulfillment, a completion, there could be nothing further to expect. But because the result is negative the next dialectical step is some sort of opposition to that negativity. Marx is right to wonder what comes after. Perhaps the theoretical mind, now freed from the world, will turn into practical energy, he suggests. Yet, even if philosophy is once more to turn its eyes to the world, its praxis is still theoretical: It is mere criticism, measuring the particular actuality against the totality of the Idea. And, to the extent that the actuality fails to measure up, philosophy once more stands opposed to the world. In this tension, the world itself becomes a philosophical entity—and this is philosophy's weakness. Thus, philosophy's supposed realization is also its loss, he says, and what it combats outside itself is really its own inner defect. As he puts it:

The consequence, hence, is that the world's becoming philosophical is at the same time philosophy's becoming worldly, that its realization is at the same time its loss, that what it combats outside is its own inner defect, that just in this combat philosophy itself falls into the faults which it combats in its opponent, and that it transcends these faults only by falling victim to them. Whatever opposes it and what philosophy combats is always the very same thing as philosophy, only with reversed factors.[7]

Philosophy's criticism of the world, Marx says, is double-edged: The philosophy that turns against the world also turns against itself. This is because, in criticizing the world, philosophy also criticizes the philosophy by which the world is inspired at the time. Then philosophy becomes split once more—one faction emphasizing the primacy of the concept, the other the primacy of reality. Each faction projects its own deficiencies onto the other: For the "idealistic" (or what he calls the "liberal") faction the world is regarded as deficient; for the "empiricist" (or "positivistic") faction it is philosophy that is deficient.

Philosophy therefore has two tasks, and they are interrelated: to overcome its theorizing isolation from the world, and to complete its "criticism of religion" (that is, its criticism of culture and society, whose values are accepted "religiously"). The point of all this, as we saw, is to restore to man a sense of responsibility for his condition, as well as an awareness of his freedom to change it. This sense and this awareness constitute, for Marx, the true "completion" of philosophy. One can see this as Marx's version of Hegel's last stage in *The Phenomenology of Spirit*, that of Absolute Knowledge (which is absolute self-consciousness). It is also, for Marx, a liberation of man and a restoration of man to his humanness. The motto "Atheism!" meant the enthronement of man as Supreme Being, not merely the dethronement of God.[8] If, as the Young Hegelians held, God is man, then man is God—and then all things are possible for man.

The step that Marx had to take from here was the step from possibility to necessity—from a conception of what the time offered to what the time required. This he expressed in the view that philosophy "completes" itself only in praxis—a praxis that completes philosophy by transcending it and by getting one out of the study and into the street. The Young Hegelians would not follow Marx on this. He therefore broke with them. Any number of important questions can be raised about Marx's idea. "Praxis" is a merely formal term. What content can that term be given, such that it is intrinsic to the very idea? Just what praxis is involved in the concept of it?

Marx's answers to these questions were crystallized in the intense period of 1843–44, when he was reading and writing at a feverish pace, both at Kreuznach where he had gone to live with his bride and in Paris where he worked as coeditor with Arnold Ruge on the *German-French Yearbooks*. Ruge was one of the Young Hegelians, and he felt with Marx the need to translate Hegelian idealism into political action. For Ruge, this was to consist of a criticism of German politics and society from the standpoint of Hegel's philosophy.[9] It is important to point out that as far as Marx *and* Ruge were concerned in their coeditorship, Hegel's philosophy still provided a basis for concrete social criticism (although this did not mean that Hegelianism itself was above criticism).

In February of 1844, the one and only issue of the *Yearbooks* appeared. Among Marx's contributions was his short critique of Hegel's *Philosophy of Right*,[10] as well as his more extended article "On the Jewish Question."[11] We shall now discuss both these important essays. The latter was written at Kreuznach and was intended as a review of two works by Bruno Bauer on this subject. Marx used the occasion, however, to launch a thoroughgoing criticism of civil society and its inherent self-interestedness.

Let us recall Hegel's distinction between "state" and "civil society":

Only the state can be the vehicle of the collective cultural spirit; civil society is the apparatus serving individualistic goals and interests. The phrase "bürgerliche Gesellschaft" means both "civil society" and "bourgeois society." Marx exploits this double meaning, finding a new use for the phrase as a basis for negative criticism. Of necessity, civil society is the society of bourgeois interests, and this is what is wrong with it. The interests of the bourgeoisie, as a class, are essentially the private interests of the atomic individuals who make up that class. To speak of bourgeois interest, therefore, is to speak not of a class interest but of an individualistic selfishness turned against the collective interest of society as a whole. This selfishness is another way for man to alienate himself from his human nature, which is why bourgeois society must be overcome. Let us see how Marx connects the Jewish question to his criticism of civil society, particularly of civil society in Germany.

According to Bauer, the oppression of Jews is merely a part of the wider-ranging oppression of mankind in general and of the German individual in particular. How then (he asks) can Jews expect a special emancipation for themselves? They ought rather to work for the political emancipation of Germany and of mankind at large. Jews ought to give up their religion altogether and thereby remove the basis of religious antagonism. After all, Judaism and Christianity are merely different stages in the evolution of spirit, "different snakeskins shed by history." In Marx's characterization of Bauer, Bauer maintains that the whole thing comes down to the prejudice on the part of the Jews themselves in holding on to their religious ties. The individual Jew's self-emancipation from Judaism is therefore the precondition of his political emancipation.

Marx reverses all this and thereby goes deeper to inquire into the meaning of emancipation itself. The German state itself is not yet emancipated from religion. The state is not really *political*, that is, secular, democratic, atheistic (Marx takes North America as an example). Rather, the German state is still a part of the alienation that created religion in the first place. As long as this is so, as long as state and religion are two symptoms of one disease, it is easy for the state to function as a church: The state takes a theological attitude to its problems, so that politics is an imperfect religion and religion an imperfect politics; in addition, the citizen adopts a religious attitude to the state, and his loyalty is a "faith."

The point, therefore, is not necessarily to ask the individual to give up his religion but rather to ask the state to give up *its* "religion." It is a mistake to say that the individual must emancipate himself from religion as a precondition of his political emancipation. On the contrary, because the state and religion are related symptoms, the individual will overcome his religious limitations only as a result of, not as a precondition of, his political emancipation.

Religion and civil society (the false state) are expressions of individualistic and materialistic interests. Opposed to this there is the concept of man's "species life" in the true political state. Here he overcomes his selfishness and approaches universality. This is the true spiritual "heaven," against which the civil society is "earth." In the true political state man is a communal being. In the civil society he is a private individual, relating to others as mere means; the individual is himself reduced to a means "and becomes the plaything of alien powers." The difference between the state and civil society, therefore, is the difference drawn by Hegel—between freedom and determinism.

There is an echo of Kant in the way Marx equates morality with universality and sees immorality in the use of another person as a mere means. There is a stronger echo of Rousseau in the way Marx says that in the true political state there can be no possible conflict between a man's religious life and his social life. In the civil society, the role of citizen clashes with every other interest—not only with the religious interest of the individual but as well with his interest as shopkeeper, laborer, landowner, or whatever. One possible result is that religion becomes entirely a private affair, as in North America with its countless denominations. So long as there is a difference between bourgeois society and true social life, it will be impossible to overcome the difference (and conflict) between private and communal interests, or between political "earth" and "heaven." So long as politics is nothing more than imperfect religiosity looking to religion for its completion, it will be impossible to abolish religion, the imperfect politics.

The true state is a secular fulfillment. "The basis of the democratic state is not Christianity but the *human ground* of Christianity."[12] If the ultimate aim of Christianity is humanitarian, the truly democratic state achieves that aim, where Christianity cannot and never can. For Christianity that aim remains an ideal. In the democratic state this becomes an actuality: Man is the supreme value. Religion can only go so far as to present an image of man in his "uncivilized and unsocial" aspect, alienated from himself, oppressed by society, not yet fully humanized, not yet a species-being.

The failure of religion, therefore, is that it seeks man's fulfillment *apart* from society. There is considerable despair in Jesus' remark, "Render unto Caesar the things that are Caesar's; render unto God the things that are God's," because man is thereby separated from all possibility of an earthly fulfillment, even a secular fulfillment in society with other men. Traditional liberalism has regarded this remark in a positive light, as the basis of religious freedom in the separation of church and state. Marx goes to some length to point out that societies avowing religious freedom are civil societies to the core, even though they may regard themselves as revolutionary—for example, the France of 1791, the America of 1776. Libertarians speak of rights as pertaining to individuals, as limitations upon what the state may legitimately do to the individual—whether in Locke, in Mill, or in Isaiah Berlin's notion of "negative freedom."[13] The American Bill of Rights promulgates freedom of speech in the words "Congress shall make no law . . ." Important as this is, there is no overlooking the point that such negative freedom sets the individual in opposition to the state and gives the state no positive role to play in individual lives. As Marx says, such liberty is "not based on the association of man with man, but rather on the separation of man from man."[14] This is the major weakness of bourgeois society.

The "man" whose freedoms are to be promoted and protected (in libertarian theory) is not fully a man at all in Marx's view. Such a man is still egoistic and self-alienated—and therefore is still religious. He may have received religious freedom, but he has not been freed from religion! So long as such an "individual" is regarded as authentically human, society will look upon real man, the citizen, as something abstract. Human emancipation will be complete only when men overcome the divisiveness of individualistic pursuits and when their collective social power becomes their political power. This involves the need to change human nature (that is, if we insist that selfishness and individualism are the prevailing human characteristics). Marx quotes with approval a passage from Rousseau to the effect that whoever dares to undertake the founding of a nation must feel himself capable of changing man's human nature, transforming the isolated individual into a member of something greater than himself, into someone utterly dependent upon society.*

* "On the Jewish Question," in L. D. Easton and K. H. Guddat, eds., *Writings of the Young Marx on Philosophy and Society* (New York: Doubleday, 1967), p. 231 (hereafter referred to as EG). The Rousseau passage reads: "One who dares to undertake the founding of a people should feel that he is capable of

The conclusion to be drawn is that just such a Rousseauian change in human nature is what is required for the completion of philosophy! Let us savor the impact of this: Philosophy, theory, is realized and fulfilled to the extent to which *man* is fulfilled. And this is what is brought about by praxis. This fulfillment involves the overcoming of man's self-alienation in all its forms. We must now see what this theoretical development means in the way of practical effects.

**Praxis and Democracy**   So far we have seen man's self-alienation in two of its main forms: religion and civil society. Here man is an individual, standing alone before God and against other men. The required change in man's nature involves a change from individual man to generic man, from the self-sufficient unit to the collectively oriented being who is responsible to his fellows. Marx employs a special terminology for this Rousseauian change: Man is a "species-being" (*Gattungswesen*), which means that he is in essence a "collective being" (*Gemeinwesen*). Man fulfills his species life only in collective life, when his most intense interests are those of Man, the species.

Another item of terminology is the "universal class." For Hegel this is the bureaucratic class, supposedly universal because it mediates between private and public interests. For Marx, however, the truly universal class is the class whose liberation would liberate *all* classes and therefore would liberate all mankind. One class alone, the proletariat, could meet this requirement. If the bourgeoisie were to be emancipated, it would emancipate only itself and remain bourgeois

changing human nature, so to speak; of transforming each individual, who by himself is a perfect and solitary whole, into a part of a larger whole from which this individual receives, in a sense, his life and his being; of altering man's constitution in order to strengthen it; of substituting a partial and moral existence for the physical and independent existence we have all received from nature. He must, in short, take away man's own forces in order to give him forces that are foreign to him and that he cannot make use of without the help of others. The more these natural forces are dead and destroyed, and the acquired ones great and lasting, the more the institution as well is solid and perfect. So that if each citizen is nothing, and can do nothing, except with all the others, and if the force acquired by the whole is equal or superior to the sum of the natural forces of all the individuals, it may be said that legislation has reached its highest possible point of perfection." *On the Social Contract*, trans. J. R. Masters (New York: St. Martin's Press, 1978), Bk. II, chap. vii, p. 68.

(with its outlook still individualistic). But, if the proletariat is emancipated, it is freed from all class distinctions; and when all class distinctions fall, *all* classes are emancipated.

To recapitulate: The realization of philosophy is a continuous path that begins in the overcoming of man's self-alienation and ends in the restoration of man to his collective humanness. In the overcoming of alienation, not only is civil society transcended but philosophy is transcended as well. The completion of philosophy is to be found not in more philosophy but in the translation of philosophy into the political action that alone can bring to concretion the philosophic aim of man's restoration as a fully political being.

Marx's *Yearbook* attack on religion and civil society has two prongs: One of these is the essay on the Jewish question; the other is his short essay, "Towards the Critique of Hegel's *Philosophy of Right:* Introduction."[15] The essay begins with the statement to which I have alluded, that the criticism of religion is the premise of all criticism. The struggle against the illusion of religion is the struggle against a world in which such illusions are needed. The way to overcome the illusion is to eradicate the need for it, to eradicate the social conditions that make it impossible for man to live in this world and thus lead him to the illusion of a world to come. (It is in this essay that Marx makes his well-known remark that religion is the opium of the people.) Feuerbach has uncovered man's self-alienation in its sacred form, Marx says. What remains to be done is to uncover it in its wordly form—so that the criticism of heaven becomes a criticism of earth, the criticism of theology a criticism of politics.

In this radical criticism, man comes to see himself as his own creator, his own supreme being—and this entails the categorical imperative to overthrow the situation in which he is degraded, Marx says. Only the proletariat, the most degraded of classes, can overcome the general degradation of man in modern society. This is the only class that can stand up for society as a whole. It says, "I am nothing, and I should be everything." (This is Marx's response to Feuerbach's characterization of religion: "that God may be all, man must be nothing.") The proletariat is *within* civil society but is not *of* it. In emancipating itself from civil society it also emancipates the rest of society. The recovery of *its* humanity is the gain of all humanity. The essay ends with the words: "The head of this emancipation is philosophy, its heart is the proletariat. Philosophy cannot be actualized without the raising up of the proletariat, the proletariat cannot be raised up without the actualization of philosophy."

Here we have another multiple meaning, which Marx exploits. "Raising up" (*Aufhebung*) is a Hegelian term that also means "transcendence," "negation," "dissolution." Something is *aufgehoben* when it is raised to a higher level of reality and its former identity is nullified, that is, when it is absorbed in a broader concept and its former limitation is overcome. Thus, the identity of the individual is negated, transcended, *and* fulfilled in the collective. His individualistic identity is given up, and he is thereby raised up. Thus, also, the identity of the proletariat, as one class among others, would be *nullified* in a classless society, and with this the proletariat would be elevated, raised up. The raising up of the proletariat is therefore the transcendence of the proletariat as a distinct class, because all class distinction would thereby be eliminated.

These early works of Marx are already a powerful intellectual performance. At the age of twenty-five, he has formulated his unique grasp of the world: He has delineated the world's problem in a way that attempts to be comprehensive and all-embracing, and he has pointed to a solution of that problem. All this emerges out of a style of thinking that begins elsewhere but that he makes entirely his own. (That style of thinking includes, besides its profundities, facile seesaw sentences—for example, "As philosophy finds its *material* weapons in the proletariat, the proletariat finds its *intellectual* weapons in philosophy"; or, speaking about Luther, "He shattered faith in authority by restoring the authority of faith." Both sentences are from the "Introduction." As an example of his more substantial thinking, but expressed in this seesaw style, see the passage from his dissertation, quoted above.)

What he lacks at this early stage (1843) is his more fully developed theory of property, the use of the concept of alienation as a tool of social description, the complete theory of communism, and the materialistic theory of history. Marx will get to these in short order; his thought grows explosively. Commentators have remarked that Marx does not grow in his philosophic outlook. This is a mistaken view, fostered by the fact that most of his "philosophic" work was produced in the comparatively short period between 1841 and 1846. If by "growth" is meant a change in attitude, then there is no growth between Marx's earliest and later philosophic writings. Even a "late" concept like the abolition of the state is already expressed in his extended *Critique* (which we shall be discussing presently). But if by "growth" we mean the amplification and deepening of one's views, the adding on of new facts and the exploration of further implications, then there is undeniable growth in Marx's thinking. It is in this sense of deepening and amplification that we can see how his concept of democracy leads to his concept of communism. I think we could say that at this early stage Marx is a democrat who advocates the control of the state by the people. I do not intend to imply that he was a democrat as opposed to a communist. Some commentators have suggested this sort of opposition in the early Marx.[16] What I shall try to show is how his communism emerges out of his democratic outlook.

As we have seen, the self-imposed task confronting Marx at this stage is that of emerging from philosophy into praxis. A lesser thinker could simply have abandoned his intellectual activities and entered the arena of political action. For Marx, however, the challenge was not to abandon philosophy but rather to convert philosophy itself into praxis, so that political action becomes an extension of philosophy, its "categorical imperative." It would be hard to imagine a more intellectual yet less academic approach to action. This is why it is so vitally important for him to go back to philosophy and to reinterpret it. To help philosophy overcome its self-imposed illusions—this, he feels, is the first step in helping mankind overcome the wider illusions generated by society.

This requires (once more) a rethinking of Hegel (and we should stress again that, in Marx's way of thinking, this requirement is intellectual but not academic). Hegel had said: "What is rational is real, and what is real is rational." We may take this as Hegel's *cogito*. As far as Marx is concerned, the problem is to rethink the relation between thinking and being, between *cogito* and *sum*. I daresay that Marx saw Hegel's statement as a twofold problem: grasping reality in a thoroughly rational way so that all mystification is cut away; and reshaping that reality so that it can at last satisfy the demands of rationality. These two projects are so close, for Marx, that they are not even the opposite sides of one coin. Rather, they involve the translation of reason itself into reality.

The *Critique* is Marx's extended criticism of Hegel, embodied in a discussion of paragraphs 261 to 313 of *The Philosophy of Right*.[17] Some scholars hold that Marx did not intend this early work for publication in its present form and that it is merely a rough commentary intended by Marx to clarify his study of Hegel.[18] Whether or not this is true regarding the original manuscript, Marx did decide to produce a larger version for publication. The "Introduction," which we just discussed, was intended by him as the introduction to this larger, amended version of the *Critique*. Yet even such a larger work would have been too confining for all that he wanted to say (as he tells us in the preface to the Paris Manuscripts of 1844). He therefore decided to write separate pamphlets on each of the subjects under discussion. The immediate result was the group of Paris Manuscripts. Eventually, the projected first "pamphlet" was expanded into the four volumes of *Das Kapital!*

The *Critique* was too long overlooked by scholars. The first full English translation appeared in 1970, and thus it has not yet received all the attention it deserves. The editor of this translation brings evidence to show that Marx considered it to be far more important than a mere student work and that he regarded it as his definitive evaluation of Hegel. I am not certain that the editor is correct in saying that the *Critique* contains "the whole program of research and writing which occupied Marx for the remainder of his life."[19] It does have the merit of showing the actual development of Marx's thinking in this period, and it contains many of the themes to be found in his later work. The claim has also been made that despite its chaotic arrangement the *Critique* is the most systematic of Marx's writings on political theory.[20]

From the evidence of Marx's notebooks, we know that he was reading very intensely in Rousseau at this time and that he accorded to the *Social Contract* an importance second only to Hegel's *Philosophy of Right*. The problem to which the *Critique* addresses itself is the problem to which Rousseau gave so much attention: how to make the public interest a matter of the deepest private interest to the individual, thereby turning *l'homme privé* into *le citoyen*. As we saw, for Rousseau this involves a change so fundamental as actually to transform our human nature. The whole of Hegel's political philosophy is a direct response to the challenge raised by Rousseau. Marx responds to the challenge in his own way, by trying to circumvent the response of Hegel. Marx does this by emphasizing and radicalizing the idea of two different human natures, as distinct as though they were related to two separate species: On one hand, there is bourgeois man, isolated and self-alienated, the man who has lost and never regained his humanity. On the other hand, there is the collective man, the political animal of Periclean Athens.* For Marx the col-

---

* In the Funeral Oration, Pericles says: "That man who takes no part in public affairs, we have no use for." See Thucydides, *The Peloponnesian War*, Bk. II,

lective consciousness is not merely a matter of man's *needing* other people. In civil society, a man can need others yet be cut off from their *interests*. It is a question, rather, of how a man attains his humanity and whether he does so by means of the collective life. In attaining his humanity by means of the collective life, man fulfills his potentialities as a member of the species (that is, as a *Gattungswesen*) through his role as a communal being (a *Gemeinwesen*). In the Paris Manuscripts, this will become the explicit theme of the recovery of man's humanity through communism. Here in the *Critique*, however, Marx merely lays the groundwork for that solution by showing us the severity of the problem. In addition, he must show that Hegel's solution is inadequate: The political structure, intended by Hegel to produce the political unity Rousseau sought, is—in its effects—entirely divisive. This leaves the way open to the solution proposed by Marx.

It is certainly true, as so many commentators have pointed out,[21] that Marx arrives at his own political theory by way of a negative criticism of Hegel. Hegel's solution is intended to show that the conflicts inherent in civil society are overcome in the state, which is an external structure involving the political participation of all social elements. Social unity is therefore achieved with the help of a political apparatus; it is this apparatus that is to change *l'homme privé* into *le citoyen*. What Marx shows, however, is that the structure fails to produce the desired effect because its elements remain isolated as mere elements, divided against one another. Thus, the state that Hegel describes cannot restore man's collective humanness; rather, the state is another symptom of man's self-alienation.

Hegel spoke of the state as "the actuality of concrete freedom,"[22] meaning that the individual achieves in it the fullest expression of his individuality while identifying himself with the universal. The opposition of interests is still there, and it is this very opposition that—because it must be overcome by rational means—leads to the rationality of the state itself! Can such a unity be achieved while the diversity of interests persists? Yes, says Hegel, for the following reasons: There is a hereditary monarch who is politically independent; there is a class of civil servants (the "universal class") who have

---

chap. IV, par. 40. See also Aristotle, *Politics*, Bk. I, chap. ii, 1253a28: "But he who is unable to live in society, or who has no need because he is sufficient for himself, must be either a beast or a god: he is no part of a state. A social instinct is implanted in all men by nature."

identified themselves completely with the interests of the state; and finally there is the deliberative body, the Assembly of Estates, which includes representatives of the crown and the executive power, the bureaucracy, the landed gentry and aristocracy, and the commercial class. The influences contributing to social unity are, chiefly, the bureaucracy; the Assembly of Estates, where the various social strata are represented *as* strata; the corporations (or guilds) that make up the actual structure of civil society; and the law of primogeniture, whereby land cannot be divided among inheritors but must be passed on in its entirety to the eldest son.

Marx takes Hegel to be describing the actual Prussian state, and it is with this assumption in mind that Marx attacks each of these institutions in turn, showing that their overall effect is socially divisive. The solution Marx will eventually propose is: (*a*) that the proletariat take the place of the "universal class"; (*b*) that private property be abolished, together with the system of primogeniture; (*c*) that universal suffrage be instituted in place of the Assembly of Estates, so that the voter can overcome the division of class interests by a direct participation in political life. I shall comment on each of these points in turn.

*a.* Marx puts the proletariat in place of Hegel's universal class: Only the proletariat can identify itself with the sufferings of all mankind. As we saw, this theme was developed in the "Introduction" and "On the Jewish Question," both of which followed immediately after the *Critique.* Here in the *Critique,* however, Marx does not yet speak of the proletariat, nor does he yet put it forward as the class whose interests are universal because it suffers universal deprivation. His aim here is only to show up Hegel's bureaucracy (and thus, for Marx, the Prussian bureaucracy) for what it is. It operates as though it stands above the law, as a law unto itself. It is within the state but not *of* the state (this is the way he later characterizes the proletariat in capitalist society), and the state becomes nothing more than the material for bureaucratic manipulation. The state creates a bureaucracy that soon becomes its own raison d'être, so that the state serves it, rather than it the state. The interest served is bureaucratic alone. In the same way, the corporations (which are the civil counterpart to the bureaucracy) stand opposed to the state and to its common interest. The same mentality is at work here: The corporate structure becomes an end in itself, serving its own interests. Accordingly, bureaucracy and the corporations cannot be said to serve the interests of the state as a whole. The conclusion is that they actually stand in the way of man's collective life and humanization.

b. The *Critique* affords Marx the first opportunity to discuss the notion of private property. For Hegel the political independence of the landed gentry derives from its inalienable property. Because this cannot be sold or divided but must be passed on as a whole, it is impervious to political or family influences. Yet, for this very reason, Marx says, such property is completely cut off from all political and social responsibility. In this way, such property is the epitome of private interest—and therefore the interests of the landed property owner are opposed to the interests of the state as a whole. And, in view of the fact that private property is the basis of the modern state, it can be said that the state is the extension of private property and is its objectification. The result is not a unification of social life but its dissolution, with the state serving as little more than the tool of private interest.

We see here the typical reversal of the subject–predicate relation, the Feuerbachian reversal that Marx sought to extend to all other areas of Hegelianism and Hegelian thinking. Instead of property being the instrument of the will of its owner, the law of primogeniture makes property inalienable so that the owner becomes the instrument of his own property. Instead of his being free to dispose of it or possess it, it possesses him. Instead of his inheriting it, it inherits him. This is the general character of man's relation to property, as Marx will show in the Paris Manuscripts. Not because of the law of primogeniture but because of the institution of private property itself are men compelled to pursue private interests; and because these interests are opposed to the common interest, they are opposed also to men's own best interest. The institution of private property is therefore the villain of the piece, forcing men to act in ways that are the most destructive socially. This is why Marx says, in the essay "On the Jewish Question," that in civil society man is forced to treat others as means, to become himself degraded to a means, and to become a plaything of alien powers. The abolition of private property is essential if man is to attain his collective being and his humanity.

c. The Assembly of Estates was intended as another way of overcoming the division of interests. Yet it is divided into classes or estates, each of which is an element of civil society, not of the state. Each member participates as a member of *his* estate, because his mandate comes from the class that elects him. He cannot overcome that fact, and this is the weakness of any parliamentary system. This is why Rousseau was so strongly opposed to factions and parties: They inevitably stand opposed to the interests of the state as a whole. This divisiveness cannot be overcome within the system. The system itself must be overcome. Hegel believed that the state supersedes civil society; the state is the higher, more inclusive and spiritual social form. For Marx, however, both are essentially bourgeois and individualistic in their purposes; they are equally materialistic. The bourgeois state and bourgeois society must therefore be superseded together in favor of collective interest. In effect, Marx is saying that the true political entity is neither the state nor civil society but the people as a self-conscious unity. The people as a whole are to be the source of political decision; this alone is consistent with their species-being. Only democracy can make possible the complete participation of the people in their political life, the overcoming of all division of interest, as well as the dissolution of both civil society and the state. Both disappear in true democracy.

**Alienation and Communism**  We saw Marx pointing to the ideal of complete and fulfilled democracy. Yet he could not have remained with this idyllic Rousseauism. To criticize Hegel from the democratic standpoint may be all to the good, but it hardly can bring men to the barricades. What is needed is a theory of revolution. And, in order to arrive at a theory of revolution, Marx first formulates a theory of materialism in opposition to Hegel. Even before he gets to his fully developed materialism, however, he evolves his theory of alienation.

What is remarkable is that he arrives at his anti-Hegelian standpoint from within the framework of Hegelian thinking itself. As Avineri has so aptly put it, Marx "built his system out of the internal difficulties of Hegel's thought."[23] His criticism of Hegel does not remain on one level but goes deeper and deeper as his own thinking progresses. We have already begun to trace that progression. When all its links are in place, this progression will form a chain of interdependent ideas leading back and back to a unique idea of philosophy itself, thus: revolution—history—materialism—alienation—democracy—philosophy. In true Hegelian fashion, Marx seeks to show the logical connection between the links. Ultimately the end is in the beginning, because philosophic praxis *is* the making of revolution. As we saw, Marx's concern for the fate of philosophy stems from an awareness of the excesses of Hegelian absolutism, its hubris and failure. Philosophy cannot produce its own cure; only revolution can do that for it. If philosophy is to be overcome and fulfilled in revolution, the idea of alienation is the connecting link between them; that is, between theory and act, between the problem and its solution.

The concept of alienation is Marx's most significant contribution to social theory, and it occupies a place of central importance in his thinking. If Marx had not relied so heavily on that concept, it would have been necessary to invent it for him. This is indeed what did happen, in a manner of speaking. The concept of alienation in Marx was first discussed by Georg Lukács (in 1923),[24] long before anyone knew of Marx's Paris Manuscripts, which were first published in 1932. Lukács saw the role that the concept of alienation *must* play in Marx's theory, thus "reading the Hegelian issue of alienation back into Marx's later writings," as Avineri says.[25] The subsequent discovery of the Paris Manuscripts fully confirmed Lukács's views.[26]

According to Lukács, one expression of the phenomenon of alienation is the way human beings and human relations are converted to things as a result of the commodity system of modern economy. This reification is such that "a relation between people takes on the character of a thing and thus acquires a 'phantom objectivity,' an autonomy that seems so strictly rational and all-embracing as to conceal every trace of its fundamental nature: the relation between people."[27] It is possible to see this as part of a broader process, an extension of the Renaissance idea of man as the center of everything. In discussing, for example, Kant's "Copernican Revolution" (according to which the objects of our experience conform to our subjective psychic apparatus, rather than the other way around), Lukács shows that modern philosophy characteristically "refuses to accept the world as something that has arisen (or e.g. has been created by God) independently of the knowing subject, and prefers to conceive of it instead as its own product."[28] In a series of brilliant essays, Lukács shows how this secularizing and humanizing trend runs through all of modern philosophy and culminates in Marx. Reification is a failure of that attempted humanization; Marx seeks to overcome this reification and to restore man's lost humanity by political means.

Lukács shows how the humanizing trend leads inevitably from Kant to the absolute idealism of Hegel, for whom the world in its *entirety* is the "product" of man—in the sense that human reason is identical with the world's logic in the realms of both spirit and nature. But Hegel is the extreme exaggeration of this trend. Marx already saw the trend beginning in the division between the spiritual and the natural, as expressed in Vico, who says that men can understand their human world because it is men who have made their world; their truth is a *made* truth (*verum factum*) in contrast to the unknowable truth of nature. We can visualize this as a line of tension between two figures: Prometheus is technological man, *homo faber*, man the maker, who feels at home in the world because he fabricates its machinery and operates it; Epimetheus is the rational man of Descartes' *cogito*, man the knower, *homo sciens*, for whom the world is an extension of his own reason. Somewhere between the two, man has lost his humanity. The machine man has made—on the basis of his knowledge—has turned around and made man its creature. A comic result of this situation is Charlie Chaplin in *Modern Times*, who goes mad as the only way out. A tragic result is the crushing poverty and dehumanization of industrial work, to the point where man is himself converted to a commodity of even lower value than the commodity he creates. Any solution short of the ultimate one can only be piecemeal. Capitalist democracy cannot be the ultimate answer. If it is man's humanity that has been lost, nothing but the restoration of that humanity will satisfy.

We have seen something of the complexity of Hegel's version of alienation in his *Phenomenology of Spirit*. We saw the ambivalence of the *thing* for master and slave: The master appropriates what he does not himself produce; the slave produces but does not possess the thing. Because the slave is not free to reject the thing, his labor is only an incomplete negation of it. By contrast, the master has interposed the slave between himself and meaningful work—thus between himself and the natural world. Master as well as slave, each in his own way, is alienated from the world. Yet even more fundamental is the thinker's estrangement from his world. Beyond all this, Hegel also speaks of the estrangement of culture from its sources in the human spirit. This is reality estranged from itself, opposed to itself: The created world becomes the mind's "object" and is thereby opposed to the mind that has created it. In the same way the social world is estranged from its human creators. It is a "self-estranged reality."[29]

Hegel and Marx look upon the world as a reality in process. The world, for Hegel, begins in a simple unity; eventually it becomes divided against itself (nature versus spirit, consciousness versus world); and finally it returns to unity, the self-awareness that is the highest level of spiritual realization. Seen from that highest point, the political state is merely an intermediate stage. Hegel and Marx agree (for utterly different reasons) that the state must be transcended, superseded. Hegel's reasons are metaphysical: Man must transcend his need for the state in order to get to the higher levels of spirit. (This is not to say that Hegel urges us to leave our political milieu; he merely believes that that milieu is not the highest rung of spirit man can attain, namely, philosophic self-consciousness.) Marx has political reasons for saying the state must be transcended: The state is the instrument of oppression, an instrument serving a primitive stage of human development.

Hegel says I overcome the estrangement of the object from myself by means of self-awareness: I *realize* that the object is a product of my own self, my own mind. For Marx this is no solution at all, because it points to an intellectual realization rather than a realization in praxis; in this self-awareness the objects remain mental products and therefore are still alienated from their creator.

A further difference between Hegel and Marx is that Marx speaks not about the alienation of culture from its source in the Absolute Spirit, as Hegel does, but rather about the alienation of man from himself, from the natural world, and from humanity in general.[30] For Marx, the cause of alienation is not (as for Hegel) in the intrinsic logic of culture as the expression of spirit; rather, the cause of alienation is entirely accidental and external to human nature—that is, it is in the current socioeconomic system. For Marx, therefore, the idea of alienation reveals the actual process of dehumanization in modern industrial life.

The Paris Manuscripts of 1844 are more formally known as the "Economic and Philosophic Manuscripts."[31] The first of these manuscripts begins with three essays that take up in turn the three basic components of economic theory—labor, capital, and land—as well as their returns in wages, profit, and rent. Yet, although the division is classical, the content of these essays is entirely polemical and humanistic, with the aim of showing the dehumanization prevailing in these areas. These three essays lay the groundwork for the criticism presented by the fourth essay in the first manuscript, concerned with the alienation of labor.

Marx does not discuss the classical theory of wages but rather uses the occasion to launch a criticism of the wage system. Thus, he begins with the challenging statement: "Wages are determined by the bitter struggle between capitalist and worker."[32] The struggle is all on the side of the capitalist. Competition between workers drives wages down to the level of barest subsistence. The worker is pressed into a situation of complete dependence, because he must work each day or starve. Classic economic theory deals with the worker as an entrepreneur selling his labor. Yet it ignores the difference that the entrepreneur who sells a commodity can sell it today or tomorrow; the worker must sell his labor today, and what is not sold is lost. Moreover, the classic entrepreneur sells his commodities and remains a human being even if prices fall; the worker, in selling his labor, sells himself and his human identity, thereby becoming a commodity himself, an object. He sells himself—and what happens if he himself falls in value?

The objectification of the worker comes in addition to his grinding poverty. We might be tempted to regard that poverty as an accidental or temporary condition; Marx shows that, although it is "accidental" in the sense of being external to human nature, it is a logically necessary result of the wage system. He had a direct concern with that system in some of its more barbaric forms. Engels had been doing some important research into living and working conditions in Manchester.[33] Those conditions now seem unbelievable, yet they are confirmed by numerous other observers. At the end of Marx's essay on wages, he quotes from a work by Eugène Buret, *De la misère des classes laborieuses en Angleterre et en France* (1840): "The longer, more arduous and more wearisome the work which they are given, the less they are paid; one can see workers who work strenuously and without interruption for sixteen hours a day, and who barely manage to earn the right not to die."

Instead of a man's wage being proportional to the amount of labor he expends (as classic economic theory has it), it is *inversely* proportionate to the amount of labor expended. Let us, for the moment, give this condition a dry, technical name—say, "indirection"—so that its technicality may make it all the more bizarre. This theme becomes the leitmotif of the Paris Manuscripts. In addition to Marx's shock and rage at the injustice of all this, he also emphasizes this indirection (as I call it) as a dialectical feature that is part of the very existence of *homo faber*. The "indirection" can be seen as follows:

In classical economic philosophy, what characterizes any action *as* an action is that it is related to a goal that is rationally chosen and fulfilled. If I want some firewood, I go and chop some; if I want some bread, I bake some. The more I do of these actions, the more I have of the product, and the quantity of the product is directly proportional to the amount of work I put in. Now Marx contends that in modern industrial life this relation is reversed; the more the laborer works, the *less* he gets. Regarding the relation between work and material product, the proportionality still holds; with more work there is more of the product. But, if we are speaking about the connection between work and *wages* the relation is reversed; with more work there is less of wages. The worker gets poorer, the more work he puts in. It is a crazy irreality whereby his increased activity only starves him the more. This is because his own productivity (fostered by technological advance and what is weirdly called the "rationalizing of industry") makes the worker cheap and replaceable. He must therefore compete with other workers, thus driving wages down. The result is nightmarish: Whatever I may try to do to improve my condition only impoverishes me all the more. I cannot slow down, for then I will be fired; and if I speed up, I earn less. Thus, the very idea of work as a productive activity loses all sense.

In discussing other processes related to the capitalist system, Marx describes a process of polarization (a theme he will expand upon in subsequent writings). This process, too, has its dialectical character. Economic activity is competitive in its essence. The result of competition among capitalists is that they become fewer in number but richer, as wealth is concentrated in fewer and fewer hands.[34] In contrast to this, the result of competition among workers for the limited number of jobs is that the number of workers increases and they grow poorer.[35]

The same sort of struggle occurs in regard to land and rent. "The right of landownership has its source in robbery," Marx says,[36] quoting the classical economist, Jean-Baptiste Say. As in the case of wages, rent is established on the basis of a struggle—between tenant and landlord. As Marx says, "In all political economy we find that the hostile opposition of interests, struggle and warfare, are recognized as the basis of social organization."[37] Ultimately, the capitalist and landowner merge their functions and become one class. As a result, society eventually contains only that one class and one other: the workers. The consequent warfare is all the more severe and extreme. As wages are forced down to the minimum required for subsistence, rent is driven upward. The inevitable outcome is suffering so intense that it leads to revolution. In addition, Marx maintains that the same monopolistic tendencies exist in regard to land as are found to exist in regard to capital—with the same destructive consequences. We can reasonably conclude, therefore, that these institutions will eventually destroy themselves by their own inner tensions and processes, perhaps even before a revolution gets to them. Marx declares, laconically, that both—landed property and industry—must achieve their own ruin in order to arrive at faith in man.[38]

The now famous essay, "Alienated Labor," summarizes these processes,[39] all of which occur as a matter of logical necessity:

(a) The worker is reduced to a commodity, and to a most miserable commodity.

(b) The worker's misery and poverty increase with his output.

(c) Competition among capitalists leads to the monopolistic concentration of wealth in a few hands.

(d) The distinctions between capitalist and landowner, between agricultural worker and industrial worker, eventually disappear, so that only one distinction remains: that between owners of property and propertyless workers.

These are not merely temporary symptoms or contingent aspects of alienation. What they point to is a whole system of alienation—of which the alienation of labor is the most prominent feature. In addition, Marx points out that alienation is also characteristic of private property and acquisitiveness, capital and land, exchange and competition, value and the devaluation of man, monopoly and competition—all of it based on a system of *money*, a false representation of value.

We have seen something of Marx's view that the worker produces his own impoverishment in direct proportion to his production of goods. Yet he produces more than his impoverishment. Let us recall that in Hegel's view of the master–slave relation it is the slave who turns inward and develops the Stoicism by means of which he conceives of his freedom and humanity, thereby reinforcing his idea of himself as a man and thus overcoming his enslavement. In the view of Marx, however, modern industrial slavery (and he has no hesitation in calling modern labor "forced" labor)[40] has no such redeeming effect. The modern industrial slave does not inevitably come to a realization of his essential freedom as a man. Rather, in addition to producing his own impoverishment, he produces his own devaluation as a person and comes to think of himself as anything but a man. Like material poverty, that spiritual devaluation is deepened as the value of *things* increases.

To the extent that the thing, the inert material object, acquires an independent existence it stands opposed to the worker. It is an alien being, Marx says, a power that the producer must serve. Here we see the direct extension of Hegel's master–slave discussion. His slave tries to overcome the object by working on it. For Marx, the thing is itself an objectification (the term he uses is *Verdinglichung*: literally, "thingification") of labor. Not only does the worker have less of the object as he produces more of it, but his increasing productivity leads to there being less and less work. Finally, work itself becomes a commodity, ever harder to find—until the worker starves and dies.

We also saw Marx's view that the actual physical process of work, day by day and hour by hour, is a process in reverse of all rationality: Work produces the diminution and devaluation of the worker; production of the object leads to the loss of the object for him and his enslavement to the object; and, finally, the appropriation of things for oneself is a process of one's alienation from oneself. Accordingly, the worker is alienated from the product, "an alien object which dominates him," with the result that the world itself becomes alien and hostile to him. There is also the alienation *in* the work, so that one's work is no longer one's own: Strength becomes impotence, creativity leads to emasculation and to alienation from one's own self.

To show that this is no merely local or contemporary phenomenon but rather something implicit in the very *phenomenology* of production and creativity as such, Marx connects it immediately to the broad process of alienation that produces culture and religion: The more man attributes to God, the less there is of man himself. In industrial work it is the activity itself that is alienated, and the product is merely the *résumé*, he says, of this activity. One thinks again of the quotation from Buret, with a bizarre feeling—as though the one and only aim behind all this were human enslavement and as though the production of things (no matter what) were deliberately devised as a mere means to that end. It is "indirection" with a vengeance.

In addition to the worker's alienation from the object he produces and from his own activity, Marx considers a third form of alienation: man's separation from his life as a member of the human species. Man becomes individualized due to his struggle with others and thereby loses the chance of collective fulfillment. He even makes his collective life serve the purposes of his self-destructive individualization. In his competition for work, man is reduced to pursuing his self-interest as opposed to the interest of humanity as a whole. Worse, he must devote all his energies to maintaining his physical existence, so that his life is reduced to a concern with nothing more than the *means* to life. Man's essence becomes a mere means to his existence. (This distinction between man's essence and existence is of the greatest importance for Marx, as we shall see.)

All this is in stark contrast to man's human (as distinct from animal) possibilities. Man need not be limited to producing for his physical needs. He is capable of producing a world, producing beauty, and is even capable of seeing himself in a world of his own making. His labor ought therefore to be the objectification of his species life. Yet alienated labor deprives him of these possibilities. As a result, man is actually inferior to the animal, whose activity is the fulfillment of its being. Man's activity, instead of serving his species life, deprives him of his humanness and corrupts his relations with his fellowman.

Who is to blame? Marx sees a multisided relation here. Alienated labor can be seen as caused by, as well as the cause of, private property. In addition to the causal there is also a logical connection: Enslavement requires an enslaver. Alienated labor leads to a special relationship between such labor and someone "who does not work and is outside the work process."[41] The concept of private property is therefore a logical as well as an empirical consequent of alienated labor—and Marx is emphatic in stressing that multisidedness. The liberation of the worker, the restoration of his humanity, thus logically requires the elimination of private property. This is not merely the elimination of an external social institution, a minor medical operation that would leave the body politic as it was, only healthier. Rather, *all* our social relations are based on a foundation in property; and all private ownership comes down to the fact that a human being owns other human beings and thereby dehumanizes them. The worker is a chattel, "a *living* capital, a capital with needs."[42] Capital in the usual sense can remain inert; but this living capital must work or starve. And so the operation that would eliminate this condition would change mankind for good and all. The surgery would be, literally, radical.

At the end of the second manuscript, Marx goes from empirical description to abstract phenomenology. We saw how Hegel spoke of the world's process from (*a*) its material unity to (*b*) its disunity in nature and spirit to (*c*) its final reunification in absolute self-consciousness. We can see something of this in the way Marx speaks of private property as the interrelation of capital and labor. The dialectical stages through which that relation must pass are from (1) capital and labor as united and interdependent to (2) opposition to one another as each recognizes the other as a threat to its existence and seeks to limit the existence of the other to (3) the point where each becomes the opposition to itself, so that capital stands against its own profit and labor against its own wages.[43] This last point is cryptic. Perhaps Marx intends this as a stage of final unification in self-consciousness, wherein capitalism gives up the profit motive and the wage system. He speaks of the capitalist sinking into the working class and the worker becoming a capitalist. Marx ends the second manuscript abruptly with the terse sentence: "Clash of reciprocal contradictions."

In the third manuscript's second essay,[44] Marx arrives at communism as the solution to the problem of alienation. On a primitive level, private property is regarded as an entity in itself: labor is its essence, capital its existence. That is to say, we regard property as in essence the outcome of work, although it exists as an owned artifact. Yet the subsequent division between labor and capital, as two opposed interests, is as deep a division, for Marx, as the metaphysical division between "essence" and "existence"—that is, the division between the meaning of a thing and the brute fact of its being there.

There is a form of primitive communism that aims merely at overcoming the distinction between *your* property and *mine*, although the institution of property is retained. Marx compares this to the communal sharing of women, where the institution of marriage-as-ownership is not really overcome. We share our women as we share property of ours; human personality is still being denied, individuality is still not fulfilled, and we have not yet bridged the gap between human essence and human existence. The result is not a true community but merely a single owner: the community itself. As long as such ownership remains, there is a long way between the primitive concept of woman as something owned and the raising of the man–woman relation to the level of a truly human relation. For the same reason, it is a long way between the primitive communism of Fourier and Saint-Simon and the communism that Marx sees as the only method for restoring our humanness. As he points out, the real problem is that men's material needs must somehow be made to be *human* needs (just as, analogously, primitive sexuality must be made human, the basis of the recognition of the person).

Marx therefore sees true communism as the solution of the deeper human *and* metaphysical problems. He expresses this in one of his best passages (with something of the *Phenomenology's* sense of ultimate unification):

Communism is the positive abolition [*Aufhebung:* overcoming] of private property, of human self-alienation, and thus the real appropriation of human nature through and for man. It is, therefore, the return of man to himself as a social, i.e. really human, being, a complete and conscious return which assimilates all the wealth of previous development. Communism as a fully developed naturalism is humanism, and as a fully developed humanism is naturalism. It is the definitive resolution of the antagonism between man and nature, and between man and man. It is the true solution of the conflict between existence and essence, between objectification and self-affirmation, between freedom and necessity, between individual and species. It is the solution of the riddle of history and knows itself to be this solution.[45]

To reunite essence and existence is to restore the human meaning to men's lives. Yet this is not the only problem that is resolved. Marx claims that communism is the answer to the fetishism of objects that stands in the way of man's self-affirmation and return to species life. Above all, it is Marx's response to Hegel's idea that self-consciousness is the goal of history. In Hegel's version this is man's consciousness of his identity with Absolute Spirit. In Marx's version self-consciousness is the solution to the riddle posed by the gap between the fact of life and its meaning—the riddle of how we can create all that we do create and yet deprive that creation of all meaning. The fact that this self-consciousness knows itself to be the ultimate source of all free and genuine creativity—that is the beginning of the answer.

Through man's self-alienation, all his creations (religion, the family, the state, law, morality, science, and art) have been pressed into the service of private property. The overcoming of self-alienation therefore requires the overcoming of religion, the family (in its possessive aspect), the state (in its service to individualistic interests), and so on—and a return to true social life. Only then can man's natural existence become a truly human existence, fulfilling a truly human essence.

Private property has had a stultifying effect: The capitalistic modes of accumulation and consumption have been destructive, nihilistic, dehumanizing—because we have become the slaves to what we produce. It is no wonder therefore (as Marx points out) that men have created a God on whom their own existence is supposed to depend, when their real lives are beset by all manner of dependencies, chiefly the dependence on the things and the system they have created. Man can create himself anew—by his own human (and humanized) labor. This is the overcoming (*Aufhebung*) of alienation.

In the last essay of the third manuscript,[46] Marx returns to the theme of the philosopher's alienation from his world. According to Marx, Feuerbach succeeded in showing philosophy to be nothing but religion extended into thought, religion intellectualized—something to be condemned as another form of alienation. It is easy enough to think of Hegel's system in this way, with its deliberate identification of the Absolute with God. As Marx points out, Hegel begins with the alienation of substance from the absolute, the infinite; then he transcends the infinite to posit the real, the finite thing; but then he transcends the finite and returns to the absolute. This is the world's own basic process from unity to differentiation to eventual reunification. In theological terms, this process can be seen as God's creation of the world, the Fall of Man (the "alienation of substance from the absolute"), and his eventual return to God. Therefore, the "transcendence of the finite and return to the absolute" is nothing but the extension of religion in philosophic form. As Marx sees it, this is self-contradictory, because it projects a theology that is ostensibly the polar opposite to philosophy yet is the creation of philosophy itself.

The career of the Absolute in the world is, for Marx, nothing but the philosophic mind giving itself some sort of objectification; and the philosophic mind is merely the self-alienated world mind thinking of itself abstractly. Its reality is translated into the counterfeit coinage of speculative logic. "Logic is the *money* of the mind," Marx says,[47] and in order to get the fully negative meaning of this phrase we should bear in mind his view of the money system as a *falsification* of real production and real value. It may not seem a very serious objection to speak about the Absolute as nothing but an extension of the philosophic mind. Yet, as Marx points out, it is the philosopher who—as alienated man in abstract form, a shadow of a shadow—sets himself up as the measure of the alienated world. From this peculiar situation arise some of the problematic dualisms to which Marx alludes in the paragraph quoted above, the dualisms that are to be resolved by communism: essence and existence, freedom and necessity, but especially the dualism between the philosopher's thought and the philosopher's world.

Where exactly does the philosopher stand—within the world or outside it? When a philosopher says, as Kant does, that we cannot prove that we are free but that we must live "as if" this is so, must he be mad merely to be taken as sincere? When he says that we cannot prove that God exists but that we must live "as if" this is so, can the philosopher be both a believer *and* a critic? There certainly are schizoid elements in these views. Marx believes that the necessary condition for thinking in this way is the philosophic dissolution of the real world and its reconstruction in mere thought. This is one side of Hegel's error.

The other side of the error, Marx says, is the reduction of man's appropriation of the world to a merely theoretical appropriation. Thus, all of man's products are reduced to merely mental status. This allows Hegel to speak *theoretically* about man's reason and the world. But much is lost thereby. The continuity between religion and reason is not maintained but broken; to be a critic is to cease being a believer:

If I *know* religion as *alienated* human self-consciousness, what I know in it as religion is not my self-consciousness but my alienated self-consciousness confirmed in it. Thus my own self, and the self-consciousness which is its essence, is not confirmed in religion but in the *abolition* and *supersession* of religion.[48]

Marx does praise Hegel for understanding man in his self-creation, for seeing man as the result of man's own labor. But this is transformed into a mental or spiritual labor, Marx says. Further, the object of that creativity is always opposed to the consciousness that created it. (The created God is "other" than his creators!) To understand, as Hegel does, that the creative spirit is the truth of everything, we must deny the *objectivity* of that creation, because everything is the product of subjective creativity. The result of man's return to himself, therefore, is that when he sees his object as his own creation he reappropriates it—but there is the problem that although these "objects" are independent of him they are nevertheless the creatures of his subjective world and subjective needs. The sociocultural world that man creates he projects as "other" to himself; yet it is entirely his own doing. The object is taken as something in itself. But man is a being for himself, realizing himself in being as well as in thought.

The scandal of alienation is that when I see the object as *my* creation it loses its objective character and becomes the mere semblance of an object. Against this, Marx wants to show that the world is man's creation and yet that it has an objectivity of its own. Marx cannot be faulted for not having overcome this gap; no one else has succeeded in doing this either. Communist humanism does not resolve the problem. To *say*, merely, that the subject creates the object—this does not *show* us how to bridge the gap between them.

Hegel maintains the distinction yet tries to encompass both sides as mere aspects of a wider, all-inclusive reality. So Marx is not entirely correct in saying that Hegel converts everything to a mere object of thought. Hegel does say, "Self is the truth of everything." Yet he does not mean that all truth is subjective, because he seeks to strengthen the tension between subjectivity and objectivity—and overcome it. Marx is therefore wrong when he says that in Hegel's system the whole sweep, from logic to nature, is reducible to a range of mental activities from abstraction to intuition.[49] This does not fit Hegel. The objects of consciousness have to be referred to the acts of consciousness for their meaning, but this does not mean that they are reducible to such acts or are to be equated with them.[50]

What concerns us, however, is not whether Marx is correct in his critique of Hegel but how he uses that critique in formulating his own view of the world. The concept of alienation stands at the center of that critique. Further, that concept points to one of the most profound of human problems. It is enough if he contributes to our understanding of the problem, if not to its solution (as he hoped). His main contribution is to connect alienation as a social phenomenon to alienation as a philosophic predicament. In one of his pithy *mots*, he says, "The Englishman transforms men into hats; the German transforms hats into ideas."[51] Yet this shows that Marx could not leave the problem there but that he had to reveal its ramifications in man's material history. To this subject we now turn.

**The Materialistic Conception of History**   Marx's worldview is historical through and through. From his grasp of history he gets his picture of human development, as well as the conviction about the inevitability of the coming revolution. Marx's idea of historical inevitability derives its *formal* aspect from Hegel's conceptions of logic and the dialectic of history, although Marx could not accept the metaphysical *content* of Hegel's historicism. That is to say, Marx took from Hegel the idea of logical necessity in history but rejected Hegel's view that the process of history is the emergence of Absolute Spirit.

Marx replaced this idealistic content with materialism—resulting in the viewpoint that might best be called "historical materialism," although in its more deterministic version it was to be named (by Plekhanov and Lenin) "dialectical materialism."

There are those who say that in formulating his historical materialism Marx ceased being a Hegelian. Others say that this is indeed a continuation of Hegelianism but a Hegelianism inverted.[52] The Hegel–Marx relation has, in recent years, come in for renewed and intensive study. Whatever the tangled truth of that relation may be, we can safely say that Marx follows Hegel in his historicism but that he is anti-Hegelian in being a Feuerbachian materialist. If we accept this, we can see that the greatest intellectual challenge facing Marx was to reach just such a synthesis of Hegelian necessity and non-Hegelian materialism. In my view this combination is impossible: Only formal relations can be necessary, and all that exists is contingent; to try to combine a necessity of form with a materialism of content is like speaking of the "necessary existence" of God.

It can be said in Marx's favor that he may have meant "necessity" in some less than formal sense. Although he tries to introduce an air of logical necessity by speaking of "premises" and so on, his reasoning is far from syllogistic and his "conclusions" are never deductively rigid ones. His attempted synthesis could work if his historical "logic" were plainly contextual, in the sense of some metaphysical logic (such as Hegel's), but this is just what Marx wants to avoid. Perhaps, then, he meant to give the idea of "necessity" a moral sense rather than a logical or metaphysical sense. (We saw how he spoke of the "categorical imperative" to end the situation of alienation and oppression.) But if we interpret Marx's idea of necessity in a moral sense, then the combination known as "historical materialism" or "dialectical materialism" loses its strictly *logical* force. As a piece of ideology, dialectical materialism may (for all I know) have a moral justification. Yet its proponents claim for it something more: the rational authority of logic itself.

Another point to be taken into account is that Marx never confines himself to one mode of speech, so we are being unfair to him if we try to extract from his words one strict meaning or other. His language is at once empirical and moral, descriptive and prescriptive, logical as well as analogical. But this many-sidedness means that we must reject from the start the possibility of the synthesis he sought: logical necessity in form combined with materialism in content. He needed a "logical materialism" in order to justify the revolution as logically inevitable (ordained from above, as it were) and to establish his humanism on a materialist basis (from below). But, as I maintain, this combination cannot be achieved, and the search for it must be as dead as the search for the synthetic a priori.

The most concise statement of his putative Hegelian/non-Hegelian "synthesis" is in the preface to his a *Contribution to the Critique of Political Economy*.[53] In this work of 1859, Marx sums up his thinking in the 1840s and presents in one long paragraph his materialistic conception of history—which he says was the conclusion of his studies and which continued to serve him as the guiding thread of his subsequent thinking. The basic idea of the materialistic conception of history is the Feuerbachian reversal of Hegel: Instead of concrete history being the result of an idea, ideas are the result of concrete historical circumstances. As we saw at the start of our discussion of Marx, Feuerbach suggested that we read Hegel so that the subject of any given statement takes the place of its predicate and vice versa. Thus, material man is no longer the outcome of history but the source; his culture and ideas are no longer the source but the outcome. As Marx says in the preface, "It is not the consciousness of men that determines their existence, but, on the contrary, their social existence determines their consciousness."

By "social existence" it is clear (from the context) that he means men pursuing their material interests through the production of material goods. This is his basic premise, as he says in *The German Ideology*.[54] Here (1845–46) Marx and Engels state that they take as their premise "the real individuals, their actions, and their material conditions of life, those which they find existing as well as those which they produce through their actions."[55]

From this "materialistic premise" we can return to the preface and summarize the materialistic conception of history:

The production of material goods leads inevitably to certain human relations Marx calls "relations of production." These are to be seen as property relations; and, taken together, they constitute the economic structure that in turn serves as the basis of the legal, political, social, cultural, and ideological superstructure. All culture, therefore, is built up on the deeper base that is the economic-productive system existing at the time. Let us recall the *mot*: "The handmill gives you society with the feudal lord." There are, then, three layers: at the bottom, the productive base that Marx calls the "material powers of production"; immediately above, the economic structure of property relations, the structure Marx calls the "relations of production"; and above everything, the sociopolitical effect of all this, the cultural superstructure.

In his preface, Marx maintains that the material base must come into inevitable conflict with the property relations and the economic structure. This leads to an impasse and eventual social upheaval. Such conflicts are usually fought out on the cultural level, in the form of religious innovation or as changes in political ideology. But all this is illusory, the mere surface effect of the deeper material conflict.

One might, for example, "interpret" Michelangelo's *Last Judgment* and the dome of Saint Peter's as concrete symbols of the Counterreformation. Regardless of whether that symbolic meaning was part of Michelangelo's intention, one could read it in and be more or less correct.[56] *Interpretans* and *interpretandum* are here very close and almost interchangeable because both belong to the realm of the cultural, the spiritual. Yet this very closeness deprives the interpretation of its force; the interpretation might well be correct, but in Marx's eyes it would verge on the trivial. According to Marx, however, there is no triviality or conjecture about the economic-material base; here we are in the realm of the scientific and deterministic. And because *this* is the reality, then in contrast to this all culture is mere "ideology," the illusory expression of deeper socioeconomic pressures. Marx gave to the word "ideology" something of the connotation of self-deception and irreality that Freud was to give to the word "rationalization." All ideology is "false" thinking.

This model of explanation involves an ontological difference between surface and depth: Only at the depth is there substance and reality; everything at the surface is mere appearance and froth. Culture is the illusory epiphenomenon of real material forces. Therefore we are never correct, in our methodology, if we try to interpret culture from a standpoint immanent within culture itself—as though the Counterreformation, as a cultural phenomenon, were the ultimate explanation of Michelangelo's dome and painting. On the contrary, an explanation of a cultural movement or artifact must always look outside culture, to its economic base. The Counterreformation is itself to be regarded as the effect of economic forces—and only when we come to these forces do we come to the rock bottom of explanation.

Accordingly, the dialectical relation between depth and surface is such that when the economic foundation changes all else changes with it. But before such a substantial and comprehensive change takes place, society runs the gamut of its productive possibilities, as Marx points out. The various methods of production constitute productive epochs: the Asiatic, the ancient, the feudal, and the modern bourgeois methods of production. With each, there is associated a distinct social and cultural superstructure. Each epoch has its unique antagonisms, in which the social relations are in conflict with the mode of production. The bourgeois epoch is not only the latest, it is also the last, because it holds the possibility of the solution of its conflicts and thus of all conflicts.

As Marx says, "No social order ever disappears before all the productive forces, for which there is room in it, have been developed; and new higher relations of production never appear before the material conditions of their existence have matured in the womb of the old society."[57] This is as much as to say that for every problem there is a possible solution and that there are no social problems that cannot be solved (and Marx even says this in the preface). The grounds for this optimistic view are in the principle that there is no social situation that is not an *effect*, and a manipulatable effect, of man's economic arrangements.

An understanding of the passage from the preface is made difficult by Marx's ambiguous use of phrases such as "relations of production," "mode of production," "material forces of production," "social forces of production," and "methods of production." A further problem is that the passage has been regarded both as a piece of empirical social observation and as a philosophy of history.[58] These two views clash: According to the one, the passage ought to be empirically verifiable; according to the other, it is not verifiable. Yet the fact is that as an empirical observation the passage is *not* universally true; and if we want to read it as philosophy of history then the fact that it is beyond verification would render it meaningless in the eyes of some philosophers. In any case, we ought to avoid the tendency to oversimplify Marx's conception. In addition, there is the scholarly controversy as to whether, in Marx's view, it is man's productive activity or the economic framework that is more basic.[59] Marx holds both these views in turn. Both elements are complex and are probably interdependent. But it is more important to note not merely that society is *involved* in material production and in the fulfillment of material needs but also that "the *character* of production determines in general the character of social life."[60] Marx stresses this point repeatedly:

The bourgeoisie cannot exist without constantly revolutionizing the instruments of production, and thereby the relations of production, and with them the whole relations of society.[61]

As individuals express their life so they are. What they are, therefore, coincides with their production, with what they produce and how they produce it. What individuals are, therefore, depends on the material conditions of their production.[62]

And then there is the handmill/steam mill epigram:

In acquiring new productive forces, men change their mode of production, and in changing their mode of production, their manner of gaining their living, they change all their social relations. The handmill gives you society with the feudal lord; the steam mill society with the industrial capitalist.*

Regarding the inevitable conflict between the "material powers of production" and the "relations of production," the examples are endless. There is the current conflict brought about by the automation of industry as against the outmoded "relations of production," which entitle the worker to job security by virtue of his membership in a labor union organized earlier on, on the basis of a different mode of production. For another example, it is well known that the introduction of a new "mode of production," the rifle, destroyed the clan structure of many American Indian tribes, because men no longer needed to hunt in groups. Another well-worn example is the Calvinist idea of God, whose mysterious grace befits capitalist conceptions of acquisition and profit. To try to give these phenomena a meaning that is independent of their material base—for example, as though the worker, in abstracto, had an inherent right to work, or as though American Indian societies fell apart because of some mysterious spiritual failure, or as though the Calvinist conception of God were fully explicable as the expression of a new individualism, and nothing more—is fallacious.

* EG, p. 480. For some reason, the translators have chosen to use the word "windmill" instead of "handmill." The German text reads: "Die Handmühle ergibt eine Gesellschaft mit Feudalherren, die Dampfmühle eine Gesellschaft mit industriellen Kapitalisten." Marx himself had reservations about this way of characterizing his economic determinism. Yet, if we realize that with a phrase such as this we are not characterizing his view but only giving it a schematic form that he himself provided, the danger of oversimplification can be avoided.

That is, to explain such phenomena as nothing more than expressions of "culture" is in itself a symptom of alienation in the intellectual who is doing the explaining. Thus, it tells us little or nothing to be told, say, that the Reformation was the product of the "culture" of the time. Worst of all, such "explanation," far from being value-neutral and objective, tends to argue in favor of whatever situation exists, a mistake Marx condemns as "ideology." For Marx, cultural creation becomes ideology when it exists in the interests of a particular class in opposition to the interests of society as a whole. In one way, Marx is perhaps endowing these creations with a special importance by calling them ideological. Yet this is also in a sense to trivialize them, as though, say, the dome of Saint Peter's were *nothing but* a sublimated expression of class interests in a devious form, an expression that is blind to its real source and meaning. Marx regards ideology itself as a false consciousness[63]—false, not in the sense that it is mistaken in what it says, but in the sense that it is the unwitting vehicle for the expression of some class aims and class interests against the interests of society at large.

We may not want to agree with the very disturbing conclusion that culture is of necessity and in essence *nothing more than* the illusory justification of class interests in their eternal struggle against one another. Marx shares with Nietzsche and Freud the aim of showing that all culture is devoted to promoting illusion, illusion that includes culture's blindness to its real sources. Marx believes not only that culture is the effect of deeper and hidden economic causes but that its blindness to that fact also has its economic source. The forces engendering illusion aim at the dehumanization of man. To uncover the illusion, therefore, is to restore man to his human dignity. Marx had enough faith in the perfectibility of human nature to feel that it is both possible and inevitable that men should liberate themselves from illusions of all kinds, once the illusions had been exposed. Yet he felt that the liberation could not be accomplished by the intellect alone. Indeed, it is precisely this misconception he sets out to attack in *The German Ideology*.

This massive work was the first joint effort of Marx and Engels. They had intended it merely as a study that would help them to focus their attacks on the Young Hegelians, particularly on Feuerbach, Bauer, and Stirner. Moreover, the book would (presumably) enable Marx to reconcile himself to the Hegelian sources from which he felt he had already emerged and thus to square accounts with (as

he called it) his "philosophic conscience." He was apparently not
disappointed when the book was rejected by the publishers. Yet it is
one of his central works. Although it is largely polemical and tendentious in character, the first part, which is devoted to a criticism of
Feuerbach, presents Marx's most sustained account of the materialistic conception of history.

The illusion of religion, Marx says, is not to be cleared up by substituting one set of beliefs for another (as the Young Hegelians maintained), even if the old beliefs are false and the newer ones are true.
One cannot move history in that way. If a change in ideas were
enough to move history, then one could say that whole empires have
been overthrown between 1842 and 1845—when "more of the past
was swept away in Germany than in three centuries at other periods."[64]
But this is the irony, that nothing has really changed, nothing has
been swept away in any concrete sense—it has all happened in the
realm of pure thought. The only kind of thought Marx finds acceptable is the thought grounded in the material world. In this connection, his problem is to show that the dichotomy between material
nature and man is not a genuine dichotomy and that the history of
man is explicable *only* in terms of man's natural and material circumstances and activities.

As we saw, Marx takes as his basic premise the material condition
of life: the fact that human beings exist and are engaged in producing
the means of their own subsistence—actions that affect most fundamentally the form of human life, because they require a social organization and interaction determined by the mode of production. Production leads to a division of labor, a term that Marx takes in its
usual sense as well as in the wider sense of a social division, a division
of classes and a consequent division of their interests. The division of
labor is so inexorable an effect that it can be seen as the yardstick
of technological development. "How far the productive forces of a
nation are developed is shown most evidently by the degree to which
the division of labor has been developed."[65]

Each new productive force will bring about a further division of
labor. This leads to the division between industrial/commercial labor
and agricultural labor and thus to the clash of interests between town
and country. Ultimately there is the division between industrial and
commercial labor, that is, blue-collar and white-collar interests—and
all these divisions and clashes, along with all further divisions, are
impelled by differences in the mode of production. The question is

whether the mode of production is the most basic cause or whether this is in turn the effect of something still deeper known as culture. Earlier, I raised the caveat against relying on the blanket concept of "culture" as the ultimate explanation. Yet this only makes us rely all the more on a blanket concept such as the "division of labor."

To regard the division between Paleolithic and Neolithic, for example, as nothing more than a technological distinction in the ways of making tools and getting food but yet as an *ultimate* explanation of the sociocultural arrangements based on that distinction—this (in very general terms) would be Marx's way of looking at society. But we might also wish to regard the Paleolithic/Neolithic distinction as reflecting a deeper distinction between types of world outlook or "culture"—this (in very general terms) would be Hegel's way of thinking about society. The risk in the first view is that we might be led to overlook Marx's rich grasp of the complexity of the problem and thus to oversimplify our understanding of him. The risk in the second view is that we might be led to postulate an entity known as "culture," which (despite its pervasiveness) cannot be grasped empirically, and thus to approach mystification. For Marx, the answer lies in the enrichment and deepening of the concept of the division of labor itself.

The stages in the actual development of the division of labor constitute, for Marx, different forms of ownership. As he says, "Division of labor and private property are identical expressions."[66] The connection may be hard to see. What he means is that the stages of development in modes of production determine the relations as well as the divisions between individuals in regard to the materials, instruments, and products of labor.[67] Marx discusses certain forms of ownership (the tribal form, an extension of the family; state ownership in the ancient town community; feudal ownership of large country estates), and in tracing the evolution and interconnection of these stages he shows that the ideas formed in these stages (whether they be ideas about men's relation to nature and to one another or ideas about man's own nature) are the expressions, real or illusory, of men's actual relations and activities. The only alternative to this sort of explanation, Marx says, is to posit a separately existing world spirit as the cause of it all—and this would be the equivalent of an ephemeral and all-inclusive concept such as "culture."

The dependence of modes of thought on modes of production is strictly causal, for Marx. And, if men's thoughts are illusory, this is because their social relations (engendered in connection with production) are themselves inverted and illusory.[68] For this reason, morality, religion, metaphysics, or any of the other creations of culture are no longer to be regarded as *sui generis*, as independent entities to be evaluated in their own terms, but are rather to be understood as "necessary sublimations of man's material life-process." In this light, Marx's most serious criticism of Feuerbach is that Feuerbach's conception of "Man" has become something abstract and independent of man's own activity. There is no "Man"—man is what he *does*, and this is the only way to understand him. This is why Marx says that Feuerbach fails to understand history in materialistic terms, although Feuerbach is a materialist.[69] Even to understand a stick, Marx says, involves an understanding of the activity of *producing* a stick.

Now the concept of "division of labor" comes into play in connection with Marx's materialistic premises:[70]

*a.* Men make history, but in order to do this they must be able to live, and this requires the satisfaction of certain needs.

*b.* The satisfaction of needs involves the acquisition of certain instruments, leading to the development of new needs.

*c.* In making their lives, men also make other lives, and this in turn leads to new needs and new social relations.

*d.* The forces of production determine the nature of society and history.

*e.* Consciousness is not "pure" but is determined by productive activity.

These premises are themselves not "pure" in any formal sense. The concept of "division of labor" is really what holds them together in a quasisystematic unity. That division of labor is to be understood as a form of alienation, leading to disharmony wherein needs are *not* satisfied, social relations are *not* constructive, and consciousness takes on its counterfeit form: ideology. As a result of that division, therefore, it becomes possible for production, society, and consciousness to come into conflict with one another, leading to conflicts of interest between individual, family, and community.[71] The overall phrase "division of labor" thus stands for the many ways in which man's own acts turn against him and become an alien power controlling him. The concept carries an extraordinary amount of freight for Marx: It is *descriptive* of certain socioeconomic conditions, but he also uses it *prescriptively*, in a moral sense. It is meant to characterize the current mode of production as well as to condemn existing property relations. Finally, Marx also uses the concept as an *analogy*, beyond its descriptive and prescriptive uses, when he speaks of man frustrated by his own acts, controlled by a power he himself produced, and thus "divided" against himself—a "division of labor" in the most profound sense.

At one point, in speaking about the division of labor, Marx gives us one of his best-known (though rather naive) pieces of imagery. The division of labor, he says, means that each of us is confined to a particular area of activity. A man is a hunter, a fisherman, a herdsman, or a "critical" critic (à la Bruno Bauer and the Young Hegelians). Communist society, however, is to break down this division, "making it possible for me to do one thing today and another tomorrow, to hunt in the morning, fish in the afternoon, breed cattle in the evening, criticize after dinner, just as I like, without ever becoming a hunter, a fisherman, a herdsman, or a critic."[72]

Still another use that Marx makes of the concept of the division of labor is to equate it with the divisiveness of civil society. The form of interaction, he says, that determines the productive forces and is in turn determined by them is civil society—and he therefore speaks of civil society as "the true focus and scene of all history."[73] He has similar words for the division of labor: "one of the chief forces of history up till now."[74] Once he equates the division of labor with the division of interests, he sees the bourgeois pursuit of private interest as transcending even the state. That pursuit may clothe itself in the guise of the state, but this only shows that the state's interest, up till now, has been identical to the individualistic monetary interests of bourgeois civil society. The immediate and concrete effect of the division of man against man is the division of class against class. The division of labor is directly expressed, therefore, as a division of classes— and it is a basic Hegelian principle that any such division, being partial, must be a hostile division. This is why he can say, in the *Communist Manifesto*, that all history is the history of class struggles—namely, of the struggles engendered by the social "division of labor." In *The German Ideology* he puts it this way:

Out of this very contradiction between the interests of the individual and that of the community the latter takes an independent form as the *State*, separated from the real interests of the individual and community, and at the same time as an illusory communal life, but always based on the real bonds present in every family and every tribal conglomeration, such as flesh and blood, language, division of labor on a larger scale, and other interests, and particularly based . . . on the classes already determined by the division of labor, classes which form in any such mass of people and of which one dominates all the others. It follows from this that all struggles within the State, the struggle between democracy, aristocracy and monarchy, the struggle for franchise, etc., etc., are nothing but the illusory forms in which the real struggles of different classes are carried out among one another.[75]

Accordingly, the real revolution, together with the withering away of the state, can only come about as the result of a substantial change in men's underlying interests. Only then will the superstructure change or fall. In the meantime, however, the initial revolutionary attack can arise from those same individualistic, bourgeois interests— that is, from the hard fact that the *private* interests of a great many individuals are not fulfilled! Workers will revolt because they are propertyless—not necessarily because they want to overthrow the institution of property. They will revolt, namely, when their *bourgeois* desires have been utterly frustrated.

The communist revolution will occur as a response to already existing conditions, even though its true aim must be to transcend those conditions. It will be the outcry of the propertyless—and although their aim may be to acquire property the true aim of the revolution will be the transcending of property itself. Thus, it must be emphasized that for Marx the communist revolution entails a fundamental change in the relations of production that comprise property relations. Human beings, in bringing about a change in what it means to own, will be inaugurating a change in what it means to be human. It is this fundamentality that differentiates this revolution from all other political change.[76] Without such a fundamental change there is no true revolution at all. The revolution entails an end to alienation, an end to the situation in which the forces of production are alien powers beyond human control. What is gained is the restoration of humanness and of the meaning of life, work, and activity. Any revolution short of this would be illusory and would be fraught with the self-contradictions that *must* generate further change!

Just as a true revolution cannot occur without a change in the economic base, neither can it occur without a change in popular consciousness. Yet that consciousness, too, has its economic base. The overcoming of local and national loyalties, of social divisions, and of psychological enslavement to the prevailing system—all this requires a change in the system of property relations. The prevailing ideology, whatever it may be, is *always* the expression of the values of the ruling class.[77] The dominant ideas are the expression (in idealized form, as "eternal laws") of the dominant material relations. When the aristocracy is dominant, the predominant values will be honor, loyalty, and so on. When it is the bourgeoisie that is dominant, the main values will be freedom, equality, and so on. Because each class mistakenly regards its interests as the interests of society as a whole, it must try to give its values a universal scope. The proletariat, however, is already a "universal class"—which is why it is peculiarly fitted for the making of revolution.

Marx draws certain conclusions from his theory of history:[78]

1. The dialectical nature of economic development is such that the productive forces inevitably become destructive. As a direct consequence, a class is formed that is oppressed, excluded from society, and therefore in opposition to all other classes. This class comprises the majority of the people, and as a result of their plight they must, in the end, come to see the need for revolution.

2. The utilization of forces of production is based on the existence of a class whose social power is based on property and whose power finds its practical and idealistic expression as the state. This is why a revolutionary struggle is always directed against the class in power— and thus against the state.

3. All previous revolutions have left the mode of production unchanged and have merely led to a new division of labor. The communist revolution, however, is to change the basic mode of production, abolishing the system of wage labor as well as class rule—and thus abolishing the state.

4. Communist awareness entails a change in man on a mass scale. This can come about only in revolution, in which the revolutionary class overthrows the ruling class and establishes society anew.

We began this book with the implicit challenge raised by Machiavelli, the challenge to which all subsequent political philosophy has had to address itself in one way or another: How can we derive a true picture of man's social existence from a view of man's nature as an individual? That nature was variously presented as "eternal," "natural," even God-given. What Marx has done has been to demythologize our picture of man. Man is only what he makes of himself; he gives himself his own "nature." Moreover, that nature is not individualistic but social, not selfishly self-interested but *in essence* collective. (Here is Marx's supreme debt to Rousseau.) Modern society has corrupted man's nature by fostering man's individualistic self-interest. This must now be put aside, to be replaced by a "second nature," which is man's *true* nature. Behind all this is a rational imperative. (Here is Marx's debt to Hegel.) Man *can* remake his society along fully rational and secular lines. He therefore *must* do this.

There are areas of Marx's thinking I have not even touched: monumental and monolithic works such as the *Grundrisse* and *Das Kapital*, which I could never have got around in so small a space; themes such as that of surplus value and the dialectics of capitalist production, as well as the theory of capitalist crisis, which I could not even begin to consider, although the picture of Marx's thought is truncated without them. I cannot even pretend to have discussed adequately the themes I did take up. Yet, in focusing on praxis, alienation, and the materialistic conception of history, I have tried to shed light on Marx's most centrally *philosophic* contributions.

It is clear that in bringing this discussion to a close I am in no way completing it. On the contrary, any discussion of Marx opens onto a world of further questions, different viewpoints, and newer interpretations.

**New Interpretations**   In the light of the fact that Marxism has become the official ideology of millions on the earth's surface and that that ideology (in all its versions) has become perhaps the most powerful historical force of the twentieth century (if we consider what it has been able to *initiate* and sustain), we might feel a sense of presumptuousness to be discussing anything so academic as "recent commentary" on or "new interpretations" of Marx. Yet Marx was himself a scholar (as well as a prodigious reader and commentator) whose intellectualism is taken as the guiding force behind that historic phenomenon. We may therefore hope that an academic commentary on Marx (but not on the political ideology known as Marxism) will not be altogether out of place here.

Let us say only this about Marxism: Ideas are what move the world. Although Marx denied this, he is one of the most prominent examples of it. If he *is* correct, however, and history is moved only by material forces, then if the true revolution has not yet come about in the Marxist countries, this can be explained only by saying that the proper economic and social basis has not been prepared in those countries. And if the Marxist countries are not founded upon the socio-economic conditions that Marx laid down as essential, then *this* is why Marxism has become their "false consciousness." What Marx condemned as "false consciousness" and "ideology" are those ideas that are out of tune with their socioeconomic reality and are therefore destructive of man's real interests. The Soviet experience—especially in the era of Stalinist industrialization, forcibly imposed *post factum*—is a further example of history being moved by ideas (although all this was quite inauthentic, because the guiding theory of the time stood quite a distance away from the prevailing economic reality). There seems to be little doubt that Marx would have condemned it all, as "ideology" and worse—that is, as the illusory justification of the interests of one part of society against the interests of society as a whole, or of humanity as a whole. Just as surely, Marx the humanist–democrat would have shuddered at the dehumanization perpetrated in his name.

This serves to explain why it is only we in the West who can distinguish between Marx and "Marxism"—between the boldly original thinking of that Promethean individual and the official pedantry of the Soviet system (and the ideologues who are its creatures). It also explains why the really vital interpretation of Marx is that which is carried on in the West. Lenin himself discussed Marx in the light of the influences of "classical German philosophy, classical English political economy, and French socialism."[79] We must not forget what Lenin so often chose to ignore—that Marx was thoroughly a West European, thinking in German, reading German, English, and French, as he sat for years in the Reading Room of the British Museum. His roots are in no sense Eastern; he is completely one of us.

The Marx literature (not the diatribe but the mass of serious contributions) is by now so extensive—running into thousands of books and articles—that a special term has been coined for Marx scholars and commentators: they are "Marxologists." (One shudders to think of corresponding terms for scholars of Machiavelli, Hobbes, Locke, Rousseau, Hegel.) Marxology has gained a new respectability in the United States and Britain in recent years. And we may expect that Marx's writings will continue to be interpreted and newly reinterpreted in years to come.

The publication of the Paris Manuscripts in 1932 led to a whole new way of reading Marx—namely, in the light of his very obvious connection to Hegel—even though the Soviets have tended to regard Marx's early works as less important than the later ones. More recently, the problems of the Hegel–Marx connection, as well as Marx's relation to the Young Hegelians, have come in for considerable reinterpretation.[80] There are new applications of Marx's concepts to contemporary problems—in works ranging from the profoundly obscure to the provocatively tendentious.[81] These contributions revolve mainly around new ways of regarding the phenomenon of alienation in modern capitalist society.[82] It is a mark of the vitality of Marx's vision that today's writers have disclosed ever-deeper implications in the concept of alienation. In addition, there are new views about Marx himself: Is he a philosopher or a scientist, *un homme engagé* or a neutral observer? Does Marx have a "philosophy of man," a view of man's nature?[83]

I would suggest that any attempt at a "comprehensive" presentation of "new interpretations" would have to embrace at least the following:

1. writers of the early twentieth century, such as Eduard Bernstein, Karl Kautsky, Antonio Gramsci, and Rosa Luxemburg—all of whom attacked the severely deterministic view of Marx, with its concept of communism's historical inevitability

2. the Hegelian Marxism of Georg Lukács, Max Horkheimer, Herbert Marcuse, and Theodor Adorno—all of whom sought to reestablish the link between Marx and Hegel, emphasizing the importance of ideology and class consciousness, and to account for the absence of class consciousness, which Marx had depicted as indispensable for revolution

3. the attempt to reconcile Marx's thinking with Freud (as in the writings of Marcuse) and with existentialism (via Jean-Paul Sartre and Maurice Merleau-Ponty)—leading to possible bridges between Marx's standpoint and other theorists whom Marx would undoubtedly have rejected

4. the effort on the part of democratic humanists from Eastern Europe—notably Adam Schaff and Leszek Kolakowski—to attack the notion of centralized state power, and to attack it on the basis of Marx's own thinking

5. "others" who do not fit easily into any of these broadly regional or temporal categories, yet who are important and/or interesting for the light they shed on Marx interpretation—writers such as Karl Korsch, Walter Benjamin, Ernst Bloch, Lucien Goldmann, Louis Althusser, Galvano Della Volpe, Lucio Colletti, and Jürgen Habermas[84]

6. still others who, although espousing no doctrinaire position, have

contributed substantially to recent Marx scholarship—writers such as John Plamenatz, Bertell Ollman, David McLellan, Zbigniew Jordan, George Lichtheim, Shlomo Avineri, and Robert Tucker.

Of course, I have deliberately ignored here the voluminous works on and by writers such as Plekhanov, Lenin, and Trotsky, who have contributed to "new interpretations" of Marx if anyone has, but any attempt to do them justice would require another book. From this vast array, I have chosen to discuss only Lukács, Sartre, and Schaff— because they represent views so disparate and polar as to display something of the variety and diversity to which Marx's ideas can be put.

*a.* As long as Georg Lukács opposed the Soviet orthodoxy (that is, until 1923), he was the most original, exciting, and germinal thinker produced by Marxism in this century. But what is perhaps more significant is that he succeeded in presenting a meaningful (and perhaps anti-Soviet) interpretation of Marxism even within the framework of Soviet orthodoxy.[85] We have already referred to his book of 1923, *History and Class Consciousness* and to his "discovery" of the concept of alienation, along with the realization that it must play a central role in Marx, almost a decade before the Paris Manuscripts were published (although the concept of alienation is fully there in *Das Kapital*). Lukács was also able to show how Marxism, especially in the contributions of Engels and Lenin, suffered from the very faults that Marx had attacked in classical political and economic theory.

In order to grasp the full impact of all this, we must begin by realizing that neo-Marxism arose because the current generation felt the need to reinterpret Marx in the light of new realities. For Lukács, the most disturbing new reality was the fact that proletarian class consciousness had not grown to revolutionary class consciousness, although Marx predicted it would. That is, where communist revolution has occurred it has not been the result of the industrial workers' oppression, alienation, and resentment. Indeed, to regard the process (as constituted of oppression, followed by class consciousness, followed by revolution) in this inevitable and deterministic way is to give it precisely the kind of reification Marx had attacked.

We know that Marx accepted the idea of the formal necessity of the historical process, and Lukács sought to show that this idea leads to internal conflicts within Marx's system of thought. In addition, Lukács saw in the theories of Engels and Lenin an overemphasis on the element of dialectic, so that they arrive at the same sort of automatism that Marx had criticized in the classical economists. That is, the classical economists regarded human relationships in mechanical terms, as though they were relationships between things and as though such factors as supply and demand, labor and wages, and so on, were governed by Galilean forces beyond human control. Indeed, the classical economists insisted on depersonalizing economic activity in order to arrive at what they regarded as scientific objectivity. For them, this meant that these forces could not be altered or interfered with, any more than could the laws of inertia or gravitation.

Yet we now take it as a truism that social laws are not like physical laws. Marx saw the difference between them and knew of Vico's distinction between the human, or made, truth and God-created natural law. Lukács was influenced by philosophers such as Dilthey,[86] who laid down a similar line of division between the humanities and the natural sciences—that is, *Geisteswissenschaft* and *Naturwissenschaft*. Primarily, what distinguishes the realm of the humanities is that it is noncausal and deals with the *particular* phenomenon (for example, this historical event, this work of art), whereas the approach of the natural sciences is to seek *general* laws and to deal with evidence on a causal basis. (In a nutshell, we can say that a humanistic science, such as history, deals with something that happens no more than once; physics deals with things that can happen at least twice.) If we amalgamate the realm of spirit, culture, and ideas to the realm of physical law, we fall into the error of thinking that one and the same determinism pervades both areas—and that therefore no social situation can be changed by human effort. In preaching revolution, therefore, Marx had to oppose any attempt at such an amalgamation of the two realms.

The trouble is, however—and this point is emphasized not only by Lukács but also by more recent critics such as Horkheimer and Adorno—that the same sort of reification and false consciousness occurs in Marx's own theorizing when he speaks of certain unalterable processes such as the rise of proletarian class consciousness. Indeed, the Leninist/Stalinist brand of authoritarianism and oppression can be explained by saying that because the expected class consciousness did not arise spontaneously a revolutionary regime had to be forcibly imposed from above. In this light, Leninism and Stalinism are seen as distortions of Marx's spirit. Marx felt that a *genuine* revolution could not be imposed on an unripe population. But, because he also insisted that all consciousness was the product of material circumstances, it was possible for Lenin and Stalin to interpret this as meaning that, if the revolution were to be initiated (imposed as a "material" circumstance), then the requisite consciousness would inevitably follow.

This shows up an implicit contradiction in Marx's theory: If the revolution is logically inevitable, then the intellectual conviction that it is so is of secondary importance in making it happen; its inevitability therefore seems to render our activity unnecessary, our praxis redundant. Yet Marx could not merely let his readers sit back and wait for the revolution to happen. His view of praxis demands the intellectual's active participation in the making of revolution—as though the revolution will not take place unless he and others of like conviction bring it about. Thus, the intellectual must have a two-sided view: The revolution cannot happen without me; the revolution will happen, no matter what. Accordingly, the materialistic conception of history (in its stress on history's logical necessity and inevitability) clashes with the idea of praxis (in its stress on the freedom and contingency of individual action). Further, there is an implicit tension (if not a contradiction) in the way Marx's materialistic conception emphasizes economic determinism as universal yet points to the possibility of mankind's release from that determinism. Marx never resolved these conflicts, and we can say that Lukács and the Frankfurt School dealt with them as their main themes.[87]

The 1923 book aroused so violent a reaction from the communist party that Lukács repudiated his work and went on repudiating it to the end of his days. Despite this, the book continued to exercise an immense impact, so influential that it led to the founding of the Frankfurt School (which is the unofficial name of the Institute of Social Research of the University of Frankfurt).[88] The institute comprised a remarkable group of thinkers, of whom the best-known in the English-speaking world are Herbert Marcuse, Erich Fromm, Theodor Adorno, and Max Horkheimer. With the advent of nazism, most of the members moved to the United States, and some of them returned to Frankfurt in the decade after the war. The general outlook of the school is continuing in writers such as Jürgen Habermas.

Through the years the Frankfurt School undertook numerous intellectual tasks, ranging over social criticism and discussion of the theory of the social sciences. In addition, there was a concerted effort on the part of the Frankfurt School to achieve the de-Leninization and de-Stalinization of Marx. There has also been the aim (already mentioned) of accommodating Marx to social thinkers such as Freud and others who are anathema to orthodox Marxism. From our viewpoint, however, the most important contribution of the school has been to expose the internal conflicts in Marx's theorizing, such as those mentioned two paragraphs above. The school has minimized the role of historical necessity and has emphasized the part played by free action. Yet the neo-Marxist emphasis on free intellectual discussion as a way of raising class consciousness cannot be seen as having resolved *Marx's* problem, however much it may have clarified the position of the school.

In all this, the part played by Lukács was extremely complex and ambivalent.[89] As early as 1920, he published an article in which (contrary to Marxist orthodoxy) he spoke of consciousness as the source of historical movement, not as a mere epiphenomenon of history. This was part of his generally Hegelian and rationalist orientation. Yet in the same article he made a complete about-face and spoke of the free revolutionary will of the people as being expressed and embodied in the Communist party. If class consciousness does not yet exist as a matter of fact, yet is the essence of what the workers *would* think if their potentialities were somehow fulfilled, then this leaves the way open for the party elite to think of itself as the surrogate of the absent class consciousness. And then it becomes permissible for the elite to employ any tactic that will lead to the historic goal, even if this means suppressing the workers' revolutionary impulses when the party finds it politically appropriate to do so! Ironically, Lukács himself was to suffer under this principle: His work was condemned by Moscow as being "ultra-Left."[90]

Lukács' many turns into and out of party approval and banishment make a tale of Byzantine intricacy.[91] As McInnes says, after Lukács' book *The Young Hegel,* the book that remains to be written is *The Young Lukács.* I would not agree with the metaphor that it was Lukács himself who buried the young Lukács in 1924; rather, I would say that he repeatedly disinterred him in order to bury him again. His frequent acts of self-recrimination were almost abjectly comic. Yet these do not minimize his outstanding contributions to aesthetics, literary criticism, social theory, and interpretation of Marx and Hegel. It was, for example, a stroke of genius on his part to show that in the *Realphilosophie* Hegel was an embryonic Marxist, just as he had shown that Marx was essentially Hegelian.

Lukács' lasting effect on the Frankfurt School has been, first, what we may call the Hegelianization of Marx—to the point where it is no longer possible for any of us to speak intelligently about Marx apart from his initial orientation as Marx the Hegelian. Second, Lukács' influence has led to a liberalization of our conception of Marx—to the point where Marx has become so definitely identified with democratic humanism that we can invoke Marx against the horrors of Leninist/Stalinist repression and authoritarianism.

From the viewpoint of the widest perspective, Lukács' contribution has been that in stressing the Hegel–Marx connection he was led to point out numerous contradictions within Marxian philosophy and Marxist ideology—and this had all the greater impact because it came from within the Communist camp. For the noncommunist reader of Marx, this had the healthy effect of provoking a deeper study of Marx. The influence of Lukács extended over Western neo-Marxists such as Sartre and Merleau-Ponty, who read *History and Class Consciousness* as perhaps the one piece of contemporary Marx literature that could be taken seriously as a work of philosophy and could make possible a bridge between existentialism and Marxian thinking.[92]

*b.* Marxist existentialism would seem to be an impossible combination: Marx emphasizes the determinism of socioeconomic forces in shaping men and society; existentialism (especially Sartre's version) emphasizes man's freedom from all determination. The amalgamation of the two would therefore appear to constitute at least a puzzle and a challenge—if not an outright contradiction. The two were utterly irreconcilable when existentialism made its popular debut after the war: Sartre pictured man as burdened by his freedom and seeking to escape it; and any escape such as is provided by culture or religion (or Marxist ideology) was seen as a trip into bad faith and inauthenticity.

And yet there were affinities between them: Marxism and existentialism both stressed the fact that human beings become reified. Marxism said that this happens as the result of the capitalist mode of production; existentialism said it is because men choose depersonalization as a way of eluding the burden of their freedom and subjective life and seek an automatic and anonymous existence. In other words, both could agree that there are forms of impersonal reality that in fact compose human existence (the "is") yet disagree on what directions might be taken to alleviate or eliminate this condition (the "ought").

Despite the deep differences between Marxism and existentialism, Sartre had always identified himself with the proletarian cause and even went so far as to praise the Soviet Union as the last great hope of mankind. (This was in the last years before Stalin's demise.) Existentialism never became a *political* force, and Marxism always had been. The need to act, politically, was therefore provided by Marxist ideology, where existentialism left *l'homme engagé* high and dry. Further, existentialism concerned itself mainly with the individual and lacked a social philosophy; Marxism had always been a social philosophy but had ignored the individual as a scientifically unintelligible datum.

A synthesis of the two was aimed for and supposedly established by Sartre's *Critique de la raison dialectique*[93]—but at the cost of a total transformation of existentialism and a new but not very significant interpretation of Marxism. To begin with, Sartre now rejected existentialism as an "ideology . . . a parasitical system living on the margin of Knowledge."[94] Apart from the sea change suffered by existentialism at Sartre's hands (to the point that it was hardly recognizable), what had to be given up on the Marxist side was the element of historical determinism. Yet that determinism was merely shifted to the existentialist side: Human action was now seen to have a "social" (that is, historically determined) dimension. Did something so obvious need emphasis? Sartre had discovered the wheel. Moreover, the existential element of nature, *être-en-soi*, namely, the brute facticity of things limiting the scope of our freedom, was now seen as presenting obstacles and scarcities that lead to a Hobbesian conflict and somehow depersonalize us; and communism, in helping us to overcome such obstacles and scarcities (how?), would restore us to humanness and genuine personhood.

What this reveals is no true synthesis of Marxism and existentialism but a reciprocal sharing of themes. The fact that these themes now cross what were once lines of demarcation only blurs those lines, without adding clarity to anything. Above and beyond all this, Sartre sought to show that it is possible for free individuals to engage in concerted political action without having to set up the sort of monolithic structure that always stultifies the existence of individuals and is so characteristic of existing communist states. Thus Sartre returned to the Rousseauian theme of spontaneous communal action—a goal hardly realistic in modern technologized society (whether capitalist or communist).

The issues were clearer and the lines stronger when no synthesis seemed possible. Sartre suggested as much when he said (in retrospect): "we were convinced *at one and the same time* that historical materialism furnished the only valid interpretation of history and that existentialism remained the only concrete approach to reality."[95] It now became the task of existentialism (not of Marxism) to provide a theoretical foundation for what Sartre called the stabilizing of the status of the individual in socialist society—and this without the supposed "mystification" attached to liberalism. The individual was to be shown to be irreducible to economic categories; and though this sounds laudable it was to be but a step toward his absorption in a Marxist society. Gone was the existentialist idea that that absorption might depersonalize the individual; in that Marxist society, existentialism (Sartre hoped) would have lost its raison d'être.

This was a far cry from Sartre's earlier work, *L'existentialisme est un humanisme*. Was it not also at a far remove from the humanism of Marx? Indeed, how Marxist this "synthesis" was is still open to conjecture; and how much of Marx we recognize in it is more conjecturable still. Sartre wanted to attack the institutionalization of Marxism for its submersion of the individual. Yet it is difficult to see how he avoids it; and, where he does, it is difficult to see that he goes much beyond Lukács—and Lukács used Marx himself as the basis for his attack.

Is a Marxified existentialism possible without contradiction, then? According to Adam Schaff, the contradiction is insuperable so long as existentialism projects an individualistic picture of man while Marxism sees man as the product of society.[96] In the continuation of the foregoing quotation, Sartre admitted that he did not deny the contradiction between Marxism and existentialism, but he declared that Lukács did not see it. Yet Sartre was not right about Lukács here, because Lukács saw and polarized the difference between Marxism and existentialism before anyone did.

Schaff says that we are dealing here with two diametrically opposed conceptions that defy unification in a theoretical system, even that of Sartre. Sartre may have sought to satisfy existentialism, Schaff says, but in reality what he sought was to transform Marxism into a version of existentialism. Does this mean that he sought to stand Marxism on its head?

What has been happening, as Schaff points out, is a rediscovery of the early Marx, revealing Marx the humanist—and this means that Lenin, Plekhanov, Luxemburg, and everyone else who wrote before 1932 (when the Paris Manuscripts were published) had an incomplete knowledge of Marxism. Perhaps only Lukács understood Marx. Schaff defines humanism as "a system of reflections about man that regard him as supreme good, and aim to guarantee in practice the best conditions for human happiness."[97] This would certainly seem to be borne out by Marx's own words, as revealed in the long quotation I have given above, where Marx speaks of communism as a humanism in the Paris Manuscripts. That these early writings pose a challenge to the adherents of institutionalized Marxism is clear. And this is why, as John Plamenatz says, "It would seem to be against the interest of any Communist government in the world today to encourage a close study of Marx's early writings."[98] This is because those things that Marx could accuse capitalism of doing in 1844 are the very things we could accuse the Soviets of doing today.

We see that the underlying strategy in such humanistic criticism—from Lukács in 1923 to, say, Schaff and Kolakowski—is to widen the space between the Marx of the Paris Manuscripts and Marxism in the oppressively institutionalized form established by Lenin. The point in common to these criticisms, therefore, is to use Marx to attack Marxism—as the "ideology" and "false consciousness" that Marx's thinking has become. There could be no worse indictment of Marxism than at the hands of Marx himself.

Let us end by asking: Where does Marx stand in the history of political theory? As I indicated, the fact that no discussion of Marx closes the subject already says much about him and about his place in the history of thought. I have spoken of Marx as the inheritor of all the problems of past political philosophy—but chiefly of the problems of Rousseau and Hegel. With Rousseau, Marx makes it clear that individualism is a result, not a premise. He has thereby avoided the problem facing Hobbes and Locke of how to build a sociopolitical framework on the foundations of individualism. Yet, in avoiding this problem, Marx has evaded the issues of justice, rights, and obligation. In these areas he has nothing to say as a political philosopher. He merely takes Hobbes and Locke as examples of bourgeois, self-seeking ideology and therefore as examples of how not to construct a political philosophy. He takes from Locke the labor theory of value, but he does not use it as a basis for human rights (as Locke does); rather, he uses it as a way of deflecting the problem of rights, as a problem.

From Rousseau, Marx gets what we might call an ontology of politics: The being of man is a collective being; hence, instead of speaking of the rights of the individual against society, we must speak of the responsibility of the individual to man's collective being and to its progress to that end through revolution. This is the source of Marx's idea of praxis.

From Hegel, Marx gets what we might call an epistemology of politics: A way must be found to expose ideological illusions and thereby to overcome the situation that makes illusions necessary for life to go on. In this way, man the creator becomes the fully conscious creator, the fully rational creator. The synthesis of these views would be the moral imperative for man to take fully conscious control—at last—of his collective destiny. This is man's task as a political animal.

# NOTES

## Machiavelli

1. "in quello io ho espresso quanto io so, e quanto io ho imparato per una lunga pratica e continua lezione delle cose del mondo." *D*, dedication. In order to facilitate reference to the various editions and English translations, I shall give citations in chapters (e.g., *P*, xv, for *The Prince*, chap. xv) and in book and chapter (e.g., *D*, II:xv, for the *Discourses*, Bk. II, chap. xv). The Italian text used is the *Opere*, ed. Ezio Raimondi (Milano: U. Mursia, 1969). All the English passages quoted are my own translation.

2. "la cognizione delle azioni degli uomini grandi, imparata da me con una lunga esperienze delle cose moderne ed una continua lezione delle antiche." *P*, dedication.

3. See John Plamenatz, *Man and Society* (London: Longman, 1963), I:26.

4. See Jacob Burckhardt, *The Civilization of the Renaissance in Italy* (London: Phaidon, 1951), part I: "The State as a Work of Art."

5. *D*, I:xi.

6. *P*, vi, vii.

7. *D*, I:xvii.

8. *D*, I:ii. See Aristotle, *Politics*, III:vi through viii.

9. *D*, I:xi.

10. *D*, I:lviii.

11. *D*, I:lv.

12. *D*, I:xii.

13. *D*, II:ii.

14. *D*, I: Introduction

15. "Non sia pertanto nessuno che si sbigottisca di non potere conseguire quel che è stato conseguito da altri: perché gli uomini, come nella prefazione nostra si disse, nacquero, vissero e morirono, sempre con uno medesimo ordine." *D*, I:xi.

16. *D*, I:xxxvii.

17. "gli uomini dimenticano più presto la morte del padre, che la perdita del patrimonio." *P*, xvii.

18. *P*, xxiii; see also *D*, I:iii, x.
19. "uomo crudele ed espedito." *P*, vii.
20. *P*, xvii.
21. *P*, iii.
22. Aristotle, *Politics*, I:2 (1253a28): The man who thinks he can live without others must be either a beast or a god.
23. "un mezzo bestia e mezzo uomo." *P*, xviii.
24. "operare contro alla fede, contro alla carità, contro alla umanità, contro alla religione." *P*, xviii.
25. *fides, spes, caritas*. See 1 Cor. 13:13.
26. Plamenatz, *Man and Society*, I:29.
27. *P*, xxv.
28. *P*, vi.
29. "il tempo si caccia innanzi ogni cosa, e può condurre seco bene come male, male come bene." *P*, iii.
30. *P*, vii.
31. *P*, vi, xxvi.
32. *D*, III:xli.
33. "andar dentro alla verità effetuale della cosa." *P*, xv.
34. "colui che lascia quello che si fa per quello che si doverria fare, impara piutosto la rovina." *P*, xv.

### Hobbes

1. *Latin Works*, ed. W. Molesworth (London, 1845), I:lxxxvi. "metum tantum concepit mea mater, ut pareret geminos, meque metumque."
2. *De Corpore*, in Hobbes's *English Works*, ed. W. Molesworth (London, 1839), Vol. I, part I, chap. vi, par. 7.
3. "For my thoughts are not your thoughts. Neither are your ways my ways saith the Lord. For as the heavens are higher than the earth, so are my ways higher than your ways. And my thoughts than your thoughts." Isa. 55:8, 9.
4. See Richard S. Peters, *Hobbes* (Baltimore: Penguin Books, 1967), pp. 21, 44, 47, 49, 52.
5. Ibid., pp. 70, 84, 85.
6. Thomas Hobbes, *Leviathan*, ed. M. Oakeshott (Oxford: Blackwell, 1960), chap. ii, p. 9. Hereinafter, *Leviathan* will be abbreviated as *Lev.* and referred to by chapter and page.
7. *Lev.*, vi:39.
8. See Peters, *Hobbes*, p. 25.
9. See Leo Strauss, *The Political Philosophy of Hobbes* (Chicago: Phoenix, 1963), p. 2 ff.
10. Peters, *Hobbes*, p. 151.
11. David Hume, *A Treatise of Human Nature*, ed. L. A. Selby-Bigge (Oxford: Clarendon, 1973), Bk. III, part I, sec. 1, p. 469.
12. *De Corpore*, in *English Works*, Vol. I, part II, chap. vii, par. 1, p. 92.
13. Peters, *Hobbes*, p. 20.
14. *Lev.*, Introduction, p. 5.
15. *Lev.*, vi:39.

16. Peters, *Hobbes*, pp. 22, 78.
17. *De Corpore*, Vol. I, part IV, chap. xxv, par. 5, p. 393.
18. *Lev.*, xi:64.
19. *De Cive*, in *English Works*, Vol. II, chap. i, par. 7, p. 8.
20. But see Strauss, *Political Philosophy*, pp. 15, 16.
21. *Lev.*, xi:64.
22. *Lev.*, xiii:80 f.
23. *Lev.*, xiii:82.
24. *Lev.*, xiii:82.
25. *Lev.*, xiii:83.
26. C. B. Macpherson, *The Political Theory of Possessive Individualism: Hobbes to Locke* (Oxford: Clarendon, 1969), p. 22. See also Howard Warrender, *The Political Philosophy of Hobbes* (Oxford: Clarendon, 1970), p. 143.
27. Peters, *Hobbes*, pp. 53, 54.
28. Strauss, *Political Philosophy*, p. 104.
29. Macpherson, *Possessive Individualism*, p. 101.
30. J. W. N. Watkins, *Hobbes's System of Ideas* (London: Hutchinson, 1965), p. 78.
31. *De Cive*, in *English Works*, Vol. II, chap. i, p. 2, n.
32. Ibid., pp. xiv, xv.
33. *Lev.*, xvii:110.
34. *Lev.*, xiii:83; xiv:85.
35. *Lev.*, xiii:83.
36. *Lev.*, xiii:83.
37. John Plamenatz, *Man and Society* (London: Longman, 1963), I:120. See also Leo Strauss, *Natural Rights and History* (Chicago: Phoenix, 1965), p. 184.
38. *Lev.*, xiii:84.
39. *Lev.*, xiv:85.
40. *Lev.*, xiv:85.
41. *Lev.*, xv:93.
42. *Lev.*, xv:99 ff.
43. See W. D. Ross, *The Right and the Good* (Oxford: Clarendon, 1967), p. 19 f.
44. *Lev.*, xv:101.
45. *Lev.*, xv:103.
46. *Lev.*, xvii:112.
47. *Lev.*, xvii:112.
48. *Lev.*, xviii:113 f.
49. *Lev.*, xxix:218.
50. Macpherson, *Possessive Individualism*, pp. 12, 13.
51. Strauss, *Political Philosophy*.
52. Ibid., p. 106 f.
53. Ibid., pp. 170, 156 f.
54. Ibid., p. 168.
55. A. E. Taylor, "The Ethical Doctrine of Hobbes," *Philosophy*, Vol. XIII (Oct. 1938). This is reprinted in full in K. C. Brown, ed., *Hobbes Studies* (Oxford: Blackwell, 1965). It is also reprinted, substantially complete, in B. H. Baumrin, ed., *Hobbes's "Leviathan": Interpretation and Criticism* (Belmont, Calif.:

Wadsworth, 1969). A valuable collection is M. Cranston and R. S. Peters, eds., *Hobbes and Rousseau: A Collection of Critical Essays* (New York: Doubleday Anchor, 1972); see especially the essay by W. H. Greenleaf, "Hobbes: The Problem of Interpretation."

56. Warrender, *Political Philosophy*, p. 309. See also Watkins, *Hobbes's System*, p. 93.
57. *Lev.*, xv:104.
58. *Lev.*, xv:105.
59. Watkins, *Hobbes's System*, p. 86.
60. *Lev.*, xiii:83.
61. Warrender, *Political Philosophy*.
62. Watkins, *Hobbes's System*, p. 87.
63. *Lev.*, xviii:116.
64. *Lev.*, xiii:83.
65. *Lev.*, xv:104.
66. Watkins, *Hobbes's System*, pp. 76, 82, 83.
67. *Lev.*, xv:93 f.
68. *Lev.*, xv:103.
69. *Lev.*, xxxi:234.
70. Plamenatz, *Man and Society*, I:154.
71. Ibid.

## Locke

1. John Locke, *Two Treatises of Government*, ed. P. Laslett (Cambridge: Cambridge University Press, 1960). References will be to the *Second Treatise* only, and by paragraph, thus: *ST*, 109.
2. *ST*, 4, 5.
3. *ST*, 6.
4. *ST*, 7, 8, 9, 11.
5. *ST*, 14.
6. *ST*, 19.
7. *ST*, 20.
8. *ST*, 102.
9. *ST*, 109.
10. J. W. Gough, *Locke's Political Philosophy* (Oxford: Clarendon, 1956), p. 89. The opposite view is held by Aarsleff (see below, n. 11).
11. Hans Aarsleff, "The State of Nature and the Nature of Man in Locke," in J. W. Yolton, ed., *John Locke: Problems and Perspectives* (Cambridge: Cambridge University Press, 1969), pp. 99, 103.
12. *ST*, 49.
13. *ST*, 6, 172.
14. John Locke, *Essay concerning Human Understanding* (London: Dent, Everyman's Library, 1964), Vol. II, Bk. IV, chap. xvii, sec. 4, p. 264.
15. Ibid., Bk. III, chap. i, sec. 1, p. 9. See also *ST*, 77.
16. Ibid., Vol. I, Bk. II, chap. xxviii, sec. 8, p. 296.
17. See Aarsleff, "State of Nature," p. 134.

18. John Plamenatz, *Man and Society* (London: Longman, 1963), I:220. See Jules Steinberg, *Locke, Rousseau, and the Idea of Consent* (London and Westport, Conn.: Greenwood Press, 1978), chap. 3.
19. *ST*, 25–51.
20. Plamenatz, *Man and Society*, I:216.
21. Gough, *Locke's Political Philosophy*, p. 73.
22. *ST*, 27.
23. *ST*, 28.
24. *ST*, 31, 32.
25. Plamenatz, *Man and Society*, I:245.
26. *ST*, 47, 48.
27. *ST*, 222, 124, 131.
28. Gough, *Locke's Political Philosophy*, p. 82.
29. *ST*, 23.
30. *ST*, 40.
31. *ST*, 87 f.
32. *ST*, 90, 91.
33. *ST*, 93.
34. *ST*, 95 f.
35. In addition to Steinberg, *Locke, Rousseau, and Consent*, a good discussion of problems surrounding consent is in Plamenatz, *Man and Society*, I:220–41. See also John Plamenatz, *Consent, Freedom, and Political Obligation*, 2nd ed. (London: Oxford University Press, 1968).
36. Plamenatz, *Man and Society*, I:228–30.
37. *ST*, 135.
38. *ST*, 240, 243, 242, 219.
39. *ST*, 232, also 222, 214 f.
40. Leo Strauss, *Natural Right and History* (Chicago: Phoenix, 1965), pp. 202–51. See also C. H. Monson, "Locke's Political Theory and Its Interpreters," in *Political Studies*, Vol. VI (1958); reprinted in C. B. Martin and D. M. Armstrong, eds., *Locke and Berkeley: A Collection of Critical Essays* (New York: Doubleday Anchor, 1968).
41. *ST*, 4, also 6 and 12.
42. *ST*, 6.
43. *ST*, 7.
44. Willmoore Kendall, *John Locke and the Doctrine of Majority Rule* (Urbana: Illinois University Studies in Social Sciences, 1941), Vol. 26. A good discussion of Kendall is Gough, *Locke's Political Philosophy*, pp. 23–46.
45. *ST*, 14.
46. *ST*, 130.
47. Gough, *Locke's Political Philosophy*, p. 40 f.
48. *ST*, 149, 211 f.
49. Gough, *Locke's Political Philosophy*, p. 44.
50. C. B. Macpherson, *The Political Theory of Possessive Individualism: Hobbes to Locke* (Oxford: Clarendon, 1969). See also his article, "The Social Bearing of Locke's Political Theory," *Western Political Quarterly*, Vol. VII (1954); reprinted in Martin and Armstrong, *Locke and Berkeley*. A good critique of Macpherson is Alan Ryan, "Locke and the Dictatorship of the

Bourgeoisie," *Political Studies*, Vol. XIII (1965); reprinted in Martin and Armstrong, *Locke and Berkeley*.
51. Macpherson, *Possessive Individualism*, pp. 221, 227. See also his "Social Bearing," in Martin and Armstrong, *Locke and Berkeley*, p. 203.
52. Macpherson, *Possessive Individualism*, p. 199 f.
53. Macpherson, "Social Bearing," in Martin and Armstrong, *Locke and Berkeley*, p. 219 f.
54. Ibid., p. 228.
55. Ryan, "Dictatorship of the Bourgeoisie," p. 233.
56. Macpherson, *Possessive Individualism*, p. 221.
57. Ryan, "Dictatorship of the Bourgeoisie," p. 240.
58. Ibid., p. 253.

### Rousseau

1. "L'homme est né libre, et partout il est dans les fers" (the opening sentence of chapter i in Book I of *On the Social Contract*). See the edition of R. D. Masters, trans. J. R. Masters (New York: St. Martin's Press, 1978), p. 46. All subsequent references, hereinafter cited as *SC*, are to this edition. The Masters translation is: "Man was/is born free . . ." For an elaborate justification of this locution, see *SC*, pp. 10–11.
2. "Tout est bien sortant des mains de l'Auteur des choses, tout dégénère entre les mains de l'homme." See *Emile*, trans. Allan Bloom (New York: Basic Books, 1979), p. 37.
3. "que la nature a fait l'homme hereux et bon, mais que la société le déprave et le rend miserable." *Rousseau juge de Jean-Jacques*, Troisieme Dialogue (Paris: Hachette, 1911), IX:287.
4. *The First and Second Discourses*, ed. R. D. Masters, trans. J. R. Masters (New York: St. Martin's Press, 1964), p. 93.
5. Ibid., p. 103. The French text reads: "des raisonnements hypothétiques et conditionnels, plus propres à éclaircir la nature des choses qu'à en montre la veritable origine." *The Political Writings of Jean Jacques Rousseau*, ed. C. E. Vaughan (Oxford: Blackwell, 1962), I:141; this edition hereinafter cited as CEV.
6. *Second Discourse*, p. 117.
7. Roger D. Masters, *The Political Philosophy of Rousseau* (Princeton, N.J.: Princeton University Press, 1968), p. 10.
8. Ibid., p. 254.
9. Ibid., p. 49 f. See also John Plamenatz, *Man and Society* (London: Longman, 1963), I:371.
10. *SC*, II:iv, pp. 62–64.
11. "d'un animal stupide et borné, fit un être intelligent et un homme." CEV, II:36. See *SC*, I:viii, p. 56.
12. "l'obéisance à la loi qu'on s'est prescrite est liberté." CEV, II:37. See *SC*, I:viii, p. 56.
13. Introduction by R. D. Masters, *SC*, p. 10.
14. See Rousseau's letter to Philibert Cramer (1764), quoted in Masters, *Political*

*Philosophy*, p. 3. See also Leo Strauss, *National Right and History* (Chicago: Phoenix, 1965), p. 270.

15. *Emile*, p. 92.
16. Ibid., p. 288.
17. Ibid., p. 289.
18. Ibid., p. 290. See Plamenatz, *Man and Society*, I:383–85.
19. "Chacun de nous met en commun sa personne et toute sa puissance sous la suprême direction de la volonté générale; et nous recevons en corps chaque membre comme partie indivisible du tout." CEV, II:33. See *SC*, I:vi, p. 53.
20. "que quiconque refusera d'obéir à la volonté générale y sera contraint par tout le corps: ce qui ne signifie autre chose sinon qu'on le forcera d'être libre." CEV, II:36. See *SC*, I:vii, p. 55.
21. *SC*, III:xv, p. 102.
22. *Emile*, p. 289.
23. Plato, *Protagoras*, 358d.
24. *SC*, IV:i, p. 109. See Ernst Cassirer, *The Question of Jean-Jacques Rousseau* (Bloomington and London: Indiana University Press, 1963), p. 76.
25. *Emile*, p. 235.
26. *SC*, II:i, p. 59.
27. From "A Discourse on Political Economy" (1755), in G. D. H. Cole, ed., *The Social Contract and the Discourses* (London: Dent; New York: Dutton, 1963), pp. 243–44. This happens to be clearer, at this point, than the Masters translation, *SC*, p. 217.
28. *SC*, II:iii, p. 61.
29. Masters, *Political Philosophy*, p. 325, n. 93.
30. *SC*, II:ii, p. 59, n. Also *SC*, II:iii, p. 61.
31. *SC*, III:xv, p. 102.
32. "Mais ôtez de ces mêmes volontés les plus et les moins qui s'entre-détruisent, reste pour somme des différences la volonté générale." CEV, II:42. *SC*, II:iii, p. 61.
33. "L'homme est né libre, et partout il est dans les fers. . . . Comment ce changement s'est-il fait? Je l'ignore. Qu'est-ce qui peut le rendre légitime? Je crois pouvoir résoudre cette question." CEV, II:23–24. *SC*, I:i, p. 46.
34. "on n'est obligé d'obéir qu'aux puissances légitimes." CEV, II:27. *SC*, I:iii, p. 49.
35. *SC*, III:i, p. 79; III:ix, p. 95.
36. *SC*, II:vii, p. 68.
37. *SC*, III:i, p. 79.
38. *SC*, III:iv, p. 85.
39. *SC*, III:x, p. 96.
40. *SC*, III:xi, p. 98.
41. *SC*, III:xii–xiv, pp. 100–101; III:xviii.
42. *SC*, III:xvi.
43. J. W. Chapman, *Rousseau: Totalitarian or Liberal?* (New York: Columbia University Press, 1956), p. 139.
44. J. L. Talmon, *The Origins of Totalitarian Democracy* (New York: Praeger, 1960), p. 43. See also Plamenatz, *Man and Society*, I:435. And see Andrew

Levine, *The Politics of Autonomy: A Kantian Reading of Rousseau's Social Contract* (Amherst: University of Massachusetts Press, 1976), p. 72 f.

45. *SC*, IV:ii, p. 110.

46. Jules Steinberg, *Locke, Rousseau, and the Idea of Consent* (London and Westport, Conn.: Greenwood Press, 1978), chap. 5.

47. See Bertrand de Jouvenel, "Rousseau's Theory of the Forms of Government," in M. Cranston and R. S. Peters, *Hobbes and Rousseau: A Collection of Critical Essays* (New York: Doubleday, 1972), p. 488.

48. *SC*, III:xv, pp. 102–3.

49. See John McManners, "The Social Contract and Rousseau's Revolt against Society," in Cranston and Peters, *Hobbes and Rousseau*, pp. 306, 303–4.

50. Ibid., p. 314, where McManners speaks of the General Will as "that instrument of equality, of civic, social liberty."

51. Stephen Ellenburg, *Rousseau's Political Philosophy: An Interpretation from Within* (Ithaca and London: Cornell University Press, 1976), p. 149 f.

52. See Judith N. Shklar, "Rousseau's Images of Authority," in Cranston and Peters, *Hobbes and Rousseau*, pp. 333–36. See also J. N. Shklar, *Men and Citizens: A Study of Rousseau's Social Theory* (Cambridge: Cambridge University Press, 1969), pp. 44, 127.

53. Ellenburg, *Rousseau's Political Philosophy*, p. 120.

54. Ibid.

55. Levine, *Politics of Autonomy*.

56. Cassirer, *The Question of Rousseau* and *Rousseau, Kant, and Goethe* (New York: Harper & Row, 1963). See Ellenburg, *Rousseau's Political Philosophy*, p. 118, n.

57. *SC*, I:iv.

58. *SC*, I:vi, p. 53.

59. Ellenburg, *Rousseau's Political Philosophy*, pp. 19, 20.

60. John Charvet, *The Social Problem in the Philosophy of Rousseau* (Cambridge: Cambridge University Press, 1974).

## Hegel

1. G. W. F. Hegel, *The Philosophy of History*, trans. J. Sibree (New York: Willey, 1944), pp. 11, 9; *The Philosophy of Right*, trans. T. M. Knox (Oxford: Clarendon, 1967), par. 31.

2. *Philosophy of History*, pp. 72, 17.

3. Ibid., p. 18 f.

4. Ibid., p. 19. The German text reads: "Die Weltgeschichte ist der Fortschritt im Bewusstsein der Freiheit." *Werke* (Frankfurt am Main: Suhrkamp, 1970), XII:32.

5. *Philosophy of History*, p. 41.

6. *Philosophy of Right*, par. 270, p. 166.

7. Ibid., par. 257, p. 155. The German text reads: "Der Staat ist die Wirklichkeit der sittlichen Idee—der sittliche Geist, als der *offenbare*, sich selbst deutliche, substantielle Wille, der sich denkt und weiss und das, was er weiss und insofern er es weiss, vollführt." *Werke*, VII:398.

8. *Philosophy of History*, p. 38.

9. Ibid.
10. G. W. F. Hegel, *The Phenomenology of Spirit*, trans. A. V. Miller (Oxford: Clarendon, 1977).
11. Ibid., pp. 21, 11.
12. J. N. Findlay, *Hegel: A Re-examination* (New York: Collier, 1962), p. 83. See also Shlomo Avineri, *Hegel's Theory of the Modern State* (Cambridge: Cambridge University Press, 1974), p. 65: "This biography of the spirit is thus, for Hegel, the philosophical history of man."
13. *Phenomenology*, par. 166, p. 104.
14. Ibid., pp. 111–19.
15. Alexandre Kojève, *Introduction to the Reading of Hegel*, trans. A. Bloom (New York and London: Basic Books, 1969), p. 46. See also Jean Hyppolite, *Studies on Marx and Hegel*, trans. J. O'Neill (London: Heinemann, 1969), pp. 26–29. See also John Plamenatz, *Man and Society* (London: Longman, 1963), II:154 ff. See also G. A. Kelly, "Notes on Hegel's 'Lordship and Bondage,'" *Review of Metaphysics*, Vol. XIX (1966).
16. Kojève, *Introduction*, p. 47 f.
17. Ibid., pp. 50–52.
18. *Phenomenology*, pp. 119–38.
19. Ibid., pp. 252–62.
20. Ibid., pp. 267–78.
21. Plato, *Apology*, 30e; Avineri, *Hegel's Theory*, chaps. 3, 5; *Philosophy of Right*, p. 10.
22. G. W. F. Hegel, *Encyclopaedia of the Philosophical Sciences*, part III, trans. W. Wallace as *Hegel's Philosophy of Mind* (Oxford: Clarendon, 1894), par. 433.
23. *Phenomenology*, pars. 11–12, pp. 6–7.
24. Ibid., par. 484, pp. 294–95.
25. Ibid., par. 486, pp. 295–96. But here the quotation is from the older translation by J. B. Baillie—Hegel, *Phenomenology of Mind* (London: Macmillan, 1931), p. 511.
26. *Philosophy of Right*, p. 10.
27. Ibid.
28. Ibid., par. 33, p. 36.
29. Ibid., par. 4.
30. Herbert Marcuse, *Reason and Revolution: Hegel and the Rise of Social Theory* (Boston: Beacon, 1960), p. 185 f.
31. *Philosophy of Right*, par. 7; S. Kierkegaard, *Sickness unto Death* (Princeton: Princeton University Press, 1954), p. 146.
32. *Philosophy of Right*, par. 35.
33. Ibid., par. 36.
34. Ibid., addition to par. 37, p. 235.
35. Ibid., pars. 41, 43, 44, 45; additions to pars. 41, 44.
36. Ibid., par. 75, last paragraph.
37. Marcuse, *Reason and Revolution*, p. 200.
38. *Philosophy of Right*, additions to pars. 108, 134, 135, 136, 141.
39. H. A. Reyburn, *The Ethical Theory of Hegel: A Study of the Philosophy of Right* (Oxford: Clarendon, 1967), p. 197.

40. Ibid., p. 201.
41. *Philosophy of Right*, addition to par. 158.
42. K.-H. Ilting, "The Structure of Hegel's 'Philosophy of Right,'" in Z. A. Pelczynski, ed., *Hegel's Political Philosophy: Problems and Perspectives* (Cambridge: Cambridge University Press, 1971), p. 102.
43. Marcuse, *Reason and Revolution*, p. 201.
44. *Philosophy of Right*, par. 258, p. 156.
45. Ibid., addition to par. 145, p. 259. The phrase is "objektive Sittlichkeit"— better translated as "objective morality."
46. Marcuse, *Reason and Revolution*, p. 201, has a very good way of putting this, in the passage immediately following the sentence quoted in the text two paragraphs back.
47. *Philosophy of Right*, additions to pars. 260, 261; also par. 146.
48. Ibid., par. 260, p. 160; italics mine.
49. Ibid., pars. 243, 244, 246, 248, and addition to par. 248.
50. Ibid., addition to par. 258.
51. Ibid., par. 183. Z. A. Pelczynski, "The Hegelian Conception of the State," in Pelczynski, ed., *Hegel's Political Philosophy*, p. 10.
52. See *Philosophy of History*, p. 452, where Hegel equates atomic liberalism with the bourgeois outlook. See also Hegel, "The German Constitution," in his *Political Writings*, trans. T. M. Knox (Oxford: Clarendon, 1962), pp. 190–91.
53. Cf. E. A. Abbot, *Flatland* (New York: Dover, n.d.).
54. *Philosophy of Right*, pars. 259, 273.
55. Ibid., par. 257.
56. Ibid., par. 258, p. 155 f.
57. Ibid., par. 260, p. 161.
58. Ibid., par. 260, p. 160. See also addition to par. 260, p. 280.
59. Ibid., addition to par. 260, p. 280.
60. Ibid., par. 261, p. 161; addition to par. 155, p. 261.
61. Ibid., par. 261, p. 162; addition to par. 265, p. 281; addition to par. 268, p. 282.
62. Ibid., addition to par. 261, p. 280. The phrase "eo ipso" is introduced in the English translation, although it is only roughly suggested by the German word "unmittelbar."
63. Ibid., par. 269; addition to par. 269, p. 282; par. 276; addition to par. 276, p. 287.
64. Ibid., par. 270, p. 167 f.; par. 270, p. 173.
65. Ibid., par. 272; addition to par. 272, p. 286.
66. Ibid., par. 273.
67. This was suggested by W. T. Stace, *The Philosophy of Hegel* (New York: Dover, 1955), p. 432.
68. *Philosophy of Right*, par. 273, p. 176.
69. Ibid., par. 273, p. 178.
70. Ibid., addition to par. 274, p. 287.
71. Ibid., par. 274.
72. Ibid., par. 275.
73. Ibid., par. 279, p. 181, addition to par. 275.
74. Ibid., par. 279, p. 183; addition to par. 276; addition to par. 280, p. 289.

75. Ibid., par. 280, p. 184, and addition to par. 280.
76. Ibid., par. 281; p. 185; par. 279, p. 182.
77. Ibid., addition to par. 279.
78. Ibid., par. 280, p. 185.
79. Strongly suggested in ibid., addition to par. 298, p. 291.
80. G. W. F. Hegel, *Jenaer Realphilosophie*, ed. J. Hoffmeister, Vol. I: 1803–4 (Leipzig: Felix Meiner, 1932), Vol. II: 1805–6 (Leipzig: Felix Meiner, 1931). Improved and annotated editions of both series are in Vols. 6 and 8, *Gesammelte Werke*, issued by the Rheinisch-Westfälischen Akademie der Wissenschaften (Hamburg: Felix Meiner, 1976).
81. Stace, *Philosophy of Hegel*; Findlay, *Hegel*; Plamenatz, *Man and Society*; K. Löwith, *From Hegel to Nietzsche* (New York: Doubleday, 1967); Marcuse, *Reason and Revolution*, p. 73 f.; Avineri, *Hegel's Theory*, p. 87 f.
82. *Realphilosophie*, I:203 ff.
83. Marcuse, *Reason and Revolution*, p. 77.
84. *Realphilosophie*, I:237; II:197 f.
85. Marcuse, *Reason and Revolution*, p. 80.
86. *Realphilosophie*, II:232–33.
87. Ibid., p. 249.
88. Avineri, *Hegel's Theory*, p. 104 f.
89. Ibid., p. 98 f.
90. Ibid., p. 90.
91. Ibid., p. 108.
92. Karl Popper, *The Open Society and Its Enemies* (London: Routledge & Kegan Paul, 1963) II:78, 29. See Marcuse, *Reason and Revolution*, pp. 177 f., 409–19.
93. Hegel, *Political Writings*.
94. Avineri, *Hegel's Theory*, pp. 34, 45, 57, 69–72, 79 f.; Hegel, *Political Writings*, p. 158.
95. Rudolf Haym, *Hegel und seine Zeit* (reissued in Hildesheim, 1962); Avineri, *Hegel's Theory*, p. 115.
96. Avineri, *Hegel's Theory*, p. 57.
97. See Walter Kaufmann's introduction to his anthology, *Hegel's Political Philosophy* (New York: Atherton, 1970).
98. Ibid., p. 4.
99. *Philosophy of Right*, p. 279, addition to par. 258. The German text reads: "es ist der Gang Gottes in der Welt, dass der Staat ist, sein Grund ist die Gewalt der sich als Wille verwirklichenden Vernunft. Bei der Idee des Staats muss man nicht besondere Staaten vor Auge haben, nicht besondere Institutionen, man muss vielmehr die Idee, diesen wirklichen Gott, für sich betrachten." *Werke*, VII:403.

## Marx

1. G. W. F. Hegel, *Lectures on the History of Philosophy*, trans. E. S. Haldane and F. H. Simson (London: Routledge & Kegan Paul, 1955) III:551–52.
2. Ludwig Feuerbach, *The Essence of Christianity*, trans. George Eliot (New York: Harper & Row, 1957). See also *The Fiery Brook: Selected Writings of*

*Ludwig Feuerbach,* trans. Zawar Hanfi (New York: Doubleday, 1972), for the text of the *Theses.* The statement quoted three paragraphs below, about the enrichment of God at the expense of man, is on p. 26 in *The Essence of Christianity* and on p. 124 in *The Fiery Brook.*

3. Karl Marx, *A Contribution to the Critique of Political Economy,* trans. N. I. Stone (Chicago: Kerr, 1904), p. 11.

4. Karl Marx, *The Poverty of Philosophy,* observation 2; reprinted in L. D. Easton and K. H. Guddat, eds., *Writings of the Young Marx on Philosophy and Society* (New York: Doubleday, 1967), p. 480. This anthology will hereinafter be referred to as EG.

5. EG, pp. 51–66.

6. EG, p. 402.

7. Notes to the doctoral dissertation, EG, p. 62.

8. R. C. Tucker, *Philosophy and Myth in Karl Marx* (Cambridge: Cambridge University Press, 1967), pp. 73–77, 82–84.

9. Shlomo Avineri, *The Social and Political Thought of Karl Marx* (Cambridge: Cambridge University Press, 1968), p. 132.

10. Karl Marx, "Towards the Critique of Hegel's *Philosophy of Right:* Introduction," in EG, pp. 249–64.

11. EG, pp. 216–48. For a valuable discussion of "On the Jewish Question" and its background, see Julius Carlebach, *Karl Marx and the Radical Critique of Judaism* (London: Routledge & Kegan Paul, 1978).

12. "On the Jewish Question," EG, p. 231.

13. Isaiah Berlin, "Two Concepts of Liberty," in *Four Essays on Liberty* (Oxford: Oxford University Press, 1969).

14. "On the Jewish Question," EG, p. 235.

15. "Towards the Critique of Hegel's *Philosophy of Right:* Introduction," EG, pp. 249–64. The German title is: "Zur Kritik der hegelschen Rechtsphilosophie: Einleitung." This must not be confused with his longer work, *Kritik der hegelschen Staatsphilosophie,* which I shall discuss below.

16. But see Avineri, *Social and Political Thought,* pp. 33–34, 38.

17. Karl Marx, *Kritik der hegelschen Staatsphilosophie* (1843). English version: *Critique of Hegel's "Philosophy of Right,"* trans. A. Jolin and J. O'Malley (Cambridge: Cambridge University Press, 1970). See EG, pp. 151–202, for a translation of Marx's commentary on Hegel's pars. 261–69, 279, 287–97, 308.

18. Avineri, *Social and Political Thought,* p. 13. Chapter 1 has the best discussion, in English, of the *Critique.* See also Avineri's article, "The Hegelian Origins of Marx's Political Thought," *Review of Metaphysics,* Vol. XXI, 1967.

19. Introduction by J. O'Malley to the *Critique,* pp. xiii–xiv.

20. Avineri, *Social and Political Thought,* p. 41.

21. See O'Malley's introduction to the *Critique,* pp. xl–lxiii. I am indebted to O'Malley for his excellent essay. See also Avineri, *Social and Political Thought,* p. 98.

22. Hegel, *Philosophy of Right,* par. 260.

23. Avineri, *Social and Political Thought,* p. 98. This "fundamentalist" thesis has been ably challenged by Bertell Ollman, *Alienation: Marx's Conception of Man in Capitalist Society* (Cambridge: Cambridge University Press, 1976), pp. 1–11.

24. Georg Lukács, *History and Class Consciousness: Studies in Marxist Dialectics*, trans. R. Livingstone (London: Merlin; Cambridge, Mass.: MIT Press, 1971).
25. Avineri, *Social and Political Thought*, p. 96.
26. For the original text of the Paris Manuscripts see Marx–Engels, *Historisch-kritische Gesamtausgabe* (referred to as MEGA), ed. D. Rjazanov and V. Adoratskij (Frankfurt–Berlin, 1932), MEGA I, Vol. III.
27. Lukács, *History*, p. 83.
28. Ibid., p. 111.
29. Hegel, *The Phenomenology of Spirit*, pp. 295–96. I quote Baille, p. 511.
30. Avineri, *Social and Political Thought*, p. 105.
31. Karl Marx, *Early Writings*, trans. T. B. Bottomore (New York: McGraw-Hill, 1964), hereinafter referred to as EW.
32. "Wages of Labour," *EW*, p. 69.
33. Friedrich Engels, *The Condition of the Working Class in England* (1845), trans. W. O. Henderson and W. H. Chaloner (New York: Macmillan, 1958).
34. "Profit of Capital," *EW*, p. 91 f.
35. "Wages of Labour," *EW*, pp. 72–73.
36. "Rent of Land," *EW*, p. 103.
37. Ibid., p. 105.
38. Ibid., p. 119.
39. "Alienated Labour," *EW*, p. 120 f.
40. Ibid., p. 125.
41. Ibid., p. 131.
42. "The Relationship of Private Property," *EW*, p. 137.
43. Ibid., p. 144.
44. "Private Property and Communism," *EW*, p. 152 f.
45. Ibid., p. 155; the italics have been eliminated.
46. "Critique of Hegel's Dialectic and General Philosophy," *EW*, p. 195 f.
47. Ibid., p. 200.
48. Ibid., pp. 210–11.
49. Ibid., p. 216.
50. Hegel, *Philosophy of Mind*, trans. W. Wallace (Oxford: Clarendon, 1976), pars. 381, 384.
51. Marx, *Poverty of Philosophy*, EG, p. 475.
52. See Z. A. Jordan, *The Evolution of Dialectical Materialism* (London: Macmillan; New York: St. Martin's Press, 1967), chap. iii.
53. Marx, *Contribution to the Critique of Political Economy*, pp. 10–15.
54. K. Marx and F. Engels, *The German Ideology* (Moscow: Progress Publishers, 1964).
55. See EG, pp. 408–9.
56. F. Heer, *The Intellectual History of Europe*, trans. J. Steinberg (New York: Doubleday, 1968), 2:55.
57. Marx, *Contribution to the Critique of Political Economy*, preface.
58. Jordan, *Evolution*, p. 289 f.
59. See John Plamenatz, *Man and Society* (London: Longman, 1963), II:274.
60. Ibid., p. 278.
61. Karl Marx and Friedrich Engels, *Communist Manifesto* (New York: Appleton-Century-Crofts, 1955), part I, p. 12.
62. EG, p. 409.

63. EG, p. 414 f. For a good discussion of this concept, see Plamenatz, *Man and Society*, II:323 f.
64. EG, p. 405.
65. EG, p. 410.
66. EG, p. 424.
67. EG, p. 410.
68. EG, p. 414.
69. EG, p. 419.
70. EG, p. 420 f.
71. EG, p. 424.
72. EG, p. 425.
73. EG, p. 428.
74. EG, p. 438.
75. EG, p. 425.
76. EG, p. 460 f
77. EG, p. 438.
78. EG, pp. 430–31.
79. V. I. Lenin, *Selected Works* (New York: International Publishers, 1935–38), Vol. XI, part I.
80. Contrast Sidney Hook, *From Hegel to Marx* (New York: Humanities Press, 1950), and David McLellan, *The Young Hegelians and Karl Marx* (London: Macmillan, 1969).
81. Contrast Louis Althusser, *For Marx*, trans. B. R. Brewster (London: Allen Lane, 1970), and Herbert Marcuse, *One-Dimensional Man* (London: Routledge & Kegan Paul, 1964). For an extensive discussion, bibliography, see the very useful three-volume work by Leszek Kolakowski, *Main Currents of Marxism*, trans. P. S. Falla (Oxford: Clarendon, 1978).
82. See the bibliography in Ollman, *Alienation*.
83. Compare Ollman, *Alienation*, and John Plamenatz, *Karl Marx's Philosophy of Man* (Oxford: Clarendon, 1975). See my "Critical Notice" of the Plamenatz book in *Philosophical Studies*, Vol. XXV (Dublin, 1977).
84. For good general discussions of these various viewpoints, see: Martin Jay, *The Dialectical Imagination: A History of the Frankfurt School and the Institute of Social Research, 1923–1950* (Boston: Little, Brown, 1973); Perry Anderson, *Considerations on Western Marxism* (London: NLB; Atlantic Highlands: Humanities Press, 1976); Neil McInnes, *The Western Marxists* (London: Alcove Press, 1972); Leopold Labedz, ed., *Revisionism: Essays on the History of Marxist Ideas* (London: Allen & Unwin, 1963); Kolakowski, *Main Currents*, Vol. III.
85 On this conjecturable point, see Kolakowski, *Main Currents*, III:253–54.
86. See George Lichtheim, *Lukács* (London: Fontana/Collins, 1970), chaps. 1 and 2.
87. Lukács, *History*, pp. 15 f., 224 f.
88. Jay, *Dialectical Imagination*, pp. 3–40.
89. Lichtheim, *Lukács*, pp. 42–43.
90. McInnes, *Western Marxists*, pp. 119, 120. See also Victor Zitta, *Georg Lukács' Marxism: Alienation, Dialectics, Revolution* (The Hague: Martinus Nijhoff, 1964), pp. 183–93.

91. See Lichtheim, *Lukács*, chaps. 3–5; McInnes, *Western Marxists*, chap. 4. See also M. Watnick, "Relativism and Class Consciousness: Georg Lukács," in Labedz, *Revisionism*.

92. See H. S. Hughes, *The Obstructed Path: French Social Thought in the Years of Desperation, 1930–1960* (New York: Harper & Row, 1969), chap. 5.

93. Jean-Paul Sartre, *Critique of Dialectical Reason* (New York: Schocken Books, 1976). The first and smaller part of this tome has been translated by Hazel E. Barnes as *The Problem of Method* (London: Methuen, 1963) and *Search for a Method* (New York: A. A. Knopf, 1963).

94. *The Problem of Method*, p. 8.

95. Ibid., p. 21; italics his.

96. Adam Schaff, *Marx oder Sartre? Versuch einer Philosophie des Menschen* (Wien: Europa Verlag, 1964), p. 40 f.

97. A. Schaff, *Marxism and the Human Individual*, trans. O. Wojtasiewicz (New York: McGraw-Hill, 1970), p. 168.

98. Plamenatz, *Marx's Philosophy of Man*, p. 4.

# INDEX